UCD WOMEN'S CENTER

To Ana, Sandy, Rebecca, Darlene, and Cora,

to the promise of a brighter future for all their children

Faces of Poverty

Faces of Poverty

Portraits of Women and Children on Welfare

Jill Duerr Berrick

Oxford University Press
New York   Oxford

Oxford University Press

Oxford   New York
Athens   Auckland   Bangkok   Bogata   Bombay   Buenos Aries
Calcutta   Cape Town   Dar es Salaam   Delhi   Florence   Hong Kong
Istanbul   Karachi   Kuala Lumpur   Madras   Madrid   Melbourne
Mexico City   Nairobi   Paris   Singapore   Taipei   Tokyo   Toronto

and associated companies in
Berlin   Ibadan

Library of Congress Cataloging-in-Publication Data
Berrick, Jill Duerr.
     Faces of poverty : portraits of women and children on welfare /
Jill Duerr Berrick.
       p. cm.   Includes index.
     ISBN 0-19-509754-8
     ISBN 0-19-511375-6 (Pbk.)
     1. Poor women—United States—Case studies.
   2. Poor children—United States—Case studies.
   3. Welfare recipients—United States—Case studies.
   4. Public welfare—Government policy—United States.
   I. Title.   HV1445.B47   1995
   362.5'0973—dc20   94-43371

10 9 8 7 6 5 4 3 2 1

Printed in the United States of America

Acknowledgments

This book honors the women and children who offered me a window into their lives, who shared their hopes and fears with me, and who spoke honestly about the struggle to live with dignity in a world that scorns the poor.

Many others assisted in bringing out their voices. I am particularly indebted to Catherine Maclay, who read every draft of the text and who helped me find words to describe each family's experience. Renee Robinson and Susan Katzenellenbogen transcribed countless hours of audiotape, and Colleen Stephens was a tireless research assistant. Neil Gilbert, my early mentor and the man who has always challenged me to think critically about social problems, was an unfailing enthusiast of this project.

The idea for this book came in a dinner conversation with my close friend Helen Noh Ahn. It could not have materialized, however, without the financial assistance of the Smith Richardson Foundation and the facilities and support of the School of Social Welfare at the University of California at Berkeley. Dean Harry Specht and Richard Barth were particularly helpful, allowing me time away from other responsibilities. Several valuable critics read all or part of the draft, commented, edited, often disagreed, but always encouraged me to continue: my parents, brother, students, colleagues, Cheryl Keller (Smith Richardson Foundation), and dear husband, Ken. I also benefited from the insight of my editor at Oxford University Press, Gioia Stevens, and from the comments of the early reviewers of my manuscript. I extend thanks to my husband, family, and friends, all of whom have taught me to question the world as it is and to embrace the principle of generosity.

Contents

Contents

Faces of Poverty

It's the money . . . if you've once had no money, and I mean no money at all, it means something always ever afterwards.

Joan Fleming, *The Chill and the Kill*

. . . the barely educated; the illiterate; women—their silence the silence of centuries as to how life was, is, for most of humanity.

Tillie Olson, *Silences*

Introduction

Living Poverty

Andrea's apartment is small and oppressive, with sagging and broken furniture and an old and stained carpet. A tired lace tablecloth covers a small kitchen table, a testament to Andrea's meager efforts at maintaining dignity in her home. On the walls, pictures of her grandmother, her mother, and her daughter provide the only color in these otherwise drab surroundings and represent three generations of women raising young girls—three generations of little education, few jobs, racism, and unrelenting poverty. Andrea talks about her life, her community, and her efforts to raise a daughter against all odds. Then she drifts off for a moment and gazes through the bars on her front window. A police car passes her house and those of her neighbors. She watches, sighs, and quietly murmurs, thinking no one will hear: "This is about as poor as I can take. . . ."

When we think of poverty in America, what is the image that comes to mind? An old, dilapidated shack in southern Alabama? Or a rat-infested tenement house in New York City? Both images are correct, for poverty exists in the backwoods of Appalachia as well as in the heart of the inner city. In homes across the country, poor women are raising poor children. Even though some seem resigned to their fate, others rage in frustration against their predicament. Most are trying desperately to move up and out and into a better life.

Most Americans do not know poor people, have never talked with them over lunch, or shared their ideas about children, politics, or their communities. This is partly a result of the growing insulation of middle-class American communities from the pockets of poverty that are becoming more pronounced throughout the United States. The likelihood that people from different classes and races will mix in churches or parks is diminishing each year, because poor people shop in different stores, travel on different streets, and eat in different restaurants, and their children attend different—usually substandard—schools.

Because most Americans are insulated from the poor, they find it hard to imagine the challenges associated with poverty, the daily fears of crime or victimization, or the frustration of not being able to provide for a child. They find it difficult to understand the courage and strength of poor people, their drive to reach a better place and a better time. News stories tell us something about the poor: "Record Number in U.S. Relying on Food Stamps"; "More Children Than Ever Are Poor, State Study Says"; "Welfare Rolls Rise 6% in a Year." But who are the poor children, the record numbers of hungry, the welfare recipients in such need? What do we know about them or how they became impoverished? Is poverty their fate for a lifetime, for generations, or for only a year or two?

Like anyone else, each poor woman has unique personal characteristics and financial and emotional reserves, and a more or less supportive family that helps her cope with her poverty. But the challenge is great. Living in poverty and raising children well are tests faced by more and more young women each year. Several women confronting that struggle are introduced in this book. Although each has a different personality, history, and character, all share one feature. That is, each woman depicted in this book is using or has used welfare at one time in her life.

This book is about the reality of welfare, designed to dispel some of the myths about the welfare population and to offer solutions to a perplexing American dilemma. It is not merely an account of numbers, facts, and figures. It is not just a fact sheet of how many women are receiving welfare this year, how many received it last year, which number is bigger, and how we should turn the tide. It is also a painting with shades and tones. It asks how welfare affects people and how they cope, and it offers some insight into living on welfare in the United States.

The women introduced here are not, of course, representative of all women on welfare, for a sample of women as small as this one could never encompass the complexity of their experience. But each woman does represent a large group of women whose pattern of welfare use bears certain similarities. Their life stories, told in their own voices, may persuade us to consider needed changes, not just in welfare policy, but in other areas of family policy as well, to enhance family life and to provide real protection for poor children.

At a time when our national leaders are turning their attention to welfare, it is important that we keep the actual conditions of poor women and children in view and not lose sight of the fundamental changes they need in order to improve their lot. Women's words, and the stories of their lives, tell us something about welfare and poverty and finding a better way.

1

What Is Welfare?

Mention the word *welfare*, and most people tune out. Although public opinion polls have consistently shown Americans' compassion for the poor, these same polls also reveal antipathy toward welfare, a belief that welfare simply does not work.[1] Women on welfare loathe a system that imprisons them in poverty; they feel that signing on requires them to give up their dignity yet getting off welfare demands that they jump impossible hurdles. People outside the welfare system have a vague notion that welfare offers too much, that it is so attractive women prefer collecting welfare to working. But the one thing on which most people agree is that welfare is unfair to children. Welfare in the United States lifts no child out of poverty.

Public perceptions of welfare have changed markedly over the past several decades. Once a program that was little noticed by either public officials or private citizens, welfare now occupies the time, energy, and frustration of policymakers, newspaper reporters, academic writers, and program operators. It is not that our attitudes toward the poor have changed; rather, our perceptions of who is poor have changed. Therefore, what we once regarded as a helpful program for destitute children and their mothers has become a focus for public reproach. Few now believe that welfare is helpful; many see welfare as part of the problem.

The establishment of the original welfare program was inspired by Americans' instinct to help people in need and also to uphold American values regarding family and motherhood. But somewhere along the line, something went astray. Times changed. Now welfare upholds few common American values. It does not encourage self-sufficiency, industry, ambition, or independence. And it barely helps support families.

The Development of Welfare

The welfare state grew out of the tragedy of the Great Depression, which began (though there were telltale signs before) with the crash of the stock market in the United States in October 1929. About one-quarter of the workforce lost their jobs; many people lost their homes; beggars became part of the urban landscape; and children across the country suffered from malnutrition. Although private charities and churches gave more assistance than ever before, the problem had become so enormous that their efforts were thoroughly insufficient to the need. In response to the massive deprivation, President Franklin D. Roosevelt initiated government assistance at a level unparalleled in the United States.

Several social programs were instituted during the depression. Some of the more prominent ones were insurance plans such as Social Security and unemployment compensation, designed to reward people who worked by providing a safety net during times of unemployment or at retirement. Other programs begun at this time were work-relief efforts, such as the WPA (Works Progress Administration) projects that helped build roads, theaters, and parks across the country. Programs such as these served more than three million able-bodied men during the depression.[2]

In the 1930s there was a group of people who desperately needed assistance yet could not be expected to work. These were women with young children whose husbands had died, divorced them, or deserted them. These women, who had to raise their children by themselves, were viewed as one of the groups commonly thought of as the "deserving poor." They were considered "deserving" because they were caught in circumstances beyond their control. For them, the AFDC (Aid to Families with Dependent Children)[3] program was established as part of the Social Security Act of 1935.[4] Rather than help them return to the workforce, women under the AFDC program were simply given cash aid.

Reflecting the social climate of that time, women were not expected to work and at the same time raise a family. In fact, women's working outside the home was thought to have an adverse effect on children, so keeping women out of the labor market was meant to protect children from the harsh realities of the outside world. When the AFDC program was begun, it was generally considered a pro-family approach to a somewhat marginal problem.[5] Caring for children was the overriding feature of the policy, which highlighted the role of women as mothers and nurturers. Early supporters of AFDC suggested that it would allow a mother to devote herself "to housekeeping and the care of her children."[6]

Although public attitudes toward these women were somewhat generous, the benefits were not.[7] Some observers of the social wel-

fare system suggest that one reason that AFDC benefits were maintained at such a low level was to create a deterrent to dependency;
that AFDC was designed as a temporary benefit to help a family
through a period of crisis. Although policymakers wanted to be per-
ceived as helping, they did not want women to become so comfortable on AFDC that they might turn down an alternative offer for their
support outside the government. In the 1930s, the obvious choice for
a woman was not support through work but the financial support of
a husband.[8]

With such minimal benefits, the many women who did not find
husbands were therefore forced to secure additional means of support.
Certainly some worked, although they were cautious about hiding this
from their welfare worker. During much of this time, the receipt of
AFDC was dependent on the suitability of the home and the parenting
practices of the women; working was anathema to good parenting and
so was considered grounds for terminating aid. Other behaviors in
women's personal lives, especially in regard to "appropriate" relationships with men, were carefully scrutinized as well.

Welfare workers were hired to oversee AFDC mothers' behavior,
but outside the welfare office's observation, AFDC was given little
public notice throughout the 1940s and 1950s. By most accounts, it
was considered a very small program under the umbrella of the larger
Social Security Act.[9] But during the 1960s, something happened to
change forever the AFDC program and American attitudes toward
women on welfare. Rather than quietly fading away or continuing only
as a residual program, the AFDC caseload began to expand. Although
unemployment remained very low in the 1960s and the country
underwent an economic expansion, welfare caseloads grew considerably. By the end of that decade, almost two million families were collecting AFDC.[10]

The growth in welfare in the 1960s continued unabated for the next
two decades, although it did slow a bit.[11] (By the early 1990s, the
number of families collecting aid had risen to more than five million,
or about fourteen million individual recipients.)[12] More women joined
the welfare rolls in the 1960s when the eligibility rules were broad-
ened and "suitable home" criteria were struck down by the courts.[13]
But much of the rapid influx of welfare recipients was, and continues
to be, a result of powerful demographic forces active in the United
States.

The 1960s and 1970s saw a dramatic shift in the composition of the
American family. More relaxed standards allowed changes in the family
to take place with somewhat less public censure than in earlier decades.

For example, single parenthood became more common. That is, whereas in 1960, 5 percent of Caucasian children were living in female-headed households, by 1980 this figure had almost tripled, to 15 percent.[14] For children of color living in female-headed households during the same period, the percentage increased from 15 to 45 percent.[15] Today, U.S. Census Bureau reports show that approximately 30 percent of all American children reside with a single parent. And among children living in single-parent households, 35 percent live with a never-married parent, and 37 percent live with a divorced parent.[16]

Divorce rates have also continued to increase. Between 1960 and 1980, the annual number of divorces tripled, from approximately 400,000 to nearly 1.2 million.[17] In addition, more women, especially teenagers, were bearing children outside marriage. Although increasing numbers of teenagers reported sexual activity during this period, the overall rate of teenage pregnancy remained fairly constant. The rate of births to teenagers who were not married rose significantly, and many of these "new" families joined the welfare rolls.

The group of women that AFDC had originally been designed to serve were no longer visible on the welfare rolls. Welfare was supposed to be used primarily by widowed or deserted women, but by 1961, the proportion of widows among AFDC recipients was only about 7 percent. By 1971, this proportion had dwindled even further to 4.3 percent, and in 1991 it was a mere 1.6 percent.[18] Although AFDC was being used by destitute women and children, the circumstances of their families had greatly changed. Over time, AFDC came to be used by women who were divorced, separated, or never married. In 1950 these groups represented 37 percent of the AFDC caseload, but by 1961 they had grown to 57 percent, and as recently as 1991 this group accounted for a full 88 percent of the welfare population.[19]

Race was also pivotal to the shift in American attitudes toward AFDC women: To imagine that race does not still play an important role in public perceptions of the poor is naive. In 1939, a few years after the AFDC program was established, more than 80 percent of all recipients were Caucasian. Twenty years later, about half the AFDC caseload consisted of women and children of color, and today that figure stands at about 60 percent.[20] Before the Civil Rights Movement of the 1960s, many states' regulations regarding AFDC had been overtly racist, with legislators and AFDC officials using the "suitable home" criteria to exclude African American children born outside marriage.[21] When these criteria were struck down as unconstitutional and eligibility was determined solely by women's income and assets, large numbers of African American families joined the welfare rolls. As more and more women of color signed on, the racist attitudes that have always plagued this country became even more apparent. The combination of race with unconventional family practices (i.e., single parenthood) created a climate intolerant of the problems faced by poor women and their children.

With this shift in the AFDC caseload, unmarried mothers—particularly unmarried women of color—became the most visible and controversial group of AFDC recipients. Although the program's original intent was to serve vulnerable children, the most noticeable recipients of aid now were women whose qualifications for public sympathy were rather dubious. Children still represented the majority of AFDC recipients, but their mothers were the primary recipients of cash aid. This tension between helping deserving children through their "less deserving" mothers became problematic. Although the widows could not help their circumstances, those women who had children outside marriage had more choice in determining their situation. Public attitudes toward single parenthood may have grown more tolerant with time, but not enough that these women's behavior was universely accepted. In contrast with the early years of AFDC, there emerged more public criticism of new welfare recipients than sympathy. Precisely because childbirth outside marriage was viewed with a considerable degree of disfavor, if not outright hostility, the shift from widowhood to single parenthood may have been responsible for the change in public attitudes toward welfare.

In only a couple of decades, women on welfare were transformed from the "deserving poor" into the "undeserving poor." To the American mind, welfare became synonymous with morally questionable behavior. Many thoughtful observers of the program noted that in an effort to provide for children, the program may have unwittingly contributed to the overall shift toward single parenthood in the United States—a condition that most Americans found difficult to support. One writer on the topic suggests that these changes in the welfare population created a kind of "moral ambiguity"[22] in our views toward welfare; how, indeed, could a program offer generous support without condoning the behavior of its recipients?

Family patterns and race were not the only factors contributing to this change in view. Other forces were the dramatic shifts in women's work patterns across the country.

This century has witnessed many changes, one of the most significant being the explosive entrance of women into the labor market. Until the mid-1960s, the participation of women in the labor force hovered around 30 to 40 percent. After the mid-1960s, this figure increased dramatically, and by 1983, more than 70 percent of women were either working or looking for work;[23] 27 percent of women in two-parent families worked full time year-round; and another third worked part time. In the early 1980s, 41 percent of single parents worked full time year-round, and 25 percent worked part time or for a part of the year.[24] In light of these changes, new expectations were levied on women on AFDC who might also be able to juggle work and family obligations.

Welfare as Intended Versus Welfare in Practice

Over time it became apparent that welfare, as initially envisioned, was unsuitable for modern families or contemporary work practices. Old standards and expectations were being applied to families who looked nothing like the original target group; the purpose of welfare as a temporary benefit for families in crisis had become distorted by the growing numbers of families who used AFDC for long periods of time. Not only did the public see this discrepancy, so did legislators. Accordingly, in the 1970s and 1980s, on several occasions, public officials modified welfare rules and regulations. Work programs, training programs, educational programs, and various incentives were introduced to "reform" the system, all in an effort to make women on welfare look more like other women in the United States.

Unlike the earlier deterrents to dependency, when women were encouraged to find a husband to support them, public officials created new "disincentives" to welfare, hoping to turn women away from the public coffers. Welfare benefits were lowered, eligibility criteria were tightened, and the application process was made more complicated. Once on the welfare rolls, many women were required to register for work or training programs and to try to find a job.

A fascinating aspect of the welfare question during this time was the interplay between policymakers and the public. Several federal work-incentive programs were attempted during the last three decades. Briefly, the Work Incentive Program (WIN) was first developed in the 1960s, later replaced by WIN II, the Job Training Partnership Act (JTPA), and eventually the current program, the Job Opportunities and Basic Skills Training Program (JOBS).[25] With each welfare reform, policymakers made certain that their efforts were well covered by the media. Headlines such as "Landmark Overhaul of the Welfare System" and "The Most Sweeping Revision of the Nation's Principal Welfare Program"[26] were routine after passage of the most recent federal legislation (the Family Support Act of 1988). The excessive attention by the media led the public to believe that these new efforts would surely move welfare recipients off the rolls and into gainful employment. Yet all these programs, designed to help women move toward self-sufficiency, have been notoriously underfunded, allowing only a fraction of welfare recipients to participate. At the peak of the WIN program, about 19 percent of AFDC recipients were actively involved in the program.[27] More recently under JOBS, funding has been available for only about 13 percent of the eligible AFDC population.[28] These figures, of course, rarely reach the media, and when they do, they certainly do not make the headlines. So instead, low-income women have continued to apply for and to use welfare and do not appear to be responding to public officials' generous offer of education and training. In turn, the public has grown increasingly frustrated with welfare women's intransigence, blaming them for not trying hard enough.

What the public has missed is that with each reform over the past thirty years, the basic premise of the AFDC program has remained intact. The reforms have essentially been symbolic gestures: efforts by public officials to look as though they were doing something about "the welfare problem." In the midst of this confusion, welfare now has few advocates and many opponents. Rather than thoroughly examining the welfare system itself, its strange incentives and disincentives, the idiosyncratic entrance and exit rules, people are quick to judge recipients for being on welfare too long, having too many children, and not trying hard enough to find work. Instead of seeing the welfare system for the mess that it truly is, the public directs its displeasure toward the women on welfare. In some cases, these petty irritations have turned to unchecked hostility. One example is a Milwaukee public official whose antagonism toward all women on welfare became apparent:

> A proposal to sell the organs of dead welfare recipients has prompted such outrage that some people fear it will undermine other plans to solve a serious organ donor crisis. Milwaukee County Board Supervisor T. Anthony Zielinski made the proposal in an effort to reduce the county's burial expenses. Zielinski had proposed selling the organs regardless of whether the welfare recipients had granted permission. "If they can't help society while they're alive, maybe they can help it while they're dead," he said.[29]

In 1992, California's governor, Pete Wilson, proposed a 25 percent cut in AFDC benefits.[30] His cavalier attitude toward the effects that this might have on women and children was apparent when he noted that at most it might mean that welfare recipients "would have less for a six-pack of beer."[31]

Sentiments such as these are common. Women on welfare have become the targets of much public debate, and the welfare system has become the dumping ground for the public's outrage over the government's inadequacy. Lost in the uproar are the real effects of poverty on the lives of children: Children make up two-thirds of the welfare population, and no matter what the faults of their mothers or the welfare system are, they are the unlucky pawns of poverty.

Myth and Reality

After several decades of dissatisfaction with the welfare system and a limited understanding of the complex problems that bring women to the welfare rolls, most Americans have settled on a somewhat simplistic notion of who uses welfare and why. These images of the welfare population, often fed by the media, have created a one-dimensional stereotype. But in reality, women on welfare are a diverse group of people unified primarily by the fact that they have very little money.

What are these common images of the welfare population, and how have they shaped our disapproval of the welfare program and the people who use it? More important, what are the facts about who uses welfare and why?

Myth 1: Welfare Payments Are Too Generous

Fact 1: Contrary to a common belief, welfare is not an attractive economic alternative. In no state do welfare payments lift a family above the poverty line, and one-half of AFDC recipients have incomes well below half the poverty standard.[32] 1970 benefit levels have fallen on average by 43 percent (adjusted for inflation),[33] and in more recent years, cuts in benefits have been severe.[34]

Welfare benefits also vary by state.[35] In 1994, a family of three on welfare received $120 per month in the state of Mississippi, whereas a family of three in Connecticut received $680.[36] (The average in all states and territories was $396 per month.)[37] Although it could be argued that the cost of living also varies by state, the differences are not great enough to justify these disparities. (Even though food stamps should mitigate the effects of low benefits, the combined income from AFDC and food stamps still leaves U.S. families below the poverty line.)[38] For example, if we assume that approximately one-third of the family budget is used for shelter, the current rates in the Deep South allot only about $40 per month, on average, for rent or mortgage.[39]

But in Birmingham, Alabama, where AFDC benefits average $164 per month for a family of three, the fair market rent for a two-bedroom apartment is $417.[40] Similarly, in New York City, where welfare benefits are $577 a month, rents average about $719.[41] These examples illustrate that it is extremely difficult to shelter and care for a family with such low payments.[42]

The public also fears that those states with higher welfare benefits will act as a magnet, drawing poor women and children from across the country,[43] although an examination of the growth of the AFDC caseload across states reveals that other factors are probably more relevant to the mobility of poor families. For example, California's welfare benefits are relatively high compared with those of many other states. California also saw an increase in its welfare caseload of 42.5 percent from 1989 to 1993. Yet adjacent states with significantly lower welfare benefit levels saw a much more rapid increase in their AFDC caseloads. Arizona, with a welfare payment about half that of California ($347 a month versus $607 a month for a family of three) saw its caseload increase by 90 percent over the same period. Caseload changes in Nevada were much the same.[44]

A better explanation of the migration of poor families from one state to another is the same as for nonpoor families: When families move, they do so in search of opportunity and employment. The unlucky ones who cannot find a job are those who turn to welfare for support.[45]

Myth 2: Most Women Turn to AFDC When They Have a Baby as a Teenager

Fact 2: A substantial number of women (about 42 percent) turn to welfare after divorcing or separating from their spouse or partner. A smaller percentage—7 percent—rely on welfare after their income drops.[46] About 38 percent of those entering AFDC are unmarried women who have just given birth.[47]

It may be surprising that divorce is linked to later AFDC use, but the economic effects of marital breakdown for women are stark: One study shows that after divorce, women's income drops precipitously.[48] That is, it is less expensive for two adults to maintain one household than to maintain two. In addition to maintaining a separate household, women's husbands or partners often contribute nothing to their children's support. According to two experts in the field of child support, "About 40 percent of absent white fathers and 19 percent of absent black fathers pay child support."[49]

The earning capacity of single mothers is also somewhat limited.

They not only must be both parent and provider (not to mention the difficulties of finding and paying for child care), but their pay, once they find a job, also is likely to be somewhat lower than men's. Although there are various theories explaining women's comparatively low wages, it is still widely recognized that on average, women make only 60 or 70 cents for each man's dollar.[50] Low wages, no child support, and the unavailability of subsidized child care all contribute to women's reliance on AFDC.

Although teenage girls do not necessarily turn to AFDC directly after the birth of a child, many teenage parents live on the margins of poverty, using AFDC as a stopgap during times of crisis. Sooner or later, many girls who have babies as teenagers eventually turn to AFDC for some period of time. Cross-sectional analyses of the welfare population indicate that about 60 percent of the welfare population are women who were adolescents at the time they had their first baby.[51] However, according to welfare researchers Mary Jo Bane and David Ellwood, "The age of the woman when she began receiving AFDC seems to have very little influence on the duration of her stay in welfare."[52] Instead, other factors, such as whether or not the woman received a high school diploma, comes from a family living in poverty, and is married, have a greater effect on the likelihood that she will remain on AFDC for a long time.

Myth 3: Welfare Causes Families to Break Up

Fact 3: Many welfare critics have noted a rise in the welfare population that mirrors the rise in single-parent families during the 1960s, leading them to surmise that one (welfare) caused the other (family breakdown).[53] Credible research on the topic shatters this assumption. Even though the number of children living in female-headed families rose from about 14 percent to 20 percent of all children, the percentage of children living in families collecting AFDC stayed constant at about 12 percent. According to welfare researchers David Ellwood and Lawrence Summers, the numbers are even more dramatic for African American families. During this same period, the number of children in female-headed households increased by 20 percent, and the percentage of African American children in welfare homes declined by 5 percent. "If AFDC were pulling families apart and encouraging the formation of single-parent families, it is hard to understand why the number of children on the program would remain constant throughout a period in our history when family structures changed the most."[54]

Although many sociological and cultural factors have probably contributed to the increasing rate of divorce, separation, and childbirth outside marriage, it is unlikely that the availability of welfare has had a significant affect on these family patterns.[55]

Myth 4: Women on AFDC Have Lots of Children

Fact 4: On average, women on AFDC have two children. Forty-two percent of recipients have only one child; 30 percent have two children; and 16 percent have three children. The remaining 10 percent have four or more children.[56]

As common sense might tell us, the fewer children that women have, the more quickly they are likely to leave welfare. With each successive child, the cost of living and the burden of care increase, making it more difficult to raise a family without assistance from other sources.

Myth 5: Once on AFDC, Women Keep Having Children in Order to Increase Their Welfare Payment

Fact 5: A growing body of evidence suggests that women on welfare are less likely to have an additional child than are women not on AFDC.[57] In fact, one study found that women on welfare were more conscientious about using contraceptives while on welfare, that they were less likely to want an additional pregnancy, and that they were less likely to become pregnant while on welfare.[58] Other studies have found that women on welfare become less interested in having additional children when they realize how great the financial strain of child rearing is.[59] In sum, there is very little financial incentive to bear further children while on AFDC. Although welfare payments do rise with the birth of an additional child, in most states, the average increase in the minimum welfare benefit is only about $70.[60]

Myth 6: Most Women on Welfare are African American

Fact 6: The majority of women on AFDC are indeed women of color, but most AFDC recipients are not African American. About 38 percent of women are Caucasian; another 39 percent are African American; and about 17 percent are Latina.[61] The disturbing feature of ethnicity and AFDC is that African American women are overrepresented in comparison to their number in the total population. That is, although African Americans make up only about 12 percent of the U.S. population, their number on the AFDC caseload is almost equal to that of Caucasians.[62]

Myth 7: Most Women on Welfare
Are Lazy and Do Not Want to Work.

Fact 7: Most women on welfare do not work in the taxed economy. According to government figures, only about 8 percent of welfare mothers work.[63] Yet other researchers have shown that large numbers of AFDC recipients work—that it is impossible to live on public assistance alone—but that these women simply do not tell the government about their outside wages. One study, conducted by Kathryn Edin and Christopher Jencks, found that although four out of five women in their sample of families worked, none felt that they could tell the welfare office about their work.[64] The welfare system has a variety of strange rules and regulations (discussed in greater detail in later chapters) that make it very difficult for women to be honest about their income. If they work without telling the welfare office and if they can do it without getting caught, they and their children will be much better off financially.

In many cases, rather than being lazy, welfare recipients are incredibly resourceful and busy women. Because they do not generally have enough money to purchase services, the only commodity available to many of these women is their time. One study found that a sample of women on AFDC spent an average of about seven hours each day managing their household, including cooking, cleaning, paying bills, running errands, and caring for children.[65] These women's behavior was not typified by indolence.

Myth 8: Once a Woman Starts Collecting AFDC,
She Stays on Welfare for a Long Time

Fact 8: Long-term welfare use is indeed a concern. No one enthusiastically supports the idea of women fully raising their children on public assistance. But the majority of AFDC recipients are relatively short term users. According to researchers David Ellwood and Mary Jo Bane, half of all women who go on welfare leave it within two years.

Two-thirds of these welfare spells end within four years, and only 17 percent last eight years or longer.[66] The unfortunate fact is that once a woman has received AFDC for at least two years, the probability of her becoming a long-term welfare user increases significantly.[67]

In addition, women with certain characteristics are more likely to fall into the "short-term" group, versus the "long-term" group. For example, women who are over the age of twenty-five, who have some work history, and who have a high school diploma are more likely to be short-term welfare users. On the other hand, younger women who have never been married are likely to collect welfare longer.[68] Although these long-term welfare recipients represent a minority of the total welfare population, their welfare use consumes over two-thirds of all welfare dollars.

Because of the expense of supporting long-term welfare recipients, there is much discussion about targeting services to women during the first two years of their welfare receipt.[69] But just as the first two years of welfare use appear to be critical, so are the first two years of independence from AFDC. Once a woman is off AFDC, the likelihood of her returning is greatest in the first two years. Therefore, the longer a woman stays off AFDC, the less likely it is that she will return. Slightly over one-third of all women who stop receiving AFDC eventually return, but repeated periods on and off welfare do not add up to a lifetime of welfare use. Even when researchers account for repeated welfare use, half of all women spend less than four years of their lives on welfare.[70]

Myth 9: Children Raised in Families on AFDC Will Become Dependent on AFDC Themselves

Fact 9: The theory of the "intergenerational transmission of welfare dependence" has received considerable discussion, but until fairly recently, few studies had analyzed the validity of these claims. Now that data are available, we know that daughters raised in welfare-dependent families are somewhat more likely to become dependent on welfare than are daughters raised without welfare, but the differences are very small. In one study, more than two-thirds of daughters from families highly dependent on welfare received no AFDC as young adults. About 16 percent received some AFDC, and about 20 percent became highly dependent on welfare as young adults.[71] It is true that women raised in families dependent on welfare are more likely to use welfare as adults than are women raised in families never dependent on welfare—indeed, avenues out of long-term poverty are few—but the relationship between the childhood use and the adult use of welfare is not absolute. As some researchers point out, other factors, such as growing up in poor neighborhoods, going to poor schools, and living in poor, nonwelfare, single-parent families, can explain later welfare use almost as well.[72]

Children raised in homes in which AFDC was the primary means of support for several years are children raised in severe, long-term poverty. To expect that the majority will experience substantial economic mobility in their lives is a naive view of American opportunities for the poor. Although most of these children will not be dependent on AFDC as adults, many will live at or near the poverty margin for many years.

Myth 10: Most Women Get off Welfare Because They Find Well-Paying Jobs

Fact 10: Some women leave the welfare rolls because they find jobs. In fact, about one-quarter of them do so because their earnings make them ineligible to receive welfare. But surprisingly, the more likely exit from welfare is based on changes in family structure. That is, almost half of all AFDC exits are attributed to women's marrying or remarrying (30 percent) or to their child's ineligibility (11 percent). Many women who leave welfare because of higher earnings may be moving into somewhat marginalized employment. Few women get jobs that pull them significantly above the poverty line, meaning that many are still at risk of falling on desperate times. Because their employment does not provide complete security, about two-thirds (65 percent) of all women who leave welfare because of higher earnings eventually return for a later period of AFDC use.[73]

What Is the Problem?

Given these facts and figures, can we conclude that welfare is a problem? This is where the disagreement often becomes fierce. Although welfare is not a major drain on the public coffers, it is a psychological liability that our society can ill afford to maintain. In 1994, AFDC cost the nation about $22 billion in federal, state, and local funds—less than 1 percent of the GNP.[74] Of all social programs, AFDC lags well behind the more popular and costly Social Security and Medicare, and although AFDC's caseload sizes have grown in recent years, cutbacks in the program in state after state have kept at a minimum the growth in program costs.[75]

Social policy is designed as much to alleviate public fears and perceptions as it is crafted to address clear and present dangers, and most Americans believe that welfare is a serious problem requiring a complete overhaul. Public opinion is, in fact, the essence of what drives the AFDC program. Drastic cuts in the welfare program in recent years have come as much because of public urging as because of the concerns of legislators and official bureaucrats. Welfare depends on public support. Changes in public attitudes toward AFDC recipients or misunderstandings about the scope of the program can therefore result in dangerous changes for poor women and children. In addition, welfare stereotypes define the users of the welfare system and leave poor women and children without a voice. These stereotypes and the mythology built around welfare shape the public's understanding of welfare as a "problem."

Perhaps the real problem, however, is not in our perceptions of who does and does not receive welfare or how long people should benefit from public assistance. Instead, shouldn't we be more concerned about the fact that welfare is synonymous with poverty and that living in poverty is what needs to be addressed? Living in poverty is not a trivial event. It is not as though the have-nots simply have less pocket change but will be all right in the end. Rather, the effects of poverty on the health and well-being of people are pernicious. Poverty is not harmless; its effects are significant, long lasting, and sometimes noxious. Mahatma Gandhi once stated that poverty is the worst form of violence.[76] This violence is regularly heaped on children, sometimes with sad and irreversible consequences:

- Poor children are more likely to be born in poor health,[77] to die in the first year of life,[78] and to show signs of poor nutrition or malnutrition.[79]

- Poor infants are less likely to have received prenatal care and are more likely to be born before term or at low birth weight.[80]

- The rates of lead poisoning of poor children are so high that an estimated three million may be at risk of impaired mental and physical development.[81]

- Poor children suffer higher rates of child abuse and neglect;[82] they also are more likely to suffer from accidental injury or death.[83]

- Poor children are more likely to have trouble in school, to repeat one or more grades, to have significantly lower IQs, and to drop out as adolescents.[84]

- Teen parenthood is most often found among young girls who were raised in poverty.[85]

- Long-term poverty has long-term consequences. The longer that household poverty lasts, the more likely that children's home environments will deteriorate.[86]

- Poverty begets poverty. Children raised in poor families are more likely to live in poverty or on the margins of poverty as adults, thereby repeating the cycle of disadvantage for their children.

The experience of poverty has many similar features, most of which are harmful. Some of the realities just listed may build character, but on balance they are stresses from which all children should be exempt.

Children of all races and ethnicities live in poverty, but some groups are affected more severely than others.[87] According to one study, "Roughly three quarters of white children never lived in poor families; only one-third of blacks escaped family-level poverty altogether." Using a nationally representative sample of children, the study's authors found that temporary poverty was more common for Anglo-American children but that among African-American children living in poverty, nearly one-half were poor for at least five out of six years of their childhood. The authors stated: "Many children and adolescents in the United States today experience poverty at least occasionally, and for blacks poverty is more the rule than the exception."[88]

Even though we know that poverty is harmful, public policy in recent years has not been friendly to the poor. In many states, programs to aid the poor have been cut back severely, and AFDC, the primary safety net for poor children and their mothers, has borne the brunt of this retrenchment. In 1990 and again in 1991, welfare conditions worsened in over half of the states.[89] According to the Center on Budget and Policy Priorities, in 1992, "benefits were frozen or cut in 44 states."[90] In six of these states, the cuts were particularly harsh. Yet the early 1990s were not the first years to see a weakening of the AFDC program. From 1970 to 1980, the average welfare benefit was reduced by more than 30 percent.[91] Today, in the lowest-benefit state (Mississippi), AFDC benefits make up only 13 percent of the poverty level, whereas even in the highest-benefit state (Alaska), AFDC still leaves families in poverty. Such policies are abandoning increasing numbers of children and families to extreme hardship.

At a time when policymakers have decided routinely to balance state and federal budgets on the backs of the poor, it is important to understand the implications of these decisions for women and children. Certainly, welfare needs reform. Most agree that the current system does little to appease the public and even less to truly serve the needy. But across-the-board cuts will not improve the life chances of welfare recipients, two-thirds of whom are children. When approximately 13 percent of all U.S. children are living on welfare and therefore living in poverty, Americans may want to ask whether they can do better for their most vulnerable citizens. Even though rates of poverty were declining among children more than fifteen years ago,[92] we have not considered recently whether the current policies, which are condemning more and more children to poverty, are fair or decent. New policies may need to provide different services, standards, rights, and obligations for women in diverse circumstances if welfare is to rise to a new level in the public debate. But minimum standards that offer children a life of decency are imperative.

Women on welfare do not fit a single mold. Each woman's experience of poverty is unique, and her ability to cope is varied. Every family has a distinctive story to tell about its own resilience, about its struggles, hopes, and fears. The reasons that families become impoverished are complex; human life is not so straightforward that it can be briefly explained and put into a single category. Poverty has a different face in each family, a different complexion, and a different set of features.

What follows are five stories of living on welfare told in part by five women and their children, to help paint a more complete picture of the welfare problem. These portraits are drawn to add depth to a picture of welfare recipients that has grown increasingly one dimensional over time. Each woman represents a group of women who use AFDC, the various reasons that they turn to public aid, and their assorted means of achieving self-sufficiency. By understanding the diversity of the welfare population, it should become clear that welfare policy and family policy must be redefined to account for these differences.

2

Ana: Caught in Circumstances Beyond Her Control

From having a lot to having nothing is very upsetting. I lost everything. I had my own business and I did terrible at it. I lost everything. I got pregnant first, had the baby, after the baby I hurt my back a year later. Then apart from that, I had a fire in the kitchen. My baby got burnt and I got burnt. So, it was like one thing after another and I lost all my money. I had a lot of money in the bank and I lost it all. I've always done well with money. I just couldn't believe it.

Ana lives on a tight budget. She is working on paying back her creditors, paying her regular monthly bills, and caring for three children. She is not on AFDC anymore, although she was for a short time. Over the past year she has received income from three different sources, one at a time. First she was working; then she received AFDC; and finally she obtained worker's compensation. Now she is working again, and all her income comes from her job. In the process, she slipped from working-class status to the bottom.

Her financial situation was not always this bad. For a long time, Ana lived a carefree life. If her children needed new clothes, she went out and bought them. If her car needed repairs, she took it to the shop. She was well paid, had excellent health benefits for herself and her family, and saved a few hundred dollars each month from her paycheck.

But financial well-being is fragile. In the United States, families who were once comfortable can easily lose their financial security. Once they do, the shock can be devastating and seemingly irreversible. Within a period of about a year, Ana lost everything, although she brought on some of her problems herself. She made some very bad choices about men, managed her money poorly, and miscalculated an important investment. But the final blow to her financial situation was caused by circumstances beyond her control. After a year of hardships, Ana is now putting the pieces of her life back together again.

Living on a Budget

Ana lives in a working-class neighborhood. The wood-frame and stucco houses are small and well kept, each with a neat patch of green lawn and clusters of bright flowers. Apartment buildings are scattered throughout the block. It is an integrated neighborhood, a mix of Latinos and Anglos. The cars parked on the streets are mostly American made: Ford Escorts, Chevy vans, and GM trucks. Though few of them look new, most are clean and polished. During the week the streets are nearly deserted, a testament to the fact that the men and women in this neighborhood work hard to make ends meet.

Ana has lived in this neighborhood, in the same house, since she was a little girl. Her parents moved to this country from Mexico with their parents when they were children, and this extended family has formed a closely-knit community ever since. As a Latina, Ana represents about one-fifth of the welfare population. She is thirty-four with blond hair and dark brown eyes, and although she has no trace of an accent, she shifts effortlessly from English to Spanish when she talks with her children or her mother.

When her parents first moved into their house, Ana lived upstairs with them and her two sisters. At seventeen, Ana married Salvador, and they had their first child. Her parents created a separate apartment in the downstairs basement of the house, and Ana and her husband moved in.

> I got married and my husband said, "You don't have to work if you don't want." But that wasn't true. It turned out I was the one working and he wasn't doing anything. He worked in construction some, and he worked until 1975 or 1976 (about two years) and then he gave up. He just stopped completely. He got his green card, and he just decided that he didn't need to help me. So I ended up paying all the bills and doing everything until 1982 and I just said, "This is it."

Ana's marriage had been loveless and unpleasant: Salvador had a drug problem and would often leave the family for weeks at a time. But his absences were more welcome than his presence, since he was not affectionate to the children and he and Ana fought regularly. Salvador was much older than Ana and had promised that he would take care of her and their son, Roberto, but it soon became apparent that she would be the family's sole provider. Ana went to summer school to get her high school diploma and later enrolled in classes at the local community college, but she did not have enough time to pursue her education and, at the same time, work. Ana got her first job as a bilingual teacher's aid in an elementary school and began the lifelong chore of caring for her children.

Ana has had an easier time working outside the home than many other women do. One of the things that made her work more manageable was the support and help she received from her mother. When Roberto (now seventeen) was two months old, Ana started working full time. When Lorena (age sixteen) was born, she took off from work for about two months, and then when Elena was born—Elena is now two years old—she took a six-week disability leave. Except for these brief episodes, Ana has always worked.

In the beginning she tried several different jobs, as a teacher's aid, a waitress, a receptionist, and a bookkeeper. But when she landed a position at the Department of Motor Vehicles, she stayed. Jobs in state government pay fairly well, and as a civil servant, a woman has good benefits and a high degree of job stability. Before her accident, Ana made $31,000 a year.

The work was physically demanding. She spent most of her days giving driving tests to truck drivers, so although she could sit much of the time, she was also required to hoist herself into the truck cab, clamber up the truck's grate, and move heavy equipment. It was exhilarating to her to know more about semis than most men did. She also liked being on the move, meeting new people every day, and she hoped to continue doing this work for several more years.

> I loved the job I was doing . . . I kept getting this image of myself in my late sixties, hobbling up on a truck. Can you imagine, a sixty-year-old lady trying to get up on this tractor?

Whenever overtime was offered, Ana would take it, as a few extra hours always meant more money in the bank. Although her attitude toward working was instilled by her father, the primary motivating factor was not the work itself but the reward. Money is a powerful influence, and although Ana was by no means rich, she had the attitude of most Americans, that "more is better."

After fifteen years with the DMV, she had accumulated several thousand dollars in savings and was considering buying a house. But because California has some of the highest real estate prices in the country, just earning enough for a down payment is an accomplishment. Over the past several decades, real estate has also been a very profitable investment. Many people have made fortunes on California real estate; others have simply ensured greater financial stability for their later years. Nonetheless, Ana decided not to buy a home. Who knows what would have happened had she done so, for even real estate is not a sure thing. But she made a different choice with her money, and that mistake still haunts her. It was Miguel who told her not to buy the house.

Ana met Miguel several years after she broke up with Salvador. After her divorce, she dated several men, but none of the relationships was serious until Miguel came along. Once involved with him, she put aside all of her common sense. Her relationship with Miguel ruined her personal life, and it also caused her to lose everything she had worked so hard to earn.

> I had a lot of money and I invested it. I invested stupidly in a restaurant—a bar. I let my heart lead my head. I listened to [Miguel] and I could kick myself twenty times over. He wanted to open a business and I said, "No"; I wanted to buy a home, and he became kind of annoyed. And you know intuition tells you to do what you want and I didn't; I did what he wanted and it just failed and I lost miserably. I kept seeing green before my eyes instead of really sitting down and doing my homework. I would ask my dad, "Should I get the bar?" and he said, "Well, it makes money, but you really need someone who knows what they're doing in there." So I would ask Miguel, "Well, do you have experience?" and he'd tell me, "Yes, I was managing this place from such and such a year to such and such a year," and I would go back and check out the places. And sure, they were doing fine, but they were franchises. That makes a difference. Because they are not the boss. They do not make the decisions. They are told what to do. There's more money backing them up and I didn't have that.
>
> So I had a lot of trouble. It was just one thing after another. I was running it [the bar] for a while and I had very nice clientele. Once he [Miguel] took it over . . . well, they looked like between street people and ruffians. He pulled in the wrong kind of people and there would be problems and the police would have to be called in. And then I found out that other people had keys, and stuff started to disappear.
>
> He's the one that helped bring it down; I didn't do it. He brought the place down. I lost everything. I was devastated. They were garnishing my wages. I lost everything. I kicked him out of the picture and just decided to start over.

But it was too late to start over. Eventually Ana sold the business and sustained a tremendous loss. Because she owed taxes and creditors, she set up a monthly payment plan to set everything straight again. One of the most important things she did at the time was to keep her job at the DMV. During the two years when the business was in operation, she kept her job, trying to work days at the DMV and evenings at the bar. Then, when everything collapsed, she still had a stable income to rely on, and so her creditors were marginally tolerant of her situation.

When Ana invested in the bar, she was trying to please her boyfriend, but more important, she was trying to capture the American dream. Like so many before her, she wanted to own her own business and create something that was uniquely hers. But owning and operating a small business is no easy task. Indeed, each year in the United States over 55,000 businesses fail. Some of these failures are due to insufficient capital; others are due to the incompetence of their owners. Although Ana had capital, she was naive about the demands of owning a business, and as she said, she let her heart overrule her head.

Before she broke up with Miguel, she got pregnant. Because she was a practicing Catholic, Ana was not willing to have an abortion, so she felt that her only choice was to carry the baby to term. The age difference between this baby and the older two was great: Roberto and Lorena were fifteen and fourteen at the time, and Ana had just begun to think that her emancipation from her children was within sight. With Elena, she had to start all over again. Ana loved Elena once she arrived, but the added financial burden made her life increasingly difficult. She continued to struggle along, but in September 1991 everything came crashing down.

One Day Can Change a Life

On September 21, 1991, Ana had an accident that changed everything:

> I was on the top stair of a truck and my foot slipped off, and I just fell over backward. I lost my balance. I was trying to break, to turn around to fall on all fours, and I fell on my side and hit my head and back. Two girls heard a crack, and I passed out.

Ana had split a vertebra and damaged three disks in her back. She saw a chiropractor and then was sent to an orthopedic surgeon and finally to a neurologist to determine whether there had been any nerve damage. Her doctors insisted that she rest for a couple of weeks and then return to work with "light duty." But because of shortages in staffing, Ana's supervisor pushed her to keep at her old work. Within a few weeks she was back on the trucks again, trying to do her original job. Very quickly, the pain grew worse. Ana tried to increase her medication, but that only made her drowsy.

Her doctors also noticed that her injury was not healing. Then one morning after a particularly heavy day at work, when Ana awoke, she could not get out of bed. Her back had gone into spasm, and she could not move. When the orthopedic surgeon found out that she had resumed her usual job duties, he reprimanded her, telling her that her daily routine was "ruining" her back.

> He said, "If you had done only light duty, your back would have gotten better." It's not your fault; it's your employer's—actually, it's your employer's negligence. He kept pushing you." The doctor said, "I cannot let you stay there because they tend to push you to do more." So he took me off work in June.

All her doctors agreed: "They don't feel I'll ever be able to do that job again." The doctors encouraged her to get out of the trucks and into training for work at a desk.

There is no question that Ana was hurt in the accident. For weeks she felt dizzy, and the pain in her back often kept her awake at night. Many people might have quit their job when they realized that they could no longer perform their required duties. But as a single mother, Ana knew that she needed to continue working to support her family. She began asking her employer to find out whether her job offered any protection from her circumstances. Since her supervisor was reticent to discuss her potential eligibility for worker's compensation, Ana called a lawyer to find out her rights.

Ana had to fight for worker's compensation. Worker's compensation is an insurance program for employees injured on the job. Employers participate by insuring their workers. Some employers use private insurance companies; some self-insure; and, in the case of state employees, the state provides insurance. Each state operates its own worker's compensation program, which varies according to what occupations they insure and how much coverage they will give the employee. Ana assumed that she would receive worker's compensation, so she left work in June and waited for the worker's comp to begin. Her doctors maintained strict supervision, insisting that she rest her back, while the worker's comp still had not been approved. With no income in sight, Ana began drawing from a meager savings account and tightened an already constrained budget. Then disaster struck again.

> I was cooking one morning. I was deep frying. I cook a lot and I was making chimichangas. The baby was close by and I don't like to cook when she's around. She was playing with the mop and she pushed the mop, and I turned around and pushed it away and then the phone rang, and I turned around and then everything came over me and it started burning. She got burned by the oil. My arms got it and the

bottom of my foot. She was burned on her leg and on her arm and on her face. I screamed and I put her in the sink, since it was hot oil, and I put cold water and I got that dishwashing liquid and put it on us, and so I got some of [the oil] off. I had second- and third-degree burns on my hand, and my arms were just first degree. [Elena] had second and first degree.

Ana and Elena spent a couple of days in the hospital and then were required to care for their burns with special lotions and bandages for several weeks.

In one year her business had failed; Ana had hurt her back; she and her daughter had been severely burned; and she had no income. Ana held a garage sale and sold all but the most precious and the most basic of her belongings. But after two months of living on her savings and the proceeds from the garage sale, Ana had nothing left. Her parents tried to help, but they also had very little money to share. Friends sometimes brought a meal or clothes for the baby, but that did not cover the daily expenses. The shock for Ana and for her children was remarkable. She could not quite believe that they had nothing left, and her older children were even more incredulous. Frustrated, they blamed her for their poverty.

> My son would cry out, "Mom, you used to give us money for everything! We ended up with nothing!"

As Ana tells it, she finally reached the point of surrender:

> I was desperate and I realized somebody had to help me. [My boss] was not helping me, so I went over to welfare and I asked them for assistance. I said this is happening, I am owed money, but nobody wants to pay me. This is the situation and I showed them. I had birth certificates, I had everything. [The worker] said, "No problem," and I said, "All I have is $37. That's all." Within two weeks I had money, and I had food stamps a week after I walked in.

I Don't Belong on Welfare

> [The people at welfare] were very helpful. They tried to work with me, and that was surprising. But I didn't want to go in there [to the welfare office]. First of all, I really thought I would be belittled. I expected them to look at me and say, "There's a dork, good-bye. You don't belong here." I just kept saying to myself, "I don't belong here." And I felt a little bad. You really do. You feel real depressed. I thought people were staring at me. And the people. . . . It was like they were very loud. I had this feeling that they didn't really want to get out of it. It's almost like they were

always going to be there, you know? No matter what day of the week you'd go in there, you'd find them in there.

[The worker] asked me a lot of questions, but that was good. I don't believe they police people well enough. They were very thorough with me. I think they're very thorough before you get through the door, but once you are in, the door locks. They were thorough, and they were quick about it.

When I got the food stamps I stocked my shelves and put stuff away. In fact, I gave some stuff away. My son's girlfriend's mother is on welfare. And I tried to explain to her how to go to use [food] coupons to get off the system and she was kind of like, "OK." Do you know how I felt? She didn't really want to get off, and it's like she'll always do the same thing and she'll always be there. I would think that you'd want to better yourself and that's how I am, I want to better myself, but she seems like she's stuck.

From the moment Ana got on welfare, she began looking forward to the day that she would get off it. She felt that it was not right to be taking welfare when she was supposed to be getting worker's compensation. And she did not feel good about worker's comp, either, except that she knew that it, too, would last for only a limited time before she had to go back to work. Ana's feelings for other women on welfare ranged from anger to disdain. Although the women she saw at the welfare office were in different situations, she always focused on the few that she was sure were abusing the system.

I went to this one class for Medi-Cal and the people that were there, it was almost unreal. They were very intelligent, you could tell they didn't belong there. At the time, even listening to them speak, you could tell that the husband just sort of walked off and left them, left them with these children. And you could understand why they were there. But there were other people there—there was one lady, she had nine children, all different fathers and she was ready to go out there and have another one.

It is not just middle-class working America that resents women on AFDC. As David Ellwood, a prominent welfare researcher, states, "Everyone hates welfare." People not on welfare hate it because of the numerous abuses and inequities built into the system. But there is derision from people on the inside as well: Welfare mothers themselves have tremendous animosity toward other women in similar situations. Their feelings toward other welfare recipients usually focus on their behavior.

The women in this study almost always distanced themselves from "other welfare mothers," variously describing them as lazy, disorganized, and dirty. Many of the women noticed the number of the other recipients' children, remarked on the number of fathers of these children, and commented about the children's behavior and dress. Ana was no exception: She claimed a moral high ground the day she walked into the welfare office.

Nonetheless, her own behavior was not beyond reproach. One can imagine the feelings of the other women when they saw Ana filling out her application. She was probably well dressed, her hair curled and her nails polished. She held her head very carefully because of the pain in her back, but otherwise she probably looked as though she really did not need or deserve much help. Ana did not bring her children with her to the AFDC office that day, but had she done so, the other women would have found another reason to judge her behavior. Ana has three children with two different fathers. Her life would have been far easier if she had not become pregnant with her third child.

Ana was quick to criticize the woman with nine children and several different fathers, but what if the woman had five children? Or three? At what point and under what circumstances would Ana consider this woman's behavior to be acceptable? In a country as diverse as the United States, there are few standard patterns of family practice. Some families with three or more children may manage quite well, whereas others with only one child may struggle. Although Ana rationalized the choices she made, she was not exempt from others' blame.

Most people rationalize their behavior because life is challenging and people's choices in life can take them in many directions. People regularly make mistakes, and some people's are worse than others. Our judgment of the actions of others often is swift, and we often claim that our choices are wiser. Many of the women that Ana was so quick to judge on that day in the welfare office were watching her with equal skepticism.

Most of the women in this study remembered the first day they applied for AFDC and the other applicants in the office. Many had intense feelings about applying for welfare, yet their need for money overcame their feelings for "those kinds of women." By accepting AFDC, they too became one of "those women," even though they fought against the characterization.

Before Ana began receiving welfare, she had the same aversion to it that people outside the system feel. American attitudes toward welfare are driven in part by the fact that most women turn to welfare because of a combination of income problems and personal problems. If the problem were only one of money, the public would be far more sympathetic. But most women are on welfare because of a miscalculation in judgment or a mistaken emotion. Women are not simply victims of an unfeeling labor market or a harsh employer: Fewer than one in five welfare recipients are drawn to AFDC because of a problem related to employment. Instead, the plight of AFDC recipients can almost always be traced back to an unplanned pregnancy, a bad or abusive relationship, or a history of pathology or neglect that could not be avoided. More than 70 percent of women on welfare ask for aid because of either the birth of a child or a separation or divorce from their partner. Other women may believe that if they were placed in the same circumstances, their choices would be better, smarter, and more carefully planned. But their choices are often determined by circumstances that cannot be controlled. A more appropriate view would be one that recognizes the vagaries of life's circumstances. "There, but for the grace of God go I" is perhaps closer to the truth.

The Fragility of American Prosperity

Most people believe in the American economic myth. In essence, this myth is that if one finds a job and works hard, one will prosper. If an ordinary person were asked to draw a line on a chart tracing the economic experience for most families, he or she would draw a line from the bottom left-hand corner up to the upper right-hand corner. The line would not be horizontal, implying a constant standard of living over a lifetime, nor would the line dip until, perhaps at age sixty-five, it reached retirement. Instead, most of us believe that income is stable and that each year brings modest but progressive improvements (barring major economic upheavals such as a severe depression). But a study conducted by Greg Duncan discovered a different pattern of lines.

Duncan began his study in 1968, and it covered more than five thousand American families. The sample was representative of the American population, with slightly more low-income families participating in the study. Each year researchers contact this group to ask them a series of questions about their income and the composition and stability of their families. After the first ten years of collecting data, Duncan reviewed his findings. He discovered great volatility in family income and a constantly changing standard of living, thus pointing to the fragility of the workforce and the potential instability of income for every American family.

> When we compare the economic position of the population in two years, 1971 and 1978, we find a remarkable amount of change at all income levels. Of those who were either at the top or at the bottom

levels in 1971, only about half had remained in those relative positions in 1978. . . . Family income mobility is pervasive at all income levels. Income mobility in the top income quintile (the top one-fifth of the population) was as great as it was at the bottom.

Duncan has continued to study this population over time and regularly finds similar results. Family income can change rapidly, but dips in family income are less likely to occur as a result of unemployment or disability than as a result of changes in family composition. That is, women like Ana, whose crisis of poverty was caused mainly by the collapse of her business and then her accident, are typical of about one-fifth of poverty cases. Duncan notes, "[T]he single most important factor accounting for changes in family well-being was a fundamental change in family structure: divorce, death, marriage, birth, or a child leaving home. In other words, changes in the economic status of families are linked inextricably to changes in the composition of families themselves."

The financial mobility to which Duncan refers dispels some of the myths about the robustness of family income. Moreover it points to a weakness in the American system of public aid. We provide fairly generous assistance to those whose fate is linked to a dip in the economy or a weak attachment to the labor market. Social Security is a good example of a social insurance program that offers fairly liberal assistance to those people whose attachment to the labor market has been strong. Unemployment insurance is not generally considered extravagant—depending on the state in which one lives, benefits may replace from 28 to 45 percent of average weekly wages—but when the overall economy falters and unemployment is high, public officials are often quick to recommend expanding coverage for eligible recipients. Worker's compensation is another example of an insurance program that, depending on the state and one's personal circumstances, may provide a modicum of comfort for eligible workers. Ana received about $1,800 a month during the four months she was off work because of her back injury. If she had not had such huge bills connected with her failed business, she would have been quite comfortable.

Insurance programs such as these are certainly justified. A system of aid that protects workers from a capricious market is, at a minimum, a decent gesture. But the welfare state is a divided system: One part is generally thought of as a system of "social insurance" in which workers are given basic protection from the market. The other category of public assistance is less generous, both financially and philosophically, as it is given to people whose economic plight can be traced back to individual decisions about the makeup of their family. If Duncan's characterization of family income is correct, it suggests that our system of public assistance is the least friendly to those who are most likely to need support.

Ana was lucky to have weathered the difficulties brought about by her divorce and later by the birth of her third child. Certainly, the addition of another child put a strain on finances, but because her job was secure, she was able to survive. In Ana's case, the "insurance program" designed to protect her against the uncertainty of illness or disability on the job failed for a time, and it was because of this failure in the system that she eventually had to turn to welfare.

Managing Poverty

Welfare meant poverty for Ana, as it does for virtually everyone. Public assistance such as AFDC is a "means-tested" program that demands strict attention to eligibility based on income and assets. Ana no longer had an income, and she had sold all her assets in order to survive. The stress was hard on her family. Ana was in constant pain from her back injury and wondered when or even if she would be able to return to work. Conversations with her employer were not comforting either, as he encouraged her to find other employment. And if she were to return to work, it was not clear what she would be doing. She was not eager to return to the trucks, simply because of the movements required. But she was also unsure about her abilities as an indoor worker. Would the DMV retrain her? Would it give her a few weeks to make the transition? Would she be forced to return to her previous job?

The strain that Ana felt spread to the rest of her family. It was not just the lack of money, but also the disparity between where they were before the accident and where they were afterward. Ana's problem was not so much one of absolute poverty—although she had very little money—as one of relative poverty. Ana and her children knew they were missing out on comforts to which they had grown accustomed.

The difference between absolute and relative poverty is an important one. Certainly, most families in the United States do not experience the kind of desperate poverty seen in many Third World countries. Except for the homeless and the most indigent, families living in poverty in the United States still have simple amenities such as indoor plumbing, shelter, and food. But the disparity between the rich and the poor grows wider each year; the cost of buying shelter (as a percentage of total income) has risen considerably; and the amount of money deemed necessary for average Americans to live on continues to outpace welfare benefits. It is now well known that during the 1980s, the rich prospered to a greater degree than any other class did, thus widening the chasm between rich and poor. In addition, according to a recent Gallup poll, most Americans believe that it is unreasonable to expect families to provide for their children on an income that is below the poverty line. These same respondents also noted that the poverty line should be set at least 24 percent above its current level.

In spite of Ana's "new poverty," she and her children managed remarkably well, although their misfortune did take an emotional toll on the family. Disaster struck one too many times, and the family members had become numbed. Elena was too young to realize what had happened, but Roberto and Lorena were hit hard. Ana decided to talk to them candidly about their situation.

> I sat them down and explained to them. I said, "This is my paycheck." I showed them [the welfare check], and they looked at me with shock. That pushed my son to work harder and to get a better job. My daughter, she went in the opposite direction. She got depressed. Her grades went down in school, and she didn't do well. And her attitude was like, "I don't care." And in high school, as long as you do well, you can work. So until she brings her grades up, she can't go out and get a job. And so it was like a Catch-22, because she's trying to get a job, but they wouldn't allow her until she brought her grades up. And so it dawned on her finally, so during the summer there was a big change in her. She went back to school and she did summer school and she started hanging around with a different crowd of people, a different type of friends.
>
> It was very hard for them. In fact, my son said, "I used to say, I need $100 and you'd say "OK," and now to get $5 from you it's like pulling teeth." The older kids, they tend to want to shop at the better stores. I used to have a bad habit of running to the store with them to shop before school started [in the fall], but we had to economize. I told them they would get $200 for the whole year [for clothes] and that would be it. It's hard because they just don't know what's good for them, but I think it teaches them. My son got it right away. He began to economize and buy cheaper things.

Roberto got a job in a local warehouse and tried to help the family. He could not afford much, since he was also enrolled in a local business college that was very expensive. Except for his food, however, Roberto was essentially on his own. In that year he grew from an adolescent into a young man and began making plans to move out on his own. Although his relationship with his girlfriend was very serious—that did not change—their enthusiasm to have a baby right away diminished considerably during that year. Roberto now knows firsthand the difficulties of providing for a family.

Ana tried to teach her children new skills during that period. They often had long talks together as they devised their coping strategies, and she thinks of that period as a time of growth for herself and her children. Although Ana gave her children greater responsibility for managing their own money, she still had to oversee all the other family expenses. During the time that she collected welfare, she considered the areas in which she could cut back. First, of course, was entertainment. Although Ana had gone out with friends on weekends quite a lot before, that was the first activity to go. Next came restaurants. Eating out was a luxury, but with no income, that, too, had to go. She stopped buying clothes altogether for herself and started searching out garage sales for Elena's clothes and toys. Ana quickly realized that the one household expense she could control was her food bill. She had not been a coupon clipper before, as the task requires a degree of organization she rarely brought with her to the grocery store. But all that changed. Ana suddenly had time on her hands. While she watched TV in the evenings, she would rummage through newspapers and magazines and clip out coupons.

> I do it about three times a week and then Sundays. I do it when I'm watching TV or just sitting there talking to my mom. It doesn't take me that long; it's not that time-consuming. I ordered this box to keep them organized. They are [organized] by product: baby foods, baby items, pet food, housewares. . . .
>
> Some of the stores will take multiple coupons. Some of them won't. You have to watch, if they see you too often they're like, "you're the one . . ." so you have to switch stores, but it doesn't say on the coupon that it's against the rules. And you can use expired coupons and they don't tell you this. But I asked one of the store managers, and you can use expired coupons for up to a year after the date. Even Kmart takes coupons. A lot of people don't know that.
>
> Double coupons and triple coupons are the best. Like when Halloween's coming up, candy is $1.29 a bag, but if you've got a 50 cent coupon and then you double it, then your Halloween candy's only $0.29. When Halloween comes around, then you have all this candy and the kids love your house because you've got a whole bunch of candy and they don't even know where to start.
>
> You have to have a list. I don't like to go into stores and be diverted into the more expensive items. You have to get only what's on your list. I go to the doctor a lot, so on my way to the doctor I hit the Safeway, Walgreen's, and Thrifty. So they're on my way or on my way back. So I don't waste any gas because I have to go there anyway.

I remember one day the guys at the grocery store were watching how I shopped. He said, "You were touching everything, picking up everything, putting it back." Then I gave him all these coupons and I floored him. He said, "I can't believe this." He was surprised. I got all the managers' specials; I got all these things that were three for $5 and I had $1 off the three Joy detergents, on the coupons, so I ended up paying $2. And I also get a lot of rebate checks from products that I buy.

I'm not going to spend a fortune. I'll go to a store and I'll look at something, how much does she want for this, and they tell me, $20. Twenty dollars for that basket, OK, so I'll look for one at a garage sale and I'll buy it and I'll spray-paint it. It matches the furniture and I spend a total of $6.

And you know how people give you soap sets for your bathroom and you never use them? Well, you take those soaps and old soap and I boil them—it's a big mess—and it turns into that soap that you use—that liquid soap. And it makes my house smell good, too.

Ana was so good at economizing on food and household items that she had leftover food stamps after a month on AFDC. She got a new allotment of food stamps in the second month, and then when her worker's compensation check came through, she went to the welfare office to tell them.

I had picked up the food stamps on Friday, and on Saturday I got the worker's comp check. So I walked in with the new food stamps and the leftover food stamps and handed them to [the worker]. And she said, "No, that's yours." I said, "What? I don't have to pay you back? I was under the assumption that I had to pay everything back." So I was trying to give it to her and she said, "No, take it." It made me feel better. To this day, I still have food stamps in my purse.

The welfare worker was astonished by her thrift. She mentioned to Ana that she should come to the welfare office and give classes to welfare applicants. Nothing ever came of the suggestion, but Ana took the advice seriously. She often talked about how she would structure the lessons, and her entrepreneurial spirit was aroused as she imagined even greater ideas about setting up a business:

The amount of food stamps they give to you is not a whole lot. You have to be very imaginative. I mean you have to really work at it to stretch that dollar. So if I decided to work with the welfare department, OK, let me have a food coupon bank and I'll work with people and we will set up food menus for the week and I'll even show how the food stamps can be stretched with the use of coupons. I'd work with the computers and say you need these coupons and I'd have the coupons right there, then go shopping. Then they don't have to work at it. I do the work for them for a fee. The next person would come in and here's your shopping list and your coupons. . . . Go, see you next week. And I wouldn't be telling them what to do. You have these people from different countries. Someone might like hot dogs every day, and some person is a chicken fiend. So they would come and say, "I want to eat x, y, and z," and you would develop a menu for them as cheaply as possible. It would work. I'd need a computer. It would also be a nice service for people who were shut in. Have someone go out and shop. I wouldn't mind.

Shelter from the Economy

Although the circumstances of Ana's life are unique, her pattern of welfare use and income packaging is not uncommon. Men and women across the country use a variety of income support programs such as AFDC, unemployment insurance, worker's compensation, or local food banks to help tide them over during crises and financial strains. Ana's reasons for beginning welfare (loss of income) and her exit (regained income) also are typical of many welfare recipients.

When Ana was on welfare, she exhibited both industry and thrift. She did such an exceptional job of economizing that she even had leftover food stamps, something almost unheard of among welfare recipients. But there was never any surplus from her AFDC check. Then and now her bills are high, and any extra dollars go toward the debt she incurred with her business. Although she is working again, that debt will hang over her head for many years. In a very short time, Ana lost a business, injured her back, temporarily lost her job, and collected AFDC. She went back to work after about six months and slowly returned to a regular schedule.

Her job is different now. Instead of working with large trucks, she gives driving tests in regular cars. It is a compromise. The movement in and out of cars still hurts her back, but there are no desk jobs currently available in her office. Ana is right. Because of her accident, things will never be the same again.

Early in this century, industrial accidents were common. Coal miners, factory workers, and assembly-line workers were often exposed to extremely hazardous working conditions. Low wages and layoffs were routine; participation in the intensive capitalist economy provided little protection from a precarious market. Some of the most egregious industrial abuses gave rise to social legislation that, although modified today, provided the foundation for the modern welfare state. At a minimum, the legislation attempted to protect workers from the hazards of the market.

Ana was a short-term beneficiary of this legislation and was given a hand up during a time of crisis. Her accident represents the types of hazards that still exist in the workplace, although they are now much less common. Because she initially had difficulty obtaining worker's compensation, AFDC protected her and her family from absolute destitution. Whereas Ana lost her job temporarily, less fortunate women (and men) have to endure long periods of unemployment. Welfare provides some security against these misfortunes.

Approximately 16 percent of women begin collecting AFDC because of reduced wages or unemployment. Some unemployment results from low productivity or poor work habits. But it is now widely recognized that the capitalistic American economy actually relies on unemployment in order to keep the economy moving. From the policymakers' standpoint, unemployment guards against inflation. For the corporate world, unemployment provides a balance to the unbridled demands of workers for higher wages and benefits. By using the constant threat of unemployment, employers can freeze or even lower wages during economic downturns. Indeed, the market economy is generally not worker friendly: Workers are routinely laid off, and during recessions, they are the first to feel the pinch.

Recent events provide an example of this effect. The nation experienced a severe recession in the early 1990s, during which businesses closed and unemployment soared. In California, the recession was especially tenacious. Statewide, the average unemployment rate hovered around 9 percent, although in some counties, local conditions were even worse. But so-called average unemployment rates mask the discrepancies between men and women and between Caucasians and African Americans. The unemployment rates for people of color are usually much higher, and in the inner city (where many AFDC recipients reside) they often are double the average.

As unemployment rates rose across California, so too did the welfare caseload. This is understandable. AFDC should be predicated on the assumption that the market will change and that with change, workers will suffer. Yet the discussion surrounding welfare at the time did not recognize the role of welfare as a safety net for families marginalized by the economy. Indeed, the connection between high unemployment and rising caseloads was almost entirely ignored.

As the economic pie shrunk, legislators and the electorate made pleas to cut AFDC benefits. People argued that lower benefits might divert would-be AFDC recipients from the welfare rolls. This movement toward shrinking welfare grants was surprising in light of the role that AFDC should play in a volatile market economy. When the economy does not operate in favor of the workers, a safety net must be made available until the workers can find a place in the economy again.

Welfare plays this role. It did this for Ana, but not without exacting a toll. When Ana was on welfare, her benefits were paltry. After a month and a half on AFDC, she wanted to give the benefits back, but the welfare office had already charged her for its service—Ana had paid the price of her welfare grant in the shame attached to it in the eyes of those both inside and outside the welfare system. She had lost her unique identity and became, for a time, just another welfare mother.

Ana used the system for a very short time, and although she had to overcome a number of hardships, her return to the workforce was relatively easy. She used AFDC for about six weeks and then collected worker's compensation for four months. When she was ready to return to work, she had a well-paying job waiting for her; she also had a free babysitter in her mother. Her transition back to work was difficult in that it was physically demanding and painful, but it was relatively uncomplicated in many other ways.

Ana's misfortune taught her a number of valuable lessons:

> You have to economize; you have to in today's society. I'm making ends meet. It's a good lesson, it's a very good lesson. I've learned to economize, I've learned to use a lot of different strategies. I've learned to manage my money better.

But if the safety net were not there to catch her—or if the safety net were so inadequate that it did not protect her from her circumstances, Ana and her children might have surrendered to desperation.

> "I don't know what I would have done," she says, "I don't know what I would have done if welfare hadn't been there."

3

Sandy: Working but Poor

I'm 24 years old; I've got brown hair, hazel eyes; I like modern rock, dancing, movies, going out to dinner and beaches. And then I'm a single mother of a five-year-old; that's a big one. I like camping and shopping; I'm really easy going, I guess. My hobbies are arts and crafts. I'm pretty quiet, but I like to be loud and wild, too. I like going outside; I'm real shy; and I'm a single mother of a five-year-old.

Sandy's whole identity is caught up in the fact that she is a mother— a single mother—a single mother of a five-year-old child. She has very traditional views of love and marriage and would give anything to find the "right" man. She does not think about her career much at all. Instead, she has a job—if it lasts through the recession—that pays most of the bills. She will work as long as she has to; she does not shy away from her responsibilities. But she would much prefer to be taken care of by a man and be a stay-at-home mom who raises a family with her husband.

Sandy does not currently use AFDC. Like about 20 to 25 percent of the welfare population, she left the welfare rolls when she got a job.[1] She has worked full time for about two years now, living on the margins of poverty, just getting by, and always hoping that she can avoid economic disaster.

Sandy lives simply and plainly. Like almost half the AFDC population (42.2 percent), she has one child.[2] She and her daughter, Kim, share a one-bedroom apartment in a run-down neighborhood dense with apartment buildings. The buildings look similar, differing only in the shade of beige or gray that each is painted. A couple of blocks away, the apartments give way to small bungalows; houses built in the 1920s and 1930s that have since fallen into disrepair. The residents in this community have few valuable possessions; instead, their property is their insurance against hard times, so many home owners have constructed chain-link fences around their yards to mark the boundaries of their belongings. Like Sandy and Kim, almost all the residents in this pocket of the city are white.

Sandy and Kim have made the most of their small space in the large apartment complex. The living room of the apartment is immaculate, with a gallery of pictures adorning one wall. Each section of the wall features Kim at a different stage of her development; first as a baby, then as a toddler, then as a preschooler, and now as a five-year-old. The bedroom walls are also fully decorated. Their one bedroom has an invisible dividing line down the middle: Kim's half of the room has posters of Peter Pan, Cinderella, and Beauty and the Beast. Sandy's half looks more like a teenager's room. One wall is covered with lovely homemade crafts, woven baskets, and needlepoint, and the other features pictures of various rock bands. A large poster of a movie star looms over her bed.

Sandy would like a two-bedroom apartment, but she knows that the cost would put her over the edge. She is still recuperating from her time on AFDC, and her financial reserves are low. Sandy used AFDC for about two and a half years, from the time her daughter was a couple of months old until she turned three. Like many AFDC recipients, Sandy started using AFDC as a teenage mother, shortly after the birth of her daughter.

Teenage Pregnancy: The Fastest Way to Poverty

Sandy got pregnant by mistake as a teenager. Although she thought about abortion, she could not go through with it. Unfortunately, when teenagers make mistakes about their sexuality, the American public pays for it. Welfare is intimately tied to the problem of teenage pregnancy, as the majority of AFDC users gave birth to their first child when they still were adolescents.[3] But even if the rate of teenage pregnancy were to fall, there would always be some young women who would rely on welfare for a while.

Sandy got pregnant about the time that her parents were going through a divorce. The divorce was messy, and there was not much love and attention in their home. Sandy was not the only adolescent in the family to rebel against her parents: Her younger brother dropped out of high school at about the same time, and her older brother got a girl pregnant. Sandy felt quite alone. Not surprisingly, she was looking for the perfect relationship that would last forever, and when she became involved with Ben, she thought she had found the perfect mate.

> I wasn't really thinking about [getting pregnant]; I think subconsciously
> I wanted it and needed it for something in my life because of every-
> thing that was happening with my parents. And looking back I didn't
> see [what I was doing]. I was very insecure. Ben was there and I latched
> on to him. We knew each other three months and I got pregnant. I
> didn't consciously think that if I got pregnant I could keep him, obvi-
> ously that doesn't work.

Sandy never really thought about the consequences of her actions.
Indeed, she never considered using birth control, and in retrospect,
she now finds her behavior shocking. She got pregnant early in the
relationship, which is surprisingly common. One researcher found that
of all first pregnancies for teens, half occur within the first six months
of sexual activity, and one-fifth happen by the end of the first month.[4]
Sandy was one of the unlucky ones.

The decision to keep the baby was Sandy's, but Ben was also a willing participant. Although he did not welcome the idea of becoming a
young father, he did not renounce Sandy or encourage her to get an
abortion. (And he had never suggested using birth control.) But
Sandy's and Ben's images of fatherhood were quite different. Ben
thought about the new baby much as an athlete might think about a
trophy: After it has been won, it sits on the shelf to be viewed from a
distance. Sandy thought about fatherhood in much more personal
terms and imagined an active participant in Kim's childhood. When
the baby arrived and Ben walked away from his responsibilities,
Sandy's illusions about Ben began to crumble. She had to brave parenthood on her own, and the challenge was greater than she thought.

Low Income and Sick Children: A Bad Combination

Sandy was going to the local community college when she met Ben,
and she was also working part time at a department store. She had
held a couple of jobs earlier and was used to working. Once she became
pregnant, she had no intention of quitting her job, and when it became
apparent that Ben would play only a marginal role in Kim's upbringing, Sandy knew that the bulk of Kim's support would have to come
from her. Sandy's father reinforced her attitude toward work as well.
When he found out that she was pregnant, his first words of advice
were to work as much as possible and to avoid welfare at all costs.
Sandy's white, middle-class family was unaccustomed to welfare.
Nevertheless, her father had benefited from a university education at
public cost; he got a substantial tax break from the deduction on his

mortgage; he drove to work every day on publicly maintained high-ways; and he often spent weekends and holidays in the public parks—but that was different. Welfare was a direct handout that implied a kind of character fault. Unlike middle-class welfare benefits, in her father's eyes, AFDC compromised a person's integrity.

So Sandy worked. She continued working up until the week before the birth and went back after six weeks of disability leave. She was lucky to have her father's health insurance plan at the time. His plan covered her up through the birth, so she had good prenatal care, and the birth itself was covered by insurance. But after Kim was born, her insurance coverage was discontinued because Sandy was no longer considered a dependent. She could have continued the insurance on her own, but the monthly premium was too high. Instead she went to her employer and asked about benefits, but no one in the company except for the managers received health benefits of any kind. When Kim was three months old, she got an ear infection and Sandy could not pay for it:

> I really needed to take her to the doctor and my dad's health plan had ended and that was the only way I could get [the insurance], so I went down to the county. I was nineteen and my mother told me to go get on [welfare]. I knew there was such a thing as welfare, but I didn't know where you went or who was supposed to get it. It wasn't something I wanted to do, but I really didn't have any choice.

It is impossible to estimate how many women turn to welfare simply because they have no health insurance for their children. Generally no records are kept that would provide that kind of information, although one study estimated that the welfare caseload would drop by 16 percent if all working women had health coverage.[5] But it is obvious that no woman can raise a child without health insurance of some kind. Children get sick. Sometimes their illnesses can be life threatening, and the parent who chooses not to provide health coverage for her child would be considered negligent by most observers. For Sandy, the opportunity to receive Medicaid made welfare an attractive alternative.

In the last decade, employer-sponsored health care has declined rapidly across the country. Hardest hit by these changes are low-income working families.[6] High-income working professionals often receive health insurance through their employer, and the poorest families are eligible for Medicaid when they receive AFDC. Thus the working poor often fall through the crack between these two groups. At the time of Kim's birth, Sandy was counted among the working poor, and she and her daughter were falling quickly. But things have changed since Kim was a baby.[7]

The Medicaid program is jointly funded by state and federal contributions and is made available to all families on AFDC. Each state also has the option of extending eligibility to other families if it sees fit. The cost of such expansions is generally borne by the state government, so poorer states are less inclined to extend coverage beyond AFDC families. When Kim was a baby, eligibility for Medicaid was more limited than it is today. But since 1987 the federal government has encouraged the states to extend Medicaid to all poor children under age eight whose family incomes fall below 185 percent of the poverty line.[8] And in 1990 the federal government passed an additional law[9] that requires the states to extend Medicaid to all pregnant women with family incomes below 133 percent of the poverty level.[10] This will certainly provide a wider safety net for families who fall through the cracks of employer-provided health insurance and is a tremendous improvement.

But is it enough? What about those families that are ineligible for AFDC yet live above the threshold for Medicaid? What about the parent who is working full time for the minimum wage but has no access to health insurance from her employer? As long as some families are unable to insure the health of their children, welfare will be seen and used as an important alternative. That our system encourages families to drop out of the workforce if they have no health insurance contradicts our traditional work ethic.

AFDC as a Disincentive to Work

Some people say that being on welfare saps a woman's motivation to work,[11] that the average AFDC recipient stops working once she goes on welfare, and that welfare itself encourages her dependence. If that is true, it is the AFDC rules that determine whether or not a woman will continue working, not the pleasure she derives from living in poverty without having to work. When Sandy began using AFDC, she saw no reason to quit her job or to quit school. She and her mother swapped babysitting for each other (her mother also had a baby, having remarried, and she worked at the same store but always arranged her schedule to be the reverse of Sandy's), so child care was not initially an issue. Sandy continued to work because it seemed to be the natural thing to do.

But the fact that Sandy worked meant that she received only a partial AFDC check. Sandy was combining work with welfare, something that about one in ten welfare recipients tries.[12]

> [AFDC] varied; I never got the full amount. It all depended on how many hours I was working. And I never really understood how they calculate these things. It makes no sense. Some months [food stamps] would drop down. You never really knew how to budget your money because you never knew how much you were going to get. Sometimes it was a feast and sometimes a famine.

At first Sandy lived with her mother, but later she moved in with a friend who was also receiving AFDC. Together they pooled their money and made ends meet. But it quickly became apparent that when Sandy varied her work hours, her AFDC grant would also fluctuate. More important, if she worked too many hours, she was denied both welfare and Medicaid at the same time.

It was precisely because Sandy played by the rules that she was penalized. Most of us subscribe to the ethic that work is good and that the more we work, the better off we will be. But in Sandy's case, she was discouraged from working more hours, by being threatened with the loss of her health insurance. After several months she was praised by her employer for her good work habits and was offered a raise. Ironically, the raise, which is generally regarded as an incentive to work more, had the opposite effect on Sandy.

> I tried to govern how many hours I worked, and how much money I was making so that I could stay on the [Medicaid]. I wasn't getting benefits at work, so I needed to stay on AFDC. And then I got the raise. Well, as soon as I was making $7.50 an hour I was down to 16 hours a week or less. It was getting pretty ridiculous. And then the store moved further away (one branch closed and another opened several miles away), but for a good two years I was balancing; well, if I'm making $6.00 an hour I can work 20 hours a week. . . . I figured it all out, how much I could make a week without getting off of AFDC. And so if it was only $50.00 I got from AFDC then it was only $50.00. That didn't bother me. I was on it for the [Medicaid].

Finally the balancing act became too difficult, and Sandy decided to leave her job altogether. She was not opposed to working; rather, the system made it too hard for her to work and to feel rewarded by her work. She felt embarrassed turning down hours that her employer wanted her to work, and she dreaded the day she would have to refuse a raise. Her manager had confidence in her abilities, but the more he relied on her, the less reliable she could be for him as she regularly reduced her available work hours.

Our economic system works best when workers are reinforced for their hard work—when work pays. Most Americans share a belief in work, but few would see the value in work if it did not offer some rewards, either personal or financial. Sandy's work did not offer much personal satisfaction. Rather, she worked because she believed that everyone played by the same rules. But when she discovered that AFDC recipients were subject to a different set of rules, her attitude shifted as well. She quit work and went on AFDC full time. It is not clear how long she would have stayed on welfare; her decision certainly was not supported by her family, even though they recognized her choice as rational. But she was able to collect a full AFDC grant for about nine months. Then when Kim turned three, Sandy's time on AFDC ran out.

Carrots and Sticks to Go Back to Work

Sandy got a letter from the welfare office requiring her to participate in the JOBS program. JOBS is a welfare-to-work program, jointly funded by the federal and state government.[13] Each state has a program with its own acronym—GAIN (CA), LEAP (OH), IMPACT (IN), REACH (NJ)—and all programs are regulated by the Family Support Act of 1988, which offers job training, education, on-the-job training, or help in finding and interviewing for a job. While women are in the program, they receive a small amount of money to buy books, tools, or uniforms; some modest transportation expenses; and child care for their children.[14] Although JOBS was created to offer women an opportunity to improve their skills, the program also serves as a public symbol of our impatience with AFDC recipients. Convinced that the average AFDC mother is not aware of the public's censure of her welfare use, JOBS provides both carrots and sticks to move welfare recipients in a particular direction.[15] Most important, JOBS provides a structured setting for the public's views on welfare use, as its rules and regulations are centered on influencing women to join the workforce.

As large numbers of women across the country have gone to work, it has become increasingly unacceptable for women on welfare not to work. The prevailing public sentiment is that mothers of children over the age of three (and sometimes younger) should work to help provide for their families if they have no other means of family support. Several research studies have traced this dramatic shift in the social landscape. For example, according to one study, in 1940, about 30 percent of American women worked in paid labor.[16] But today's estimates show that roughly 70 percent of women are either working or looking for work.[17] The most striking increases in female labor force participation are among women with children. In 1950, about 28 percent of married women with children over the age of six worked, rising to almost 70 percent in the late 1980s.[18] And in 1986, about half of all women with children under six were working, in contrast with only about 20 percent who worked in 1950.[19] What is most remarkable is that before 1950, the Bureau of Labor did not even collect statistics on the number of women with children under age one in the labor force. Today, about half of all women with infants are working.[20] Demographic changes such as these have, in part, driven the new philosophy of work for welfare recipients.

JOBS provides the setting to enforce this new philosophy. Lawmakers who designed the program certainly hoped that AFDC recipients would see their required participation in the program as a message that they were no longer welcome to use AFDC. Although many women understand this, Sandy was the first woman that I have met who took this recommendation quite seriously.

> The way society is now, most kids age three are going to day care, so it's no big deal. It's not the same as when I was growing up. [JOBS] was saying I had to get off [welfare]. I personally didn't see any way around the system—I'm sure there are ways—but I personally didn't see any way around. So the law pushed me to go out and get a job. Which was good, and I'm glad. And I think I was kind of ready in a way, and it kind of helped me in an odd way to get off of it. It was time to go out and get a job.

Sandy was eager to get a job as directed, but not all women are equally successful. And what is the real determination of success? If a woman gets a job, has she satisfied the public's demands concerning how she should spend her time? If she gets a job that pays more than her AFDC grant, has she gained more comfort? More stability? More safety? Or are we looking for something else—perhaps a job that will lift her and her family out of poverty? Unfortunately, the chances for this are slim. Sandy went to the Job Club classes provided at the beginning of the JOBS program, but her experience was frustrating:

> All the jobs that the EDD [Employment Development Department] worker had listed in the computer printout or in the paper started at $5.50 and $6.00 an hour, and I'm looking at her and going, "I can't make it on $5.50 and $6.00 an hour and I certainly only have one child, how can someone with three kids?" And some of them don't have any skills. How are you going to employ these people? Unless you're in a

Section 8 house[21] in the scummiest place on earth. How can I raise a child making $6.50 an hour? You can't do it. You have to go out making $7.50 or better, with benefits.

Many women in the JOBS program do find jobs. Finding a job that reduces their poverty, however, is a challenge. Work-incentive programs such as JOBS have been attempted in various states and localities for more than two decades. With each experiment, detailed evaluations are conducted at great expense to determine the cost savings to taxpayers and to assess the programs' relative effectiveness in reducing dependence on welfare.[22] Most evaluations indicate that such programs are somewhat costly to taxpayers, with the benefits materializing only slowly over several years. The benefits to the recipients are equally ambiguous. Although many get jobs, the economic well-being of these poor women and their children is rarely improved.

Sandy found work, but it was not enough to provide real security. In fact, it raised her just above the annual poverty rate (which in 1992 was $9,467 for a family of two),[23] but it scarcely paid enough to cover her basic expenses. When Sandy found her job, she became one of the growing numbers of working poor in America. According to one study, the number of working poor adults has increased by almost 60 percent since the late 1970s, which translates into about two million adults who work full time throughout the year.[24] The problems of the working poor are particularly vexing because in many cases they are doing the very best they can but are limited by their skills, their education, or the labor market from finding real economic security. Often the working poor find jobs that do not provide health insurance, and they also must struggle with day-care costs. At first, Sandy had the support of the government to ease the burden of working poor, but many are not so fortunate:

> I went to Job Club for two weeks at the EDD office. And they tell you how to get a job and you do a mock interview and you look through the paper. I found a job through Job Club, working at a bank, making $900 a month, gross, working 32 hours a week. I got benefits, but I had to pay for part of my benefits with my pay check, about $50.00.

Sandy jumped the hurdle that put her on AFDC in the first place, finding a job that provided health benefits for her and her daughter. But times had changed since she and her mother swapped babysitting, and she now needed day care. In a way, JOBS helped her with this problem—JOBS is supposed to pay for child care while women are training or looking for work. But the program also caused her a great deal of anxiety.

Moms Cannot Work Without Child Care

While you're in JOBS attending the orientation, your day care is paid for, and then you go to Job Club and your day care is still paid for. But then there's a break, and your day care isn't paid for. So if your day care isn't paid for between now and your next module, what are you supposed to do with your child? You don't want to lose the [day care] space, and you want to keep things as stable as possible for your child. And I just couldn't believe that.

I had found this preschool for Kim, and when I walked in I immediately loved it and Kim loved it. And so I just kept taking her. I told [my JOBS worker] I got a job, so I didn't need to go to the last couple of days of Job Club, but I just kept taking her, but there was another week or so until my job started, so I kept taking her so that she could get used to it. Well I don't remember how I found out, but then they told me it wasn't covered, so what am I supposed to do with my child in between? I mean, you guys want me to find a job so bad, but you're not going to help me? What is this? Is $200 that much or do you want me to stay on AFDC and pay me $560 a month? Which is it? Give me a break.

Sandy reluctantly asked her father to help pay the difference in her child-care bill until her "transitional child-care" benefits were activated. The help was welcome at the time, but the debt still hangs heavy in her mind.

Transitional child-care (TCC) and transitional Medicaid benefits are available to women who completely leave the welfare rolls because of their earnings from work. The benefits last for one year on the assumption that after a year of work, the women's income will be stable and they will be able to pay for these services on their own. Sandy remembered the JOBS worker's telling her that she would receive free child care once she got a full-time job, but she did not recall her saying anything about medical benefits. When Sandy told her EDD worker at Job Club that she had found a job, the worker also neglected to tell her that she was eligible for health or child-care benefits. Sandy's experience is not unusual. One recent study of the JOBS program found that most women who found jobs did not take advantage of these "transitional" benefits. When asked what they had been told about their availability, most of the respondents said that they could not remember being told about the benefits at all, that their AFDC worker had discouraged them from applying, or that they did not believe they were eligible for the benefits.[25]

Despite these problems, TCC is a great concept. It is one of the first changes in welfare policy to acknowledge the need for child care for low-income working mothers. But unfortunately, the benefit is restrictive as well. First, a woman has to be completely off aid before she is eligible. Most women who participate in programs such as JOBS can find work, but few such jobs pay enough to move women completely off welfare. Instead, women often work part time and so continue to receive a partial AFDC check. Once they are working, they no longer qualify for the JOBS program, so the child-care benefit they received when they were in JOBS disappears, yet they are also ineligible for TCC because they are not completely off aid. This dilemma is remarkably frustrating for women who are trying to do what they think is expected of them. Certainly women who work part time need child care, but these women receive the fewest benefits of all. Also, as indicated earlier, many low-paying jobs—whether part time or full time—do not provide health benefits, so many of these families must continue to receive partial AFDC payments.

TCC is considered generous by many because it provides a full twelve months of child-care benefits (in the early years of the California GAIN program, women received only three months of benefits), but the fact that it ends abruptly after a year is hardly "transitional." What about those women who do not get a raise within that period of time? Or what if the raise is so small that they are still unable to pay their child-care bill along with their other expenses? Sandy began to get very nervous as the end of her benefits grew near:

> I was [at the bank] eight months. They were getting rid of my position and they were looking for another place for me to go but then the day-care thing. . . . I had to be making more money and there wasn't really a position for me to go to. At $900 a month, with the possibility of being able to move up in that year, there was a possibility that I could make it. So it got hairy when there weren't any new positions open for me to be making enough money. So what am I going to do? My day care's going to run out.

Sandy started getting telephone calls from the welfare office informing her that her transitional benefits would soon be terminated.

> And I remember saying (to the woman on the phone), "Well, do you want me to get a job, or do you want me to stay on welfare? Don't make it so tough for me to work. Don't make it that hard."

I asked Sandy how the transition might have been made easier:

> I think there ought to be more subsidized day care because if you're taking a job that's only paying $5.50 an hour, one year of day care will be fine, but what are you supposed to do when the year's over? I was like, "What am I going to do at the end of the year? I can't afford

$100 a week!" So there either has to be more subsidized day care, or else there has to be another program that says in the second year, we'll help you with 50 percent of the costs so that gradually it's not like boom you're gone, and then there's nothing.

Sandy's comments are echoed by welfare recipients across the country. Many women turn to welfare in the first place simply because they cannot make it financially. Some need health insurance but cannot pay for it. Others want to work but cannot afford the child care. Rather than providing a lifeline for low-income families who are working, the system waits for women to come to the end of their tether, to deplete all their resources, and then to turn to AFDC. Once on AFDC, welfare does not provide enough to make ends meet and so continues the drain on women's personal resources. Combining AFDC with work is problematic, however. In fact, because AFDC regulations penalize women for maintaining a savings account for either themselves or their children, they never have the chance to catch up financially.

Despite these obstacles, the American public still encourages, badgers, and cajoles women to return to work. But if they do find a job, the system offers only a minimal, short-term safety net to assist them with the transition. And when women do not return to the workplace or when they continue to cling to a partial AFDC grant, we are often surprised and frustrated by their intransigence. Do these women have much choice? One study that examined women's transition from welfare to work described the transition as comparable to "being hurled off a cliff with nothing to cushion the impact."[26]

Because of the rules determining eligibility for support services, a very small increase in pay or in hours worked can translate into huge decreases in overall income. Sandy found this out when she was combining work with welfare and then again when she found a full-time job. Working can be a costly venture for a low-income mother. Day-care costs are almost unavoidable; health care is essential; and transportation and clothing costs rise, but our transitional benefits to help these women are inadequate at best.[27]

> When I was on [AFDC] and I wasn't working, I felt like what I was getting was fine. The hard time came when I was going from AFDC to a job, when the extra $50 for day care would have been wonderful to get me through or to pay for that two weeks [of day care] between my JOBS program. They make it so hard to make the transition. It's easier to get on and fill out the book [the welfare application] than it is to get off. And that's my big grief about the system. Like with the day care. The first year, let's go ahead and pay the day care, and then we understand that you're not able to get a raise, and if I kept that

same job and everything, then we'll help you. We'll pay 50 percent or have it so that they just pay the extra.

Sandy's suggestions are good ones, but they would be expensive to implement. They are based on the assumption that the American public and welfare administrators not only want women off welfare but that they also want them to be able to provide a better, more comfortable life for their children. That is quite an assumption. Welfare administrators have experimented with a variety of welfare-to-work programs such as JOBS. Some programs provide intensive (i.e., expensive), resource-rich services to enhance "human capital." Other programs provide low-cost services that emphasize immediate job placement. The former programs often result in somewhat higher earnings by welfare recipients, but the trade-off is great: Welfare departments need to spend a lot of money to bring women's abilities up to a level that will enable them to land a good job. The latter programs result in cost savings to the welfare department, but as stated earlier, although many of these women get jobs, few pay enough to get women fully off welfare or to raise their standard of living.[28]

Not surprisingly, political attitudes toward these various approaches tend to follow party lines. In the state of California, both the current and previous governors have encouraged short-term, low-cost job placement (i.e., Job Club) services for women participating in the JOBS program. Until the public sees the value of raising the standard of living for these women, Sandy's thoughts on the topic will probably be disregarded.

Working and Just Getting By

After her job at the bank, Sandy was offered a position as a bookkeeper in a small, family-owned firm. Although she has been with this job for about a year and a half now, it does not provide a great deal of security or comfort. If Sandy had relied on the job market for her position, she probably would not be as well off as she is. When she was working at the bank, a relative of Ben's felt sorry for her and offered her a position in his company. Because of the personal relationship she has with the owners of the company and their commitment to Kim as "family," Sandy has had an easier time than many other women have. She was offered a job in this company when she still had a couple of months of transitional child care left. Her employer gave her a higher wage ($7.25) than the $6.50 an hour she was making at the bank, plus full medical and dental benefits. When her transitional child care was terminated, her employer gave her a $0.25 raise, knowing that this, plus the additional hourly rate, would be just enough to pay her monthly child-care bill. Since then, Sandy has always managed to get a raise just when her expenses increased. When her roommate moved out, Sandy mentioned what a treat it would be to be able to afford a one-bedroom apartment. Shortly thereafter she received a small raise. When her car finally gave out, her mother bought her a new (used) car but asked Sandy to pay her back at $100 a month. At about the same time, Sandy found that she had another $0.25 an hour in her paycheck.

> They're very generous. I started out at $7.25, and then I went to $7.50, and that was within a month and a half. There was a time when . . . was it the day care or my car? I can remember talking to [one of the owners] and telling her how much I needed in order to make it work [financially] and then [the other owner] two weeks later gave it to me. He didn't even say anything. He always said he hoped that would help me. And then when I moved in from living with two people, he gave me a $0.25 raise and he said, "It's not much, but I hope this will help you." But $0.25 is an extra $40 a month! And then the secretary quit because we were laying off anyway. There were two of us in the office. When she left and I took her responsibilities, I went to $9.00 an hour.

Sandy knows exactly how much money she makes every week and plans meticulously how she will spend that money. When extra money comes in (such as child support), she views it as an unexpected pleasure. Every month she tries to save a little bit in case of an emergency, but she knows that she would quickly find herself in desperate straits if she lost this job. She does not worry about it, however, in the way that she did when she was using AFDC. Although Sandy has book-keeping skills and could interview as a receptionist or secretary, she also knows that it would be very difficult to find a similar job that pays as much. With unemployment currently at more than 9 percent across California, she might also have to look for a long time before she could find another job.[29]

Sandy currently makes about $17,000 a year. That is not a lot of money, but it is enough to get by. When I looked over her expenses with her, I calculated that she has about $100 to $200 to spare every month.[30] Most of that goes into a savings account that she uses for emergencies (such as new car tires or a new head gasket) or for an occasional vacation to an amusement park with Kim.

The tax rebate she gets every year also goes directly into savings. This year, Sandy got about $300 back from the government. The rebate she receives is called an Earned Income Tax Credit, or EITC. It works like this: Working poor families qualify for a credit that functions much like a wage subsidy. If a working parent has an income of between $7,500 and $11,850 per year, she will get a tax credit of $1,324. As her income rises, the amount of the credit diminishes until it reaches zero at $22,370. Families with two or more children get a larger maximum amount ($1,384), and families with children under age one receive an additional supplement of $376. (Another $451 is available for families who need to buy their own health insurance, assuming that the costs exceed that amount.)[31] The credit is "refundable." That is, if families pay no taxes because of their income bracket, their rebate will be refunded. Sandy could get the rebate monthly if she wished, but like most low-income parents who qualify for EITC, she takes her rebate once a year. Because she receives this rebate annually, she does not think about this part of her income when she calculates her budget every month.

Sandy has grown so accustomed to living on a limited budget that she has not yet shifted her thinking to accommodate the relatively new child-support payments she receives. Child support is a recent phenomenon for Sandy and Kim. It took five years, but it is the very least Ben can do after everything that has happened.

Make Him Pay

Like all welfare recipients, when Sandy applied for AFDC she was required to tell her welfare worker about Ben. The father's name, address, and place of employment were passed on to the district attorney so that he could be found and ordered to help pay a share of the AFDC costs through child support. Sandy had tried to get Ben to pay something toward the support of their child, but he had always shirked his responsibility. When the woman at welfare asked about Ben, Sandy was glad to oblige; it seemed only fair that he help out. Sandy told her exactly where he worked, when he usually was at home, and the names and addresses of all his friends and family members. Sandy had hoped that the district attorney's office would catch up with him right away, but a year later she still had not heard anything. Sandy then began calling the DA's office regularly to tell them about changes in Ben's address or his job, but still nothing happened.

> You need to sign these papers saying that you'll do everything in your power so they can find him. Well, he lived next door to me for months! I called them. I told them, these are the hours that he works. Do they serve him? No they don't. He was in jail for four months. I told them.

They didn't serve him. He spent a month at my apartment a while ago! I called them. I said, "He's here sleeping on my couch, will you please come and serve him?" I would tell them where he worked, what times he worked, every single thing that I knew about him. When you call you get the operator. You never get to talk to a district attorney. They switch them like they switch social workers. And I called the DA's office in January of last year, and I was getting really upset with the people on the phone, and I said, "He was in jail and I can't even believe that you didn't serve him!" I get a call back a month later. "I'm returning your call. . . ." and I had no idea who this person was, and he says, "Well, I'm from the DA's office." But at that point I had already started filing restraining orders and child custody with Legal Aid. And so he says, "Well, you don't want us to serve him?" And I said, "Well not now, thank you very much. I only waited five years for you to do it!"[32]

After five years, Sandy finally took the issue into her own hands and got a child-support order. Unfortunately, the circumstances surrounding the order were devastating for Sandy and Kim.

During the first few years of Kim's life, Ben was intermittently involved with the family. He showed up for birthday parties and holidays; sometimes he dropped by unannounced. During this whole period, Sandy remained emotionally tied to Ben; on some level, she still hoped that things would work out between the two of them and that they would eventually form a perfect, nuclear family. Ben's emotions during this time went from hot to cold, so it was no wonder Sandy's hopes were high. And Ben cared for Kim. He rarely did anything to support her financially, but he was always affectionate and playful. Sandy's naive hopefulness so clouded her vision that she was unable to see Ben clearly.

We used to talk about getting married. We talked about it a year ago . . . and then something happened. It was on Mother's Day. He did it on Mother's Day, that creep! He ruined my Mother's Day forever!!

Sandy is reluctant to talk about what happened between Ben and Kim. Maybe it happened once or perhaps several times, but it was Mother's Day, a year ago, when Kim cried as she divulged the dark secret about her father. Ben had molested his daughter.

He made her make a promise and she had to break the promise. Now she says, "Daddy's mad at me because I broke the promise," Sandy almost whispers. I say, "No, he's not mad at you. You know those are secrets you have to tell." Now she cries all the time saying, "I want my daddy." And I have to say, "Honey, I'm sorry," and then I go through the whole thing again about how he's got to do certain things and it takes a long time." It's been over a year. I say, "As soon as he gets something set up, you'll get to see him." It's getting to the point where it's been so long that she's thinking in her head all these scenarios—"Well, my daddy hasn't seen me because he's mad at me, because I made the promise and I broke my promise." This last year has been a hell of a year.[33]

The proceedings went very quickly. The police came and arrested him; Ben pleaded guilty; and he went directly to jail.

> He got a nine-year prison sentence, suspended. So he was actually sentenced six months and he served four. He's a first offender: nine years' state pen suspended, six months' county, and three years' probation. Probation is definitely three years, nothing shorter, so if he messes up on probation he still has that nine-year prison sentence hanging over his head.

As a condition for his release, Ben was required to attend therapy. He was assured by the judge that after his treatment he would be allowed to see Kim again, occasionally and always under the supervision of a probation officer. Until that time, he was banned from seeing her, talking with her, or communicating with her in writing.

Ben went to a therapist once and after that claimed to "forget" or be "too busy." Ben claims that he does not need the therapy. He does not know why he molested his daughter, and he does not know how it happened, but he claims that he will not ever do it again. He knows that what he did to Kim was wrong, but now that it is over, he pretends it never happened at all. Ben still calls and asks for Kim, although Sandy has to remind him of the court order and regularly threatens to call the police.

> It would be one thing if he had died; then she would know that he's not around and she can't see him. But she knows he's alive, and she knows I can see him and everybody else can see him but her.
>
> She's so little, she doesn't understand. She keeps asking, over and over, "How did they find out? Did you tell?" And I say, "No, I didn't tell. Mommy was feeling really sad and didn't know what to do so I went to talk to somebody and they said it was against the law and they had to tell, and the therapist called the cops."
>
> I've wanted to hit him. I've wanted to kill him. I've wanted to scream, "How could you do this!?" But what happened, happened, and she will remember it for the rest of her life.

In Sandy's view, nothing can make up for Ben's actions. His jail sentence helped, but only a little. Kim does not understand what happened to her or why, and now she feels utterly abandoned by her father, who has made no real effort to see her. Sandy does not understand how it all could have happened, either. She still struggles to justify her previous feelings about Ben with her recent emotions of pain and anger.

It was during this episode that Sandy became heavily involved with the courts. The Legal Aid Society helped her get the restraining order, and it also helped with custody—Sandy now has full legal and physical custody of Kim. In the midst of all the turmoil, Legal Aid suggested that she file for child support as well.

Now, beyond his brief jail sentence, Ben's only other penalty for his actions is a child-support payment—steeper than most. Getting child support was a coup for Sandy. Many women—some with more resources and clout—never see a check from their child's father. Of those fathers who do pay child support, the average monthly payment ranges from about $150 to $250 a month.[34] Until very recently, judges could order child support, but enforcement was very lax. Certainly in Sandy's case, the DA's office was not very enthusiastic about finding Ben.

But after the long battle, the child-support payments began, and getting that first check was a terrific moment:

> We had our hearing date on June 12 and they order it right then, and then they automatically attach wages and they serve his employer right away. I got my first $300 check on August 1. The only thing is I'm really leery about relying on it because he probably won't keep his job. But I saw that $300 child-support check and I went crazy. I bought a vacuum cleaner and I bought myself a new shirt and a dress and I bought Kim some new clothes and some things for the house. I didn't book a trip to Hawaii or anything, but I did buy. Next month I'll put it into savings.

Sandy's worries that Ben might quit his job are justified. Although Ben did nothing to support his daughter for the first five years of her life, his burden quickly became onerous. After he got out of jail, he had a job at a local convenience store making $6.50 an hour. The hours varied, and he usually worked only about twenty hours a week. Once the $300 was deducted along with his taxes, he had only about $150 to $200 remaining to cover his expenses. Sandy chuckled when she remarked, "He gets about $30 or $40 a week and I get the rest . . . so he works for me!"

Several months later Ben did lose his job. He was late too many times and could not be counted on for anything. Another job came up right away, but as soon as he lost the first job, Sandy's child-support payments stopped abruptly. Long after he was working again, she still did not get any money. The original child-support order was enforceable only on the first employer, and in order to continue payments, the new employer had to be served child-support orders as well. So again,

Sandy had to take time off from work to go back to the court house, get a copy of the original order, get it signed by a judge, and then hand deliver it to Ben's new employer.

Sandy quickly learned that although politicians often use the rhetoric of cracking down on "dead-beat dads," child-support regulations are actually very burdensome to mothers. In some ways, the laws reflect the fathers' attitudes—that these children are the mothers' financial responsibility and if women want financial help, they will have to go out of their way to get it. Under the current system, men are not especially encouraged to take responsibility for their children, and women are told, implicitly, that they must bear the full burden of finding support for their child.

After five years, the DA's office called Sandy one day to tell her that they would soon be contacting Ben for child-support payments. Sandy's response to the call was lukewarm.

> I told her I'd already started the papers. "If you want to go for back child support for the time I was on AFDC, be my guest, but I'm already milking him for everything he's got."

Sandy was wrong; there was still some money to be milked from Ben. Sandy was indeed getting her child support, but the reason for the DA's involvement in child support was to recoup welfare costs from the absent father. If the DA cannot regain those costs while the mother is on AFDC, he will recover them afterward. Ben was served his orders to pay back child support, and he will be paying off that debt for years.

> He [Ben] called me Monday. He got served his papers for what the county went after him for. It was $9,800. They are going to take out $175 a month, minimum. He's going to be left with about $10 a week.

At that rate, Ben will be paying off Sandy's welfare costs for the next five years of his life. And the DA's office really means business when it finally gets around to handling a case. Ben also received a lien notice for any property he might have. Had he owned a car or other valuable property, those might have been taken, too. I ask whether he won't just quit his job to duck the responsibility, but Ben is caught between a rock and a hard place.

> If he quits he goes to jail. He's on probation, so the condition of his probation is that he stay employed. He has to have some sort of job so that he can pay his bills. And if he gets fired, he's got to make sure that he's going to go out there and look for another job. And the county can charge him interest. Eighteen percent interest on the unpaid balance.

I ask how he is taking the news—after five years of complete freedom, the new arrangement must feel strange.

> He said it sucks. I said, "Well, it's child support, Ben. It's part of life. You have a kid, you have to pay child support. This money ain't supporting her." I said, "This is the money you didn't give me when you were supposed to be giving it to me." He's like, "Well, you're not getting the money." I said, "Well, look at it this way: The state paid me the child support you ought to have been paying me with welfare." But he's just all bent out of shape about it.

After five years, the child support is a help, but it is not as though Sandy had not tried all along to recoup some of the costs of raising Kim. A couple of years earlier Ben had owed his mother some money. They made a deal that he would give his mother his paychecks for a few months and she would deduct her loan amount, giving him the remainder. One month she took out an extra $500 and gave it directly to Sandy for child support—but that did not really help Sandy financially, and it certainly made Ben angry. Because Sandy was on AFDC at the time, she reported the money to the welfare department. The department applied the money to her AFDC grant and then gave her $50 as a "reward."[35] Actually, Sandy was not very bothered by the money part of it. It was the principle that most concerned her; it was only right that Ben pay to help support Kim.

At first, Sandy was not looking for a lot of money, but a little bit would have been nice. She would devise creative means of getting money out of Ben, but it was never very much.

> One time he had gotten into an accident and I had to go up and clean out his apartment and he had the Beatles records from way back when. So I stuck them in my room and then he wanted them, so I said, "Well, you pay me $100 for child support and you can have them." And it was the same thing with his stuff. He was storing a bunch of stuff over at my mom's house and he had just let it go. He has a tendency to just kind of forget it, or he knows it's there but he just doesn't want to do anything about it. It's part of his lack of responsibility. And so my mom wanted to get rid of it, so I went through the boxes and I got his stereo. His mother was having a garage sale and I took it up there and I sold it for $30 'cause I needed diapers. So he was mad 'cause there was a sticker on it that he had wanted. But I was like, "You didn't tell me." So I sold it and I went out and I bought diapers. One way or another, you can get money.

Sandy was right. Many women devise ingenious ways of getting a few dollars out of their child's father, but the money is not very much, and it usually does not come regularly. Imagine if we had to trick our employer to get a monthly paycheck or if our paycheck fluctuated madly. Some months we might be paid for going to work and some months we might not. When women stay home to raise their young children, they are indeed getting paid to work. Yet many women resign themselves to erratic child-support payments, thinking that if they get paid something, it will be a special favor. Those women who think that men can and should pay for the support of their children grow resentful when child-support payments are irregular. They also become frustrated when the state promises to find the father and then delays indefinitely. If the AFDC recipient wanted to hire a lawyer on her own to file child-support orders, she could do that, but the average mother on AFDC has barely enough money to put food on the table, and a lawyer would be very expensive. The Legal Aid agencies that are designed for low-income people generally do not handle child support —because it is the DA's responsibility—unless the order is tied to another legal proceeding such as child custody, or to a restraining order.

In many cases, once men finally start paying for their parenthood, they also want to take a more active role in raising their children. Ben actually contested Sandy's plea for sole physical and legal custody, thinking that if he had to pay for a role in Kim's life, he might as well play a role as well. (The judge turned down his plea.)

A man's delayed realization of his fatherhood can test a woman's patience. Although many writing about welfare have decried the breakup of families and have either implicitly or explicitly encouraged young women to marry their child's father, these views are often out of step with the mother's wishes.[36] Many women are content as single parents. Although their financial standing may be seriously compromised without the father's income,[37] the emotional stability of their lives may be enormously enhanced.

Securing a Future

Although Sandy has been getting her child-support payments for several months now, she is still extremely cautious about money. If she were to lose her job tomorrow and live on her savings, she would be about two paychecks away from AFDC. Because of that, Sandy tries earnestly to keep costs down. Her conservative approach to money is obvious in everything that she says. She is constantly aware of the cost of items, is selective about what she buys, and makes sure that Kim also knows that they live on a tight budget with little room for excess.

In a conversation over the dinner table, she notes the cost of milk, vegetables, or meat. When Kim asks for dessert, Sandy usually gives her a homemade popsicle, made out of frozen juice. Or when Kim has been given a new toy (usually by one of her grandparents), Sandy admonishes her to be careful with it, noting that the toy must have been "very expensive." Where Sandy lives, summer temperatures regularly reach 90 degrees, but she refuses to use the air conditioner.

> I have air conditioning and it's just too expensive to run, so I don't run it. I use the fan.

And in the winter, her attitude is similar. She makes sure that she and Kim are comfortable, but she is sparing with the heat and instead prefers to bundle up.

> You're always thinking about your expenses. There's no cream on top. Actually, now that I'm getting child support, there is some cream. I can buy her salami now, every once in a while, which is one of her favorite foods. That's expensive. I can every once in a while buy a steak or ice cream. Ice cream used to be a real luxury. Soda was a luxury. Cable TV. I used to not go out. To go out to a movie? Well, [try] to justify spending $7 for a movie, when you can just go down to the store and rent one. But the car insurance, the rent, the utilities, and the food were number one. I always kept those up. And then everything else came after that.

Sandy is raising Kim to be especially cautious about money. Because money is a regular topic of conversation in their household, as Kim grows older, she will have a healthy respect for what money can and cannot do:

> This evening we went to the grocery store and she was showing me this cereal, and I looked at it and I'd say, "Yeah, that looks like a really neat cereal, but that's not in our budget, we can't afford it. That's $4 for a box." So she knows that we usually buy things that go on sale. [When you're on a budget] you really have to plan. If I buy this week, then I'm not going to have money on the fifteenth for my phone bill, so I really can't buy it this week. You've really got to think about when the money's coming and when the bills are coming.

In so many ways, Sandy is trying her best to raise her daughter well. Kim is warm and loving toward her mother; she is a delightful little girl with an adorable giggle and a sweet smile. When Sandy puts her to bed at night, the two of them talk and laugh—they sound more like sisters than like a mother and daughter.

Sandy and Kim are a family. They represent the growing number of families that have been redefined by traditional standards. Sandy would love to be part of a two-parent family. She watched reruns of Ozzie and Harriet as a child, and that is her ideal.[38] But the American family is changing. The "traditional" family, which has two parents, only one of whom is working, now represents about 25 percent of all families.[39] Since the 1960s and 1970s, a new wave of redefined traditional family standards have been ushered in, and it will take a massive demographic and cultural shift like that seen twenty years ago to undo the family patterns that we see today.

Sandy is raising Kim alone, and she does the best she can. It would be nice if there were someone else to help out. Family members are there for some things, but they can do only so much. Ben is irresponsible and reckless; the most she will ever get from him is a few hundred dollars a month to feed and clothe their daughter. With limited help from family and only forced help from the child's father, how can a single mother raise her child? More important, how can she raise her child without inflicting the scars that are often the result of living in poverty?

Living in poverty is hard on children. Sandy and Kim weathered their episode on AFDC, but many children who survive poverty are not so lucky. AFDC lifts no child out of poverty in the United States, but it does provide one option, one buffer against the extremes of desperation, one transition until things can turn around. Welfare is not the answer to the problems of poverty; current welfare policy barely ameliorates the most extreme circumstances of living on the margin. But it is a safeguard for the most vulnerable members of our society. For Sandy, and most AFDC recipients, welfare is not a good solution, but it is a modest cushion for which they feel enormously indebted:

> I don't like the idea of being on welfare. It's not fun to report to the state every month. I made a mistake and got pregnant, but I wouldn't change being on welfare. It was an accident. I didn't plan it. If you're going to give me a year [of AFDC] then I'm going to be grateful for a year. But it was a mistake. I know it's not the taxpayer's fault, but should my daughter have to suffer? It's not something I really regret, and sure I think about what my life would have been like if I hadn't gotten pregnant, but I couldn't not [have Kim] [she pauses]. How could you look at her and trade her for anything?

4

Rebecca: Motivation and a Fighting Spirit

The kitchen is a mad rush of activity. There are noodles everywhere. The red pin-wheel noodles are laid out on paper towels on the kitchen table. Green mostocolli cover an old tea towel on top of the stove. Blue elbow macaroni are lying in a strainer on the kitchen counter, and Rebecca is standing over the sink with a bowl of orange ribbon pasta. She has pulled her shirt sleeves up and her hair is tied back, but her apron is splashed with colors and her arms and hands have turned a strange maroon with each successive layer of food dye. "Tanya's having a friend over tonight, so I thought they would have fun making noodle jewelry."

Tanya, age six, is Rebecca's first priority; she is the center. Although Rebecca gave birth to Tanya, perhaps it is the other way around: Rebecca came alive when she became a mother, and now she is working as hard as she can to make a comfortable, stable home for her daughter.

Rebecca is a twenty-three-year-old Caucasian woman, about five feet tall, a little stocky, and full of energy.[1] Her face is long and full, with freckles spread across her nose and cheeks. Her dark eyes are circled with thick lashes, giving the appearance of eager wonder.

Rebecca never really relaxes but is on alert all the time, sitting at the edge of her chair. She is strong willed and has definite views about most things, from politics to parenting. She is easily irritated by signs of lethargy and has no patience for people with little ambition. Rebecca wants to become a schoolteacher, and she will be a good one. She is driven, she is motivated, and she is determined to succeed. But the woman I am describing here was not always like this. Friends from her adolescent years probably would not recognize her now. From an irresponsible and almost hopeless teen, she has grown into a pleasant, fairly dependable young woman.

Not Makin' It

Rebecca was a decent student in elementary school. She was well behaved and regularly turned in her homework. She had a few problems that required extra supervision, but nothing particularly out of the ordinary. It was the critical transition from elementary school to junior high that brought about some of the early problems. Many of her former friends were placed in another local junior high, and Rebecca had to find a whole new set of allies. Her mother says that she cast about for months before she finally found her niche. Unfortunately, Rebecca landed in the "wrong" crowd.

> That's when I started smoking cigarettes, smoking weed, but I don't think I was drinking that much then, and I don't know how I went on to the ninth grade. That's really when I stopped learning anything at all. I really stopped going to school most of the time. And I would get in trouble all the time. I don't even remember going to many classes there. I got suspended all the time. All the time. [The school] was just so big, and it was rough. You could do things and the teachers don't really know you that well, so you could just do things. And I would do a lot of things there like I would cuss the teachers out to impress the other kids in the class. And I knew I could cuss them out and they couldn't beat me up, so that was the perfect thing to do, and then it would show that I was really cool, too. I used to do that. I can't believe it now.

School officials attempted to turn Rebecca around with discipline and punishment. Her mother was often angry with her and tried to shame her into better behavior. At the time, Rebecca only remembers one teacher who made a positive impression on her.

> Mrs. Burke. I liked her. She knew all of her students and she was just really . . . she cared more than the other people did.

But the transition to high school was not any easier for Rebecca.

> I went there for the first quarter and I would get A's and B's, just to prove to myself that I could do it, and then I would stop going. I did that every year. I just wouldn't go. I think I was bored and I think that there was just no reason to be there. I had no idea why I was there, what it was for.

Looking back, Rebecca is amazed at the sheer absence of thought that characterized her daily life. She never thought about the future; she never thought about her behavior. She did not care what happened or what anyone thought about her. Each time when we spoke and I asked her about that period of her life she would answer, "I don't know what I was thinking." Rebecca is now so different from her former self that she often seems to be speaking in the third person. And she is not the best informant about her history because she no longer knows who that person was "back then."

Part of the reason she remembers so little about that period of her life may be because of her heavy drug use. Rebecca began using drugs when she was about twelve years old; in some ways, her development was suspended at that age level and did not progress until she got off drugs. One day she was sitting in class and began to think about the purpose of high school. Her comments resemble those of a young child:

> So why am I here? I was just trying to figure it out. I thought about it for a couple of days because I really could not figure it out, and then finally I realized that I was here to learn! It was like a big revelation. I didn't think about college or anything. I thought that I would just grow up and I would just know everything. I thought when I reach a certain age then automatically I would just know things. But I never knew that you actually had to study to learn things.

Although Rebecca was sent to the school counselor and then the school psychologist, that merely made her more hostile. The one teacher that had any influence on her was the one who made her work hard, cared about her, and had high expectations for her work.

> But he told us that he wouldn't be teaching again for anybody except seniors. So he told us that one day and then the next day I just never went back to class. I regret that.

Rebecca has disdain in her voice when she talks about the other teachers who gave good grades for little work. There is no telling what would have turned things around for her at the time, but higher expectations might have helped. Her mother says that she was "smart" but that she lacked "certain skills." Rebecca was always being told that she had trouble with reading, yet as an adult she reads very well and has no unusual deficiencies. Or perhaps help came too late. Rebecca took part in a Youth Corps program, funded primarily with state and local funds, during two of her summers in high school. She worked in specially designed summer jobs that were intended to give her good work skills and keep her in school. She thought both of the jobs were "fun," but at the time, she completely missed the point of the programs.

Rebecca grew more irresponsible, more self-destructive, and increasingly uncontrollable for school officials and her parents. She was drinking heavily, doing drugs, and quickly dropping out of society. Her reckless behavior culminated with Marty. At age sixteen, Rebecca met a twenty-three-year-old drug dealer and crack addict, Marty, an African American man living in the ghetto who picked up Rebecca at a party.

Lousy Odds for a Decent Future

In recent years the United States has had the highest teen fertility rates of any industrialized country. In 1981, there were ninety-six pregnancies per one thousand girls (ages fifteen through nineteen) in the United States. Although the rate of teen births appeared to decline during the 1970s and early 1980s, the adolescent birthrate began to rise again a few years ago. Now, each year, about one out of every seventeen teenage girls in the United States gives birth.[2] In other countries with comparable rates of sexual activity, the rates of teenage pregnancy are much lower. For example, the pregnancy rates of Great Britain, France, and Canada are about half the United States', and Sweden's is about a third.[3]

In addition, despite the fear of AIDS and sexually transmitted diseases, few teenagers practice safe sex. One study found that fewer than half of sexually active teenagers use any form of contraception. And contrary to popular opinion, many of these girls' sexual partners are not teenage boys. Rather, they often become involved with older men who father their children.[4]

> He was twenty-three and I was sixteen, and I had Tanya a month before I was seventeen.
>
> I ask, "Were you trying to get pregnant?"
>
> "No."
>
> "Was it an accident?"
>
> "No, but he was like, "I can't have babies. Nobody's pregnant yet." And I didn't really care. I don't know. I guess I wasn't trying to, but I wasn't trying not to. I don't know what I was thinking about then. I didn't plan anything then.

Marty's cavalier attitude toward pregnancy was not uncommon. Most of the women in this study readily acknowledged that the father of their child had assured them they were sterile. This pattern was clarified by Andrew Hacker, who pointed out that poor men—often African American—are eager to have a child as an affirmation of their manhood. In low-income communities in which men have few other opportunities for public approbation, fathering a child becomes an important reference point for their recognition.[5] And perhaps many men have a sense that they will be able to support the child, although the vast majority are either unable or unwilling to take responsibility for the baby's growth and development once it arrives.[6]

Despite Marty's assurances, however, Rebecca found herself pregnant, dropping out of school, and completely unaware of what the future might bring. "Wasn't it scary?" I asked.

Sometimes. Sometimes I would wake up at night and I was like, "What am I doing?" But then there was always something inside of me that was saying, "Just do this." I would think about it and wonder what I was doing, but there was no chance I wasn't going to do it.

Rebecca moved out of the house and got an apartment with Marty. The odds to do well were not in Rebecca's favor. Although she had no way of supporting herself, she was intent on keeping the baby. Babies slow women down, keeping many from realizing their economic potential and can hamper their educational achievement.[7] But even though the birth of a child can bring powerful negative forces into a woman's life, that birth can also be both life changing and life giving. After she became pregnant, Rebecca began to make the gradual change toward adulthood. On some level, something changed; her pregnancy ushered in an internal, personal commitment to life.

Beating the Odds

Teen mothers often drop out of school; about half of all school-age parents never finish high school. Without a high school diploma, a woman's earning potential also plummets. Teen mothers earn about half the income of other mothers who postpone childbearing. Some of the teens marry, but few have lasting marriages, so they often cannot count on a second earner in the home. Without their own or another's income, many are forced to turn to AFDC. Indeed, more than half of all school-age mothers will receive AFDC at some point in their lives,[8] and these are the women at greatest risk for long-term dependence on welfare.[9]

With these odds, it was no wonder that Rebecca's mother was worried. And since Rebecca was experiencing so many other problems in her life, her mother felt she was doomed. Her daughter's pregnancy so distressed her that she did everything in her power to try to persuade Rebecca to abort the baby or give it up for adoption.

> She was going to try everything to get me to give up the baby. She paid my rent for the first two months, still hoping in those first two months . . . she was like, "I'll get you an apartment. You don't have to get pregnant to leave." Then she took me to Europe! I was pregnant and it was horrible. I was sick the whole time. And she was like, "I'll buy you this stuff," and she didn't have a lot of money. We had a house and she sold it and that's where she got the money to take me to Europe!

Rebecca saw in Europe what she might be missing, but her resolve only intensified. She stopped using drugs and decided to finish high school.

> [I stopped using drugs because] I guess for the first time I had a rea-
> son to. I had something inside of me that was alive.

She enrolled in the local public high school for pregnant teenagers and finished school. She took regular classes such as English and math, but she also took a class on health, nutrition, childbirth, and parenting. After a few months she gave birth to Tanya. From that moment on, everything changed.

> When my daughter was born, it was just kind of a regrowing—just
> starting over in a way. If I didn't have her, I think I'd be on crack right
> now. I have very little doubt that I would.

I have very little doubt, too. Many of Rebecca's friends from high school are on crack and have essentially dropped out; that is, they dropped out of high school, and then they dropped out of society.

Luckily for Rebecca, Marty went to jail about a week before Tanya was born.

> That made it easier. When I lived with Marty that was depressing. We
> were fighting all the time. He thought of the baby as ours and I thought
> of her as mine. So that was different. And we talked about the things
> that he would do with her, but I don't think he really meant it. He
> would go through phases of being in and out of jail. For a while he
> was calling us all the time, and I don't think that's good for Tanya.
> Like when he first got out, he got her that Nintendo, and then he just
> gets back into smoking [crack] and then kind of loses touch. The last
> time he came out, Tanya really didn't want to see him or talk to him.
> It was hard. But right when she was born he went to jail. It was a week
> before. And then he was in jail for a year.

Marty's absence removed one of the obstacles to Rebecca's ultimate independence and to her remaining drug free, but it also left her without financial support. Rebecca turned to AFDC for help, and she spent the next two years growing up. It sounds strange, but that is exactly what the American public was paying for with those welfare dollars every month. Rebecca was essentially a twelve-year-old girl in an eighteen-year-old body who began to discover the world for the first time. She explored the world with Tanya and she found it very exciting.

They went to the park every day, and Rebecca began naming the world for her daughter. When Rebecca came across something she did not know, it suddenly mattered to her to find out about it. Tanya was eager to learn. She squealed with delight when she saw a flower, a fish, or another child in the park, and her enthusiasm was contagious. Rebecca felt the weight of her responsibility to raise Tanya well and to teach her about the world.

By the time Tanya was twelve months she used to get fascinated by things. So her first one was maps. There was this map and globe store. We used to take the bus and she would get all excited on the bus saying, "Maps, globes," and so we'd go in there and it would be better than a toy store! And my mother had this book on Turkey and it would have this one map on this page and she would just look at it and say, "Maps." I actually got her an atlas and I used to bribe her with, "Come on, we'll go home and we'll look at the maps," just to get her home. And then she got interested in pendulums, from the pendulum at the aquarium. And I didn't know what a pendulum was at the time. So she must have been about two, so then we'd talk about pendulums. I would get books, and I'd set up these little blocks in a circle and take a string and tie something to it and swing it back and forth. She would love that. I don't think she got it at all, but it was real fun. . . .

You know, you asked me how I've changed since I was seventeen and just . . . well, in every way. I'm responsible now. I do things. I'm interested in things. I don't mind working. And I think that was Tanya. Because I just watched her. That's why I say that I might want to have her again if I had to do it over, 'cause I just watched her explore everything and it was just . . . what better way to learn about human nature. You can learn so much, especially if you have the time. It makes you want to know things.

Most people do not believe that bearing a child as a teenager can bring much of anything except trouble, and in general, teenage parenthood should be avoided. But for Rebecca, having a baby turned things around. She spent those first two years focused almost exclusively on Tanya. Then after Tanya turned two, Rebecca decided it was time to turn her attention to herself. She enrolled in the local community college and started taking general education classes for an AA degree.[10] Rebecca had decided that she was going to become a teacher. It is clear that Tanya was her inspiration. She loved teaching Tanya, and she found it easy. She realized that she enjoyed learning, and if she could find creative ways of teaching, young children might have a better start in life than she did.

Rebecca's experience in community college was affirming. She got A's in almost all of her classes, and her teachers were very supportive. She was really starting from scratch when she enrolled in school, and so she had to learn, for the first time, how to be a student.

That first semester that I went back I had Mr. Garlan for writing, and that was great. And then I took a psych class and [the teacher] was great. I studied so much. I really studied. When I first started, every chapter we had to read—I read it three times. Because I was just going back to school and I didn't know. But I got all A's. What I learned that first semester; well, first of all I got confidence from that writing teacher, because I never had any idea that I could write. And then also from that psychology teacher because she was real clear. Her notes were real clear. And also I learned how to study. So now, like in biology, I didn't have to read the chapters three times because I already knew what I needed to get out of it. I just studied all the time that first semester. My mother told me that the best way to learn is to skim it once, then read it a second time and then read it again. Read it pretty thoroughly, and then skim it again. After a while I only read it twice, but most of the time I read it three times. And I did my first research paper that first semester, too. It was on the effects of child care on infants, and I got an A+ on it.

'Cause I didn't think I could do it. I had no idea. I knew I was going to [go back to school]. People were telling me that maybe I should teach, and then I started working at Tanya's preschool, so I said, "Maybe that's what I'll do." I always knew I would go back to school, but I didn't know what I would do. I just wanted to wait until Tanya was old enough.

It took Rebecca three years to finish her general education requirements. That is longer than the two years a full-time student might take, but considering that she had a young daughter, that she dropped out for a semester because of illness, and that she was also working part time, her progress was excellent. Her grades were so good that she came to the attention of a recruiter at a local private college and was offered scholarships and loans. The $15,000 annual tuition scared her off, however. Instead, Rebecca decided to attend a public state college to finish her B.A. and enrolled when Tanya was about five. Since then, the pace has been hectic.

I just want to hurry up, because I was helping my friend do this paper on teen pregnancy and there were all these studies saying that [teen parents] don't graduate college and get their B.A. by the time they're twenty-five. But I'll be twenty-five next year and I want to have my B.A. But I worry about Tanya. I feel like I'm studying a lot and one of my tutors was always saying, "Go to the private college," and I said, "No, because the most important thing is Tanya and I have to have time to pay attention to her, and if I have to work that hard, then I'll be forgetting what was important to me in the first place." Trying to balance homework with taking care of her is hard. Plus I think I should get A's. I always said that her [Tanya's] development was more important than what grade I get, but sometimes I have to remember to just slow down. It's hard to balance that, and I don't want to turn on the TV and have her just watch. It was easier when she was younger because she'd go to sleep at about 7:00 [in the evening] and I was working at her school, so I'd be with her all through the afternoon, so

I didn't have the same kind of guilt. But I want to just make her more the center—pay more attention to her education and to her.

Rebecca is right—balancing home, children, school, and work is challenging. There is always a trade-off, and sometimes the compromise is difficult. Most studies show that when women turn their primary focus away from parenting to other activities such as working or going to school, they quickly give up a significant amount of leisure time, and they also lose sleep.[11]

Rebecca has to contend with these same issues. Last semester she took fifteen units—a full course load—at the state college. Now she cleans her apartment only on the weekends, and meals are very simple. These are some of the corners she can cut without too much guilt. For her time away from Tanya, however, she pays an emotional price: Time spent away from Tanya feels like a retreat from her responsibility as a mother.[12]

Getting by on Welfare

While she goes to school, Rebecca uses welfare. How else would she get by? AFDC has been her lifeline. It has not provided a comfortable existence, but it has made things easier. In the first couple of years, welfare gave Rebecca the opportunity to raise her child and be a full-time parent. The investment was worth it. She flung herself into the role and provided an excellent foundation for Tanya. After that, she beat the odds of other teenage parents by enrolling in a community college and then a state college. Again the investment was a good one. The fact that she had financial assistance to help get her there is all the more important. Most Americans generally think that an investment in financial aid and college grants is money well spent. The earning potential of college graduates far exceeds that of high school graduates (not to mention dropouts as Rebecca might have been), and their taxes contribute to public services for all. Rebecca received both AFDC and financial aid. She represents one of a growing number of women enrolled in college in the United States while receiving public assistance. This year she will receive $3,585 in financial aid and $1,500 in loans; this, in addition to the AFDC, enables her (and Tanya) to lead a more comfortable life, but it is hardly luxurious. She may scrape by with an income just above the poverty line, but her expenses are high.

Rebecca's monthly rent is $500. She lives in a one-bedroom apartment and receives no public housing subsidy. Nationally, about 18 percent of AFDC recipients live in publicly subsidized housing.[13] In California this figure is much lower. About 12 percent of welfare recipients (all of whom live in poverty, by definition) receive housing assistance in the form of a housing voucher or a public housing apartment.[14] In Rebecca's case, she has watched her rent increase annually while her AFDC payment has been cut every year for the past three years.

> First I lived in a studio, and when I moved there it was $340. By the time I left it was $425. That was over four years. It was about $25 more a year. This place was supposed to be $475, but they said because there were two people living here . . . they wanted a reason, because first they said it was an extra $25 for a parking space, which I should have took but I didn't, so then they just said it's because there are two of you.

Rebecca's rent is not especially high for the area. According to the U.S. Department of Housing and Urban Development, California has the highest rents in the country, the average rent for a one-bedroom apartment in her city being $640 per month.[15] If Rebecca were extravagant, she would spend about $800 for a two-bedroom apartment,[16] but that would be well beyond her means. As it is, Rebecca's rent eats up 99 percent of her AFDC grant, and for that she has no space she can call her own.

When they lived in the studio, Rebecca and Tanya slept in the same bedroom. Now that Tanya is older, Rebecca feels that she should have her privacy. And indeed she does. Tanya's room is as large as the living room and part of the dining area combined. She clearly has the largest, most private space in the apartment, and she fills it completely. The walls are covered with bright posters, and the bed is a rumpled mess of pillows, stuffed animals, and bedding. Her room looks like a child's sanctuary with toys and books everywhere. But Rebecca is not as fortunate; her bedroom doubles as the living room. The couch pulls out into a bed, so her private space is also a public, family space. For now, this is probably the best she can do for the money.

With rent costing $500 a month, there is not much room to negotiate financially. I did a monthly budget with Rebecca and came up with the figures listed in the following table.

Certain numbers stand out in Rebecca's budget. On the expense side, her food bill is high. The average U.S. food stamp payment is based on the assumption that each family member in a household needs about $0.92 per meal, per day.[17] Critics of the food stamps program, however, argue that this amount is unrealistic for most families.[18] If Rebecca received a full food stamp allotment, it would equal about $171 per month in food costs. Rebecca admits that if she spent more time cut-

Rebecca: Motivation and a Fighting Spirit

Income		Expenses	
AFDC	$504	Rent	$500
Food stamps	$ 10	Food	$300
Child support	$ 0	Gas and Electric	$ 40
Financial Aid	$398	Telephone	$ 40
Loans	$166	Tanya's school	$100
Work	$100	Gas	$100
Work study	$200	Laundry	$ 30
		School supplies	$ 83
		Cleaning supplies	$ 10
		Tuition	$158
		Cigarettes	$ 75
		Entertainment	$175
Total	$1378	Total	$1611

ting coupons and planned meals more carefully, her food bill would be lower. But again, she does not feel able to make this trade-off with her time. Her days are already full, and she feels that she compromises time with Tanya just to manage the demands of school. Instead of $171 per month, Rebecca's food stamp allotment is actually $10. Food stamp payments are based on a series of calculations that include other income such as AFDC, financial aid, and work; as one's income rises, food stamps usually fall. The amount Rebecca is granted is so small that she often does not even bother to claim it. With all the other things filling up her life, it has not been worth the time.

In addition to her household expenses, Rebecca also pays for a private school for Tanya. This may seem strange, like a luxury for a welfare recipient to send her child to private school, but Rebecca has very strong feelings about education. She has a sense that the public schools failed her as a child, and she wants something better for her daughter. Given the community she lives in, Rebecca's concerns are well founded. The local school district is notorious for low test scores, overcrowded schools, demoralized teachers, and campus violence. Drug use is rampant, and the dropout rate begins to soar in junior high rather than high school.[19]

Although Rebecca's decision makes sense, it is expensive. Tuition for the school plus an hour of after-school care is $425 per month. Obviously Rebecca cannot afford that, but she has been very fortunate in the generosity she has received from the school staff. Each month she is given a $200 scholarship. Her mother also pitches in another $125. Then Rebecca trades work for money. She is respon-

75

sible for $100 each month, and so the school employs her to help out in the classrooms or in the office. Some months she cannot pay anything, so she spends more time at the school. Other months she pays what she can and continues to put in her time. Time is a commodity for Rebecca—it is the only thing she can trade, since she cannot buy services. Of course, this puts another strain on her time, another monthly worry, but Rebecca usually does not have enough cash to support her decision about Tanya's school.

Rebecca works hard and she tries to keep up with everything, but in some things you can see the shadows of her former self. The change in her character is neither miraculous nor total. Rebecca is a complex woman. Physically she is twenty-three, but developmentally she is only about eighteen. Each day she struggles to combine the careless attitudes of her youth with the more prudent beliefs she has adopted in adulthood. She is a young woman with high ideals, mixed with a perspective carried over from her past.

Rebecca gets A's and B's in college, loves to engage in political debate, and prefers documentaries to other kinds of TV shows, yet she surrounds herself with people who rarely share her interests. All her friends are low-income men and women who have had trouble with the law or with drugs. She knows that she has undergone some kind of character change, but she is unable to describe it. Rebecca is a matter-of-fact kind of person whose goal is to get through each day and on to the next. She does not spend time thinking about the meaning of her behavior, and she is not particularly reflective about the choices she makes in her life.

For example, a couple of years ago, Rebecca started dating a man named Derek. He had little to recommend him except for a warm smile and complete admiration for Rebecca's accomplishments. Tanya took an immediate dislike to the man. Part of it was jealousy, but Tanya was also aware of Derek's inadequacies as her mother's mate. Tanya hated it when Derek smoked, she hated it when he turned on music during a dinner conversation, and she felt neglected when he did not praise her artwork or her reading. Rebecca also knew that Derek was not good for her. He was a recovering crack addict who had spent his adolescence in and out of jail. He had trouble holding a steady job, and Rebecca was constantly frustrated with his indolence.

> He has a good sense of humor, and we get along pretty well. And he's real sensitive and sweet and he really makes an effort to try to be good with Tanya. And I like that he tries to do well in school and that he's really making an effort, but he doesn't try hard enough for me. It

annoys me that he doesn't take that extra initiative. He's not real interested in the things that I like. I like to watch documentaries and *Inside Washington*, every political show that comes on. And he wants to watch *Starsky and Hutch*!

When I asked her to speculate why they were still together, Rebecca would shrug her shoulders. I imagine that after a lifetime of feeling inadequate, she enjoys the sensation of feeling superior to the people around her. By Derek's standards, Rebecca has accomplished a great deal. Now she uses Derek and her other friends as a constant reminder of how far she has come. She also seems to feel more comfortable with them than with most of her classmates in college. Rebecca is filled with strange contradictions: Sometimes she appears comfortable with her new role as a college student, but often she still behaves much as she did in high school.

For example, when she talks about her obligation to work at Tanya's school, she often remarks, "Well, I haven't gotten there yet this month" or "I really need to find some time to get there." As a pattern develops and no one at the school enforces her obligation, Rebecca becomes less and less compelled to do anything. Sometimes she talks as though there is a secret understanding that her child's scholarship really amounts to $300 a month instead of $200. Her mother tries to enforce her moral obligations by occasionally refusing to pay anything toward Tanya's tuition; then Rebecca has to scramble to come up with more cash or spend more time at the school.

For Rebecca, coping—economically and emotionally—as she maintains her various roles of mother, student, and part-time worker is a delicate balancing act. A survival strategy she has developed over the past six years is ignoring her commitments when things threaten to overwhelm her. As in the case with her obligation to work at Tanya's school, when Rebecca finds it impossible to perform certain duties, she simply ignores them and hopes that they will go away.

She applies this strategy to the problem of car insurance. Driving with car insurance would cost Rebecca about $200 a month—obviously an amount she could not pay. Not driving a car would mean not having transportation to Tanya's school and to her college classes. Rebecca is a determined young woman. She plows ahead, eyes fixed on her goal of becoming a teacher and a self-sufficient provider for herself and her child. And so she drives without insurance, overlooking the danger.

In addition, Rebecca has credit card problems. In some ways, this seems peculiar, for she has never been well off; she did not slide from the middle class into poverty. So how did she ever obtain a credit card in the first place? Her naïveté was partly to blame. Rebecca never had a course in finance. She was never told how credit cards work and how to use them correctly. She did not know about the high interest rates or how a minimum payment on several credit cards could rapidly get out of hand. But as a community college student, she was approached by a number of credit card companies offering her instant credit without a background check and without any collateral. Rebecca did not know that credit cards were so easy to get.

> They come to [the college] and they give you these credit cards! And of course you're going to take them. But now the [bill collectors] are always calling me. I had Macy's, I had a Visa, Capwells, and then I got Furniture 2000 and that was a big mistake. I got that furniture (she points to the living room set). So I told them, "Come take the furniture if you want. . . . I can't pay for it." It was stupid of me. I thought I'd be able to pay it back, but I just recently stopped paying and now [the bill collectors] are driving me crazy. They had stopped for a while, and now they started again. It's like they go in sprees, and all of them get together and call. It's irritating and it's funny because they say, "Well, we're going to sue you." I'm like, "If I had something for you to sue for, don't you think I would pay you? I would pay you then!" I've been thinking about doing bankruptcy, but I don't know. What am I going to say? How do I explain?

Rebecca is in a bind. She realizes her error, but now that she has made it, she does not have enough money to make the monthly payments. She tried for a while, and then it became overwhelming to her. As usual, she ignored the problem, and now the bill collectors are trying their best to remind her of her obligation.

Surprisingly, the default on her credit does not get in the way of her obtaining new loans for school. Rebecca has taken out over $10,000 in school loans so far, and she has another couple of years of school left. By the time she has finished, she will probably owe about $15,000 there as well. Luckily her attitude toward school loans is better. She hopes that one or two of them might be forgiven, since she plans on working in the inner-city schools after graduation. But she also expects to be paying them off for the rest of her life if she must, because that is a contractual agreement she feels obligated to keep.

Rebecca cannot afford the credit card payments, and she cannot afford car insurance. Her monthly expenses total about $1,600 each month, and her income amounts only to about $1,400. Part of this difference is usually made up by her mother, who pays her telephone bill (since most of Rebecca's calls are to her mother, who lives about thirty miles away) and for her gasoline.[20]

When I last saw Rebecca, she was very worried about Tanya's teeth. She had recently taken her to the dentist and was told that Tanya badly needed braces to correct some of her dental problems. Braces will cost about $1,500, and Rebecca has no idea how she can pay for them. First, there are few dentists in her county that take Medicaid patients, and then Medicaid has been cut back so severely in recent years that orthodontics is almost never covered. Rebecca asked her mother to help with the cost, but her mother has nothing left to give; other family members are strapped as well. Incidentals such as these—financial problems that even most middle-class parents find difficult to cope with—are a nightmare for women like Rebecca.

Things would be easier, of course if Marty helped her support Tanya. But on the income side of Rebecca's monthly balance, there is a notable absence of child support. This is not unusual. Child-support payments are notoriously irregular in the United States. Only about 44 percent of all middle-class women receive any child support from the absent father, so not surprisingly, the figures for low-income and never-married mothers are even worse. Only about 11 percent of never-married women receive any child support at all from the father in a given year.[21] This includes men who pay regularly and those whose payments are erratic and minimal.

Rebecca is not sure where Marty is today. He is probably either in jail or on his way back, so in any case, his child-support potential is very low. Even when he was out of jail, he was not a good provider. He tried to support Rebecca when they were first together, but as she observed,

> He helped [financially], but he sold drugs. So, [he helped] a little bit, but he smoked them too, so there wasn't a lot of money.

Rebecca is not particularly disturbed by Marty's absence. In her mind, the less he pays, the less claim he has to their daughter. Not that he asserts his parenthood very often or very loudly, but Rebecca thinks of Tanya as her daughter alone, and the less Marty has to do with her child, the happier she is. Marty is like a bad dream for Rebecca, one of many memories she would rather forget.

Since Rebecca receives no assistance from Marty, financial aid and her school loans help pay the bills. In addition, she works at the college. Rebecca has been working since Tanya was about nine months old. At first she babysat on weekends and in the evenings. Then she began watching one or two children all day long when their parents went to work or school. When one of the little girls she was caring for started attending a preschool in the mornings, Tanya asked if she could go, too. This is when Rebecca decided to return to school, taking classes in the morning and watching the girls in the afternoons.

During her second semester, Rebecca did not work. It was a luxury in terms of her time but a hardship financially. She remembers going to school in the morning, picking up Tanya at her preschool about noon, and then studying and playing with Tanya for the rest of the day. But because Rebecca was not able to pay her bills, she went back to work. She was hired at her daughter's preschool, where she was paid about $8.50 an hour. At first she worked two days a week, but soon this increased to four. Throughout this period, Rebecca was paid under the table.

Both the child-care business and the house-cleaning industry are lifesavers for welfare recipients. Jobs are plentiful. Women are usually paid with cash or a check, so their income is rarely reported to the IRS (and thus the money is easily hidden from the welfare office). Employers like the arrangement because they do not have to worry about deducting taxes or paying Social Security.[22] They also do not have to abide by fair-employment practices, and their liability, in case something happens on the job, is almost nonexistent. Obviously these benefits to the employer can become real abuses for the AFDC recipient. Women generally do not receive benefits such as medical insurance, paid holidays, or sick leave. Although by working under the table, women maximize their current income, neither they nor their employer pays anything into the Social Security system. Then when these women grow older, they cannot collect Social Security, since that system is based on previously reported earnings.[23]

The worst feature of working under the table, however, is the element of risk. Women live in fear of being found out. They fear the unhappy employer who reports their work to the welfare office, or they fear that something in their manner will give them away to their welfare worker.

Like so many other welfare recipients, Rebecca is committing welfare fraud. The fraud itself is not unusual; it is the degree that varies. Every year some woman on welfare makes headlines for cheating taxpayers on a grand scale. Certainly, when a welfare recipient is living better than the rest of us but working half as hard, it is easy to feel moral indignation. But most welfare recipients' efforts to get by are not particularly elaborate: Women on welfare work because they have to.

It is not difficult to figure out that if Rebecca were not going to school or working, she would have a total of $4 available each month to pay for all her expenses, including food, utilities, transportation, and other incidentals. The strange and contradictory aspect of welfare is that it does not pay enough to live on, but public sympathies are offended when women do what they need to, to survive. The system promotes fraud implicitly and the woman who does not cheat—out of fear or scrupulous morals—is a woman whose poverty is probably quite desperate.

In 1988, Kathryn Edin and Christopher Jencks conducted a study to find out the extent of welfare fraud among a population of women in Chicago.[24] The study was remarkable in that the researchers were able to gain the trust of the participants and felt confident of the honesty of their answers. In this study, of fifty women (about half of whom lived in publicly subsidized housing), Edin and Jencks found that not one was able to live on her welfare grant alone. Every woman supplemented her AFDC check with either work or help from friends and relatives. About four out of five women worked either full time or part time, but none reported their income to the welfare office.

It is clear why many women do not report their income to welfare officials and also how Rebecca found herself among the welfare cheaters. All these women have the same goal in mind. They want to make ends meet, to get food on the table, and to make life just a little more comfortable for the time being. Rebecca tried to be honest with the welfare department about her earnings, but she quickly realized that it did not pay:

> I really didn't have any problems with welfare until I started working and that's when I started having a million problems. I had to send in my check stubs every month, but this one worker would send me things a day before they had to be turned in. One time she sent me something after the date that she said she needed it back. Then I would have to go back and deal with it, but I'm trying to work, and it's just a major hassle, 'cause I didn't have a car or anything, so trying to get there. . . . And I would call her, but I don't remember what she said but she was really nasty.
>
> The first two months I worked, they didn't take anything out of my grant. So you get your full amount. When I called [the welfare worker] to say the job was ending, she said, "We can't give you the full amount until two months later." I was getting about $476 [in AFDC] at the time. And during the first two months they didn't take anything out. Then after that they took out one-third [of the AFDC]. I was getting like $300. Now I was making $400 (working) so I was getting $700 total. But then after that, I'd say about two more months, they cut [the AFDC] down to $111. [So her total monthly income was $400 (work)

+ $111 (AFDC) = $511.] So I would make $35 more a month working than I would just being on welfare. And I did that for three or four months. And then that's when the job was ending. So then I was stuck with a check for $111 for two months!

So I said [to my worker], "Well, what's going to happen to me? I could be homeless." And she said, "Well, why do you think we gave you the full amount for the first two months?" And I said, "As an incentive to get people to work." She said, "Well, we don't care if you work or not. Let me rephrase that. I don't know if somebody way up there cares, but I know nobody down here in this office cares whether you work or not. All that will happen is you'll be sixty-five years old, won't have any children to draw AFDC from, and will never have worked for Social Security. So it'll be your problem."

In this one incident, Rebecca not only became fully disillusioned with the "helping qualities" of her welfare worker, but she also was rudely awakened to the backward policies of combining work with welfare. Unfortunately, our policies designed to help welfare recipients move up and off welfare (called *work incentives*) are not as helpful as we might like to think. When a welfare recipient works (and tells the welfare department about it), she is not allowed to keep both her earnings and her welfare check. Welfare is not designed to provide a guaranteed base of income. Instead, as women work, their welfare grant is either reduced or heavily taxed. For each dollar earned, their welfare grant is cut by a dollar, with some exceptions. Child-care expenses due to work (up to $175 for one child and $200 for two children) are "disregarded" each month in the calculation of the grant, and $90 is allowed in work-related expenses (such as clothing, tools, or transportation). The first $30 that a woman earns each month is not counted as income for twelve months, and an additional one-third of her earnings is disregarded for the first four months.[25]

The "disregards" are certainly better than a dollar-for-dollar tax on all earnings (although they are so complex that most welfare recipients are unaware of how they work), but for many women on AFDC, the disregards are not enough to keep them honest. Because of the difficulties of reporting earned income, in addition to the heavy taxes, official estimates suggest that very few welfare recipients (about 8 percent) work while they collect aid.[26] Yet many women realize that they can maximize their income if they continue to work but omit their earnings from their monthly report to the welfare office. This is exactly what Rebecca did. After the incident with her welfare worker, she realized that it did not make sense for her to report any of her earnings.

Before, I had told them about school, about financial aid and every month I would tell them how much I got. But now I just put "no," "no," "no," on the CA-7 [the monthly income and expenditure report], and I just send them a copy of it. You know, that's what I think is really stupid about welfare, because one of the reasons there are so many stereotypes about people on welfare is because they won't let you work. Most people, well, a lot of people that are on welfare, work. And I mean, you want to say that people on welfare are lazy, but most people do work. It's just that we can't tell you that we work!

Welfare recipients are not conniving, unscrupulous cheats out to make money off the system. Rather, they act like most Americans, trying to make a harsh economic system work in their favor. They have children, usually young children, whom they are trying to support and protect, and they will do what they can to improve their children's lives. But work and welfare combined are not enough to get by. In many cases, as Edin and Jencks also discovered in their study of welfare recipients, women must rely on friends and family to bridge the gap between income and expenditures. Rebecca relies on her mother all the time. Without her, she would have been in critical need more than once. When her car breaks down, it is her mother who pays to have it fixed; her mother gave her the twenty-year-old car in the first place. When Rebecca needs extra groceries or Tanya needs new shoes, her mother often helps. Without friends and relatives, living on AFDC would be impossible.

Conservative writers[27] on the topic of welfare often advise family members to play a larger role in the financial support of AFDC women and children, but their capacity also is limited. Rebecca's mother helps as much as she can. To do more would strain her own, already tight budget.

Welfare as a Means to an End

All the decisions that Rebecca makes about work, welfare, and her financial status are fairly practical. For Rebecca, welfare is not a lifestyle but a means to an end. She has thought about her goals and does not see any way to achieve them except by following her current path. To be satisfied with AFDC alone, or with a low-paying job, would just ensure her poverty for the rest of her life, and for Rebecca, poverty means conferring a lifetime of limited opportunities to Tanya. Poverty means fewer choices, less safety, and less respect. For Rebecca, and for many women and children on welfare, poverty is synonymous with

AFDC. And because of the premium we Americans place on wealth, being on AFDC usually feels like a shameful experience:

> When I started using AFDC, my mom was like, "People won't like it." I think that's why I'm so self-conscious about the food stamps. Because it's like people really don't like it. People judge it. It feels like everybody's respect is dependent on what you're doing and how much you're doing. It's hard to be part of a system that doesn't work. But when you're on welfare, you're part of that system, no matter how hard you try not to be. It's a system that has so many problems.
>
> When I first applied, I would just look at people and think, "Oh God," 'cause you know. . . . They were just—all of them looked like they're going to be on this for the rest of their life. Most of them did. When you start thinking of ways to get more from them . . . and start getting into lying and all this stuff, it kind of makes it seem like you're really going to be on for a long time. I'm not sure what it is. It's like you have to lie to get on it. Usually you do. But see, when you get too involved in finding out things and figuring out ways, then you get deeper into it. It's just too much a part of you. When you sit around and wait for it, it becomes you. But I don't think I ever thought that I'd be on welfare for the rest of my life.

Rebecca will not be on welfare for long; it is just a means for her to achieve what she wants. She tried the JOBS program as well, but she quickly found out that this well-meaning program was more of an obstacle than a help. JOBS is the outgrowth of a welfare policy that, like the incentives to work, was well intentioned but has had limited success. Like all welfare recipients with children over age three, Rebecca was required to participate.[28] At first she thought it would be a good way to pay for her child care, and she hoped that the welfare office might actually try to help. Once she enrolled, however, she found out that there was a two-year limit to the JOBS program in her state; that her educational goals had to be such that she would be finished and "job ready" after two years. It quickly became clear that this would not work for her at all, since her education plans would be much more complicated.

Luckily, Rebecca's JOBS worker was sympathetic to her situation and indicated on her Employment Development Plan that she would be qualified as a teacher's aide after two years of the program. When Rebecca's two years were up, the worker told her about the special loopholes in the program that would allow her a "deferral" from participation, and she encouraged Rebecca to find one that fit her needs. Accordingly, Rebecca got a deferral when she received her work—study notification from the college indicating that she would be working more than fifteen hours a week. Had her worker been less supportive, Rebecca would have faced a powerful bureaucracy at the end of her two years, pushing her to get any kind of job that would get her off welfare.

Essentially, JOBS is designed to provide just enough assistance to move welfare recipients into the labor market as quickly as possible. It disregards the needs of women to make enough money to support their families but generally encourages them to take low-paying jobs that maintain their marginalized economic existence. In California, the average JOBS participant makes about $5.90 per hour[29] when she leaves the program (or about $12,272 per year).[30] Finding a well-paying job is highly dependent on the unemployment rate in the community. As Rebecca explained:

> They want you to get jobs that you can't do anything with. It's really limiting. They send you to training programs but they [don't teach you] anything really meaningful. For me, we wrote down that I could be a teacher's aide after two years. But see, if I just did it for two years and did get a job like that, I would never be able to get anywhere, because I would never make enough money to pay for everything.

Rebecca has used AFDC for quite a long time now. Tanya is six, so she has been on AFDC continuously for more than five years: That is a long time and a lot of tax dollars. So far, Rebecca and Tanya have probably received over $30,000 in welfare payments alone. But Rebecca's strategy is sound. In another two years she will be working full time as an elementary school teacher. She will be making a good salary and will fully support her family. Unless something unexpected occurs, Rebecca and Tanya will be free of welfare for the rest of their lives. When Rebecca talks about her career choice, she not only mentions the personal satisfaction of the work, but she also talks about it in purely pragmatic terms:

> It's definitely practical. I know that I'll get a job when I finish school. There's no way that I can do all this and then not get a job. So it's secure. And then, I like kids. And I think [teaching jobs start] maybe at $20,000. Between $20,000 and $24,000. And then you get summers off. That's a major part. I plan on working in a public school at least for a couple of years and then maybe opening up a school, you know, if I could get support. Basically, I hope I can do it for economically disadvantaged children.

Rebecca will realize her goals in part because she is so motivated to get there. She works hard and holds traditional American values about the importance of work and industry.

> There's something to hard work. And I would always . . . it annoys me to see people that will not work hard.

Rebecca's feelings about work are fundamental to her character; others around her who do not share these values get little of her sympathy. Actually, her attitude toward work is the main barrier to her relationship with her boyfriend, Derek.

One day Derek and Rebecca were dreaming about what their lives would be like if they suddenly became rich. Rebecca thought that rich meant having an income of about $40,000 a year. Certainly that is a lot of money, about six and a half times more than her welfare benefits, but it is not the millions that others might dream about. Her only hope was to join the middle class—perhaps she felt that anything more would be extravagant. Derek wanted to go to an island somewhere and "just sit," but that did not appeal to Rebecca. Her response provided a glimpse of her character—her attitude toward work, industry, and adventure—and perhaps a glimpse of Rebecca's future:

> I'd still want to work. I don't know how much. But it would be boring not to work. I want to always do something, like work with kids. But if I could do anything, at least for a little while, I'd like to be an archeologist and go dig bones. That would be so fun. If somebody gave me $40,000 a year, I might do that.

5

Darlene: Complex People, Complex Problems

There's this magazine with a picture of a diver, and it's at this angle showing the diver and he looks so high. And there are all of these people standing around . . . and you can't tell where he's going, and that's what it feels like. There's this diving board and I'm walking out there, and I'm ready to come down and people are going to be looking at me.

Darlene is stuck. Somehow she got onto this diving board and now has no idea how to get off. She is stuck in a dysfunctional family. She is stuck in poverty, has known it all her life, and does not know how to get out. She is stuck in the role of a single parent and does not know how to share that responsibility. Some days she sees a way out but then becomes paralyzed by fear and indecision.

To say that Darlene is a victim of circumstances beyond her control is a half-truth. She is indeed a victim of an abusive and ignorant family and a victim of racism. But could she handle her current situation better? Darlene certainly has potential, but she probably could not do much better. When one compares Darlene with some of the other members of her family, she is a startling success. But to expect her to turn her back on her family, her past, and her class is unrealistic.

Darlene wanted to be more and to do more with her life. She had visions of going to college, getting a law degree, and providing for her son, James. But her dreams for a better future never materialized, and they probably never will. Darlene is caught in a web of poverty, punctured by a history of deep psychopathology—a legacy willed to her by her father.

Chaos Inside and Out

Darlene's small one-bedroom house is enclosed by a tall fence. Inside the fence, Prince, a German shepherd, stands guard in a yard tall with weeds. The fence, the dog, and the bars on all the windows are multiple barriers to any intruders. Still, the family never has a feeling of real security. Darlene lives in a part of town that is not safe. According to the local police, her neighborhood has consistently remained "one of the worst in the city" for twenty years. Four or five murders are reported every year, in addition to numerous incidents of aggravated assault, rape, and armed robbery. A nearby thoroughfare provides regular business for drug dealers and prostitutes, and drug users prey on the surrounding community to help support their habits.

Darlene is always aware of her vulnerability and is careful with her things. One day when I was visiting, James was playing outside with his cousins, riding bicycles up and down the street. When they finished, they put down their bikes in front of the house and walked inside for a drink. "James, the bikes cannot stay outside the gate like that," Darlene told him, "people will come by, they'll take the bikes, and we'll know nothing about it until we get outside and it's gone. When we first moved here," she tells me, "somebody stole the bike off the moving truck! We hadn't even moved into the house, and the bike was gone."

Inside the house, everything is in disarray. As with most aspects of Darlene's life, some of this is her doing, and some of it is beyond her control. The home was probably comfortable for one or two adults when it was built sixty years ago. But now, with two adults and a child—and sometimes more—the house is very crowded.

Darlene gave the one bedroom at the back of the house to James. When he was younger they could share a room, but at eight, James needs his privacy. The front room of the house is divided into a living room and a dining room. A couple of years ago Darlene put up a large sheet between the two "sections" of the room to create a bedroom for herself. This arrangement was moderately acceptable, although Darlene never had enough closet space to store her things. But a year ago she invited her sister to live with them. Rochelle was going through hard times herself and needed some temporary housing. Temporary, of course, means different things to different people, and a year later Darlene is wondering when their arrangement will end. The frustration in her voice is apparent: It would be much easier if Rochelle found a new home.

> My family is becoming very imposing. Just having Rochelle here is a real drag, actually. I sometimes wonder, what benefit is there for me? She acts like she's renting a room here. And for one thing we don't see each other enough to have any real communication. I've set up a time for meetings and we haven't made the meetings. And she's in school and I know what that's like. She requires more social interac-

tion and she has very, very late hours. She'll stay at Brenda's house [their cousin] 'til very late. And she doesn't rent a room here, you know. She lives with me. I wouldn't rent a room to anyone. You're staying in my bedroom! I have no bedroom. And I have no bed! That's what she doesn't see.

Darlene and Rochelle share the front bedroom. With one small dresser between them and no closet space, Darlene's clothes end up in the living room. Rochelle tries to keep her things on the large chair in the bedroom, but they often overflow onto the bed. Before and after a big laundry run, the clothes often tower three feet above the bed.

The disorder of the bedroom has spread into the living room. The couch, made of artificial leather, sags in the middle and is torn in several places. The clothes that cover it spill onto the floor. The living room is unkempt, unswept, and unvacuumed. Pieces of food and paper are strewn everywhere.

Beyond the obvious signs of Darlene's own neglect of her home is the smell of mildew that hangs heavy in the air. Even on warm sunny days, a feeling of dampness lingers in the house. The floor boards are rotting under the carpet; the wooden window frames are separating from the glass. Darlene has had trouble with her gas and electricity— her meter box blew up because of the water standing underneath the house. Her landlord was supposed to fix this problem. He brought in an electrical contractor to make the repairs, but the contractor wanted to wait until the end of summer, after the earth had time to dry. Now it is October. The contractor has not been back, and the house continues to settle in the mud.

The feeling of dampness is exaggerated by the dim light inside. All the windows have thick bars on the outside, and the two houses on either side of hers are so close that Darlene's home never gets any direct sunlight. This moist, dark feeling was alleviated for a time by a patch of color: The living room used to have a makeshift coffee table in front of the couch, a small plywood box painted bright red and orange that gave the room some needed warmth. Darlene used to sit on the box while we talked, but one day James used the box as a toy, and it collapsed. James was trying to annoy his mother and had readily succeeded.

Slipping from Middle-Class Dreams to the Underclass

Darlene is thirty-eight, somewhat older than the average AFDC recipient.[1] She is short and round with lovely chocolate-colored skin.

An extremely intelligent woman, Darlene is unsure about her talents, and this makes her shy and quiet at first. But once she feels comfortable around others, she is open and thoughtful, with an engaging, delightful laugh.

Like so many other AFDC recipients, Darlene began collecting welfare when her child was born.[2] That transition, from single adulthood to single parenthood, was traumatic, and she has not yet recovered.

Before James was born, Darlene was working the swing shift as a live-in nurse for an elderly woman. She was making good money ($12 an hour); she had a car and her own apartment and was getting along fairly well financially. Although the external circumstances of her life were quite stable, Darlene was depressed and had been for several years. Her bouts with depression had begun when she was young. This time she expressed her depression by overeating. Every evening after work she would stop by a newsstand, pick up a cheap paperback, and go home and eat. In a short while she gained over a hundred pounds and felt terrible. She did not like herself and could not imagine anyone paying any attention to her, least of all a potential suitor. The reactions she got from friends and family confirmed her worst suspicions about her looks:

> They act like you've been in some horrible disfigurement fire. That's the kind of reaction you get. They ask you all these . . ."What happened?! What's going on with you? You were so beautiful."

So when Reggie did pay attention to her one night at the newsstand, she was both surprised and pleased.

> I hadn't been in a relationship in three years. I'm really good at that—social anorexia—so he was a real surprise. He was clearly bent on seduction and I wasn't even aware. I'm heart battered; there's sexual abuse in my family; there's alcoholism. I don't understand relationships. I don't know what I'm doing. I quit. I had considered suicide, but I thought my mom deserved better than that. So I lived; I worked. This is what I was doing when I met him, just working and living. And so it was a surprise to suddenly be involved.

In retrospect, Darlene was very vulnerable at that time, and Reggie was taking advantage of that. Darlene had boyfriends before; four or five had been serious. But none of these love affairs could compare with her feelings for Reggie. Their relationship was stormy and passionate, lasting over two years. But Reggie was not responsible. On good days he was loving and caring, but most days he showed his true colors. He was an alcoholic; he was involved with drugs; and he was absent, both emotionally and physically, for days at a time. Darlene excused his behavior because she had never really known a man who behaved any differently. Every person she had ever lived with, including family members, friends, and lovers, had been alcoholic. Some were also gamblers, and some used drugs. Every member of her family was an addict of some kind, and the most prominent male role model in her life, her father, was also the most brutal.

So Darlene had her guard up, but only partway. When they first slept together, Reggie told her that she could not get pregnant, that he had had a vasectomy, and that he had never gotten a woman pregnant before. But Darlene did not believe him and decided to take care of her own birth control with a low-dosage "minipill." After two years, the fighting, jealousies, and misunderstandings grew worse. Reggie started seeing other women, and Darlene started to date other men as well. At one point, Darlene was sleeping with Reggie and another man on alternate nights. The results were disastrous:

> Well, I didn't have a period. I thought I was pregnant. And then I thought, well, I really didn't want to have an abortion. I had abortions before and I didn't want to have another one. And it was like, here you are thirty years old, and you are still getting pregnant, accidentally. You need to have a baby. If there's one thing I know, having a baby will cure pregnancy [laughs]. I mean, this was my logic! So I said, "Whatever happens, happens. You're just going to be embarrassed. If you don't know who the father is, then you'll just have to look at the kid when he shows up."
>
> But see, I was not pregnant. This happens to some people [not getting a period], but I didn't know this. So I'm thinking I'm pregnant, so I quit taking the pill. So Reggie calls me a couple of weeks later, and I told him I thought I was pregnant and we got back together. And then I did get pregnant. That one time. That one date. September 22, 1982. I know exactly when I got pregnant. And so I get pregnant, thinking I'm pregnant! I mean, how could you do this!? When I figured out what had happened it was like, "You got pregnant, thinking you were pregnant? Who does that?"

Darlene and Reggie broke up again shortly after that and then came the embarrassment.

> You know, I'm a nurse, I'm thirty years old, this happens to teenagers, it doesn't happen to thirty-year-old nurses. I was just very, very embarrassed. Plus I'm just thinking, "How am I going to do this socially? How am I going to manage this?"

Her feelings of embarrassment really masked other feelings that she had about Reggie. Darlene wanted things to work out with Reggie.

She wanted to have a baby, and she wanted to have a husband. She could have had an abortion. She was not opposed to abortion for religious or philosophical reasons; indeed, she had had three abortions previously. But she did not realize that she did not want to have the baby without Reggie. Like most Americans, she had traditional beliefs about marriage and family.[3] But when she realized that she would be alone, she sank into a very deep depression.

> I was about five months pregnant [when I saw him again] and he said, "Well, call me when the baby comes." He had told me to call him and I called him, and he had an answering machine and I knew it was his machine, and he had a tape and it was a standard message and I left a message and he never called me back. I said, "I'm at North Point Hospital, it's a boy, nine pounds. . . ." And he wasn't there. And I happened to be—just my luck—I really don't think there is an anthropomorphic God that punishes people, but this was very ironic. I had to have a room, it was a semiprivate room with a woman who had the most attentive husband there ever was. Ever was. "Now why am I here?" I'm thinking. "I'm here alone with this baby." And so I got out of there as fast as I could and I really had intended to stay and enjoy being in the hospital, but it was like, "I cannot watch these people."
>
> And it was just totally different to have a baby and not be married and to be around people who were married. And it was an outside-looking-in experience, and it was understanding how society views things, because it would have never occurred to me to treat anyone's child differently or anyone who is having a baby—you know, as far as giving a person showers, giving a person gifts. There were people who didn't acknowledge James. So you know that was hard. And I see people on the street and I want to say, "Do not do it. You have no idea. You have no idea the reaction you're going to get."

The birth of a child brings financial stress to most families. Although it is difficult to calculate the real cost of raising a child, there is some evidence that the average American child costs more than $100,000 before the age of eighteen.[4] The expenses are not just those associated with cribs, bottles, and diapers—there is a human cost as well. Although about half of all women with infants (under one year old) return to the workforce, the other half remain at home.[5] Thus, family income often falls sharply just as expenses rise.

For single mothers like Darlene, the financial strain of child rearing can be especially difficult. A few months into the pregnancy, she quit her job as a nurse, since she did not want her employer to find out about her situation. She took another job as a phlebotomist in a Plasma Center, but the pay was not half as good. After she gave birth, she got disability pay for about six weeks and then she went on aid.

I suppose Darlene should have known better. She should have recognized Reggie's irresponsibility. She should have known that he
would never come back to her and help raise their child. Like her father
and all the men with whom she had been involved before, Reggie was
an alcoholic and a drug addict, and he was not likely to change his
behavior. Rather than regretting that he had left, Darlene should have
been furious and demanded support for James. Instead, it was the
welfare office that demanded Reggie help support his son.

When Darlene applied for welfare, her intake worker told her that
the office would try to locate Reggie and make him pay a share of
the cost in raising James. Darlene gave her all the information she
had, including his name, address, P.O. box, and his place of employment. When the DA's office tried to contact him, however, it just
missed him. Reggie had been fired from his job a few weeks earlier
and was now collecting unemployment. But even unemployment
provides some income, so his monthly "wages" from unemployment
were garnished, and the state began to recoup some of the costs of
supporting Darlene and James. Not until Reggie realized that he was
"losing" money did he even attempt to see his son. He had never
before tried to contact Darlene and had never been interested in seeing James.

This episode brought still more pain to Darlene, and she realized
during this period that men often have a great deal of power over
women:

> He came to me and asked me to lie about who the father of my child
> was. But what I could see about it was that I was so attached to him
> that I would probably do it if he kept hanging around. I really thought
> that there was some danger that I would do this. That he could talk
> me into anything.

Reggie maintained that he wanted to support Darlene informally without the intrusion of the state but that the only way for him to do this
was for Darlene to renounce his paternity. In reality, the state would
not have simply backed out if Darlene had done this. Blood tests would
have been taken, and Reggie would have been confirmed as the father
anyway. This also would have meant that Darlene had perjured herself,
something she did not intend to do.

> So he asked me, "What did I think was fair for child support?" And at
> that time I think I was spending about $400 a month for child care,
> and that's all I asked for, was half the child care. I didn't even figure
> in food or diapers or health insurance. Just child care was all I asked
> for, and he said, "Well, this would seriously cut into my drug money."
> That hurt. It really hurt.

Darlene never lied to the authorities about Reggie, but she also never saw a dollar from him, either directly or indirectly. Reggie found a way to duck the system. Maybe he moved to another state; maybe he uses a false Social Security number when he works now; or maybe he has moved into an underground economic system that does not bother with Social Security, unemployment, or taxes. When I met Darlene, one of the first things she told me was,

> I have no idea where James's father is. I don't know if he's living or dead.

She said this in kind of a resigned tone. In time I understood that she felt the disappointment of her single parenthood every day. I learned that she had middle-class values regarding parenthood, marriage, and family but that the day that she decided to keep her baby—knowing that Reggie could never be a parent to her child—she began her slip away from the middle class. Parenthood was a life choice that would always haunt Darlene, bringing her both pleasure and great pain, yet she allowed her ambivalence about single parenting to paralyze her for years to come.

Self-Esteem, Mental Instability, Abuse, and Neglect

Darlene's ability to cope with her single parenthood is one of the principal obstacles to her self-sufficiency, as her single parenthood is partly an outgrowth of her inability to deal effectively with men. Darlene never learned how to be forthright with people, so she has countless stories of men who took advantage of her and men who were abusive to her. She also has an uncanny ability to choose lovers and housemates who are addicted to drugs, alcohol, or gambling.[6] These experiences, along with her family background, have left her with a fragile sense of self-esteem. During our time together, Darlene would tell me that she was not "good enough," or "smart enough," or "strong enough." She was not good with relationships; she was not good with her family; she was not good with her son; she was not good in school; and she was not good at work.

But Darlene's self-esteem is not her only problem. After I had known her for a while, it became apparent to me that Darlene's difficulties were not just transient or that she just needed a friend to talk to. Rather, Darlene has deep emotional scars that have left her mentally unstable. The balance she tries to maintain between emotional maintenance and disarray is precarious at best. She is often immobilized by a deep depression, a feeling so desparate that she does not recognize the importance of getting up in the morning or carrying out her daily tasks. Each social encounter, whether it be with her son's teacher, her welfare worker, or another parent in the community, is fraught with fear and discomfort. Her mental instability is not schizophrenic; she has no hallucinations, and she is not paranoid. But the emotional swings from euphoria and hope to despair and sadness impair her ability to cope effectively with the requirements of a constructive life.

Although Darlene's family members have been supportive during hard times, they are perhaps more critical of her than any other people she regularly encounters. Darlene described her father as "the most critical person I've ever known," and her sisters (there are four of them), as "supportive" and "caring" but also "very critical people."

Darlene's life is so intertwined with her family's that she has few outside friends. Her sister Rochelle lives with her, and her other sisters and cousins are regularly in and out, dropping off children, stopping by for a chat, or asking for a favor. Her mother is the emblem of strength for the family and offers a good role model for the whole family. After surviving routine abuse from Darlene's father and having raised all her children by herself for a time, Darlene's mother went back to school in her late fifties to become a preacher. Darlene's mother has opened doors for Darlene that she would otherwise have found closed, and her mother continues to provide support and inspiration.

When she was a teenager, Darlene got her first job as a volunteer in a local elementary school where her mother was a teacher's aide. Later, Darlene's mother worked in the welfare office as a clerk. Darlene soon got a job at that office through her mother's contacts. Later it was her mother who went to school to become a live-in nurse. After she completed her course, Darlene also gave it a try. Now, Darlene works as a receptionist in her mother's church a few days a week. Although her mother has always provided some buffer between Darlene and the other members of her family, when Darlene was a child her mother was blind to the terrible destruction caused by her husband. Darlene's own words best describe the story of both sides of her family:

> My parents were one step from being sharecroppers. They were virtual slaves. They owed so much that they couldn't leave the property they lived on.
>
> My father's family? I think there was sexual abuse in his family as far back as you can remember. His father was really his grandfather. I mean, his grandfather had a daughter and he raped her when she was twelve, and then my father came along and he continued to live in the house with this incest everywhere. And basically the grandfather

and his son, my dad, had sexual relations with all the women in the house.

And my grandfather was a mean man. I mean, he was dangerous. He had been put in prison before on a chain gang, and these men would have to go off and work in the fields or dig ditches connected to each other by these chains. And one day he came back and there was nobody attached to his chain. And we know he killed the man. I mean we know he was dead. But it was just another poor black man, so nobody did anything about it.

[My mother's] father was very brutal and he would whip babies. He believed that you could break a horse by beating it, so you could break human beings by bending them to your will. So my mother had never heard anything about picking up and holding children. Her mother was a schizophrenic and my other grandmother was an alcoholic.

My father drank, too. My father would get so drunk, I mean he'd be standing on his feet, but—he almost burned down the house a couple of times. He would start to cook and you'd wake up and the house would be full of smoke. A typical scene, my family. Very scary, but very typical.

Then the sexual abuse began in Darlene's own family. It began with her eldest sister and spread through the family like a disease. She does not know all the details because family members are only now sharing their own pain with one another. Darlene also does not know everything about her own sexual abuse because there are "big black spaces" in her memory—images and moments that she cannot bear to relive in the telling. Smells and sounds can bring back an image:

When my father sexually abused me, he was always drunk. So alcohol breath is something that I actually despise. People get close to me, and I get this revulsion and fear and tighten up. ·

As Darlene speaks, she grows quiet and hugs herself like a little girl:

I would put my bed against the door. I don't know why I remember the last incident—maybe because it was really violent. He didn't do anything, he just tried to come in. It was very, very strange. And I just sort of stood there and looked at him. My sister was there and we just stood there while he tried to get in. And then I don't remember anything. It's like I blacked out. And then he left us and went into my other sister's room and sexually assaulted her while my other sister watched. I think that all of them were sexually assaulted, except for one. My younger brother.

In junior high, Darlene began the first of several years of therapy.

I never knew why I was going to therapy. I mean, I knew why, but I really didn't understand. I didn't understand how she was supposed

> to be helping me. I'm sure they didn't know what to do with me at
> that time. That was a long time ago and they didn't know how to deal
> with sexual abuse. I'm sure it's like being a nurse and being stuck on
> the oncology ward, I mean, you just don't want to be there!

Her mother and father also started to see a counselor, and the whole
family had several sessions together. But nothing changed. The image
of the healthy, happy family had disappeared, and there was no way
to retrieve it.

Looking back, Darlene noted that her mother was always trying to
make the family look and feel like a different kind of family.

> My father married my mother when she was fourteen years old, and
> he was the bright spot in her life. And she always wanted to keep the
> family together, which is a good goal; it's just that they didn't have
> any fabric to hold together. I mean, it had all these big holes in it; the
> fabric was just in shreds; and how do you put that back together?

Today, Darlene's childhood experiences get in the way of her adulthood all the time. Like many adult survivors of sexual abuse, she is
easily hurt and misunderstands the slightest criticism.[7] Her inner life
is chaotic and disorganized. She does not understand who she is or
where she is going, and she is always uncertain of the next step to take.
As an adolescent she had hopes of going to college. Later, as an adult,
she thought she might become a lawyer. But neither she nor her
mother had a realistic understanding of what she needed to do to get
there.

> You know my mother, at one point, wanted me to go to college. But
> she had no idea how to work it. And I had no idea how to work it. My
> parents' family—you learned how to read, which was a jump, because
> the generation before them didn't know how to read. Middle-class
> people know. They know you've got to take SAT exams; you're going
> to have to take these kinds of courses; you need this much time to
> study, this much support. You didn't get that kind of support in our
> family.

Middle Class? Underclass? Categorizing Class

Darlene frequently compares her family with the middle class. Like
most members of the middle class, Darlene speaks clearly and expresses
herself well. She uses standard English (or did whenever we were
together) and selects her words carefully. But her language is deceiv-
ing because Darlene is not of the middle class, and she knows it. Nor
is she a member of the working class. Darlene does not work (in the

taxed economy), and few members of her family do. So where does she belong?

Christopher Jencks, a well-known researcher on welfare issues, categorizes class in various ways.[8] Sometimes class is determined by a person's income. By income standards then, Darlene is a member of the lower class. But the term *lower class* has fallen into disuse in recent years, replaced by a term that defines both a person's income and his or her behavior. Again, to use Jencks's terminology, Darlene might be defined as a member of the *impoverished underclass*, one subgroup of Jencks's *underclass*, which also contains the *jobless underclass*, the *reproductive underclass*, the *educational underclass*, and the *violent underclass*.

The term *underclass* nonetheless has its critics and has been much debated in recent years. Some claim that it unfairly categorizes whole neighborhoods as "violent . . . or outside politics and social structure."[9] Michael Katz has been a particularly vocal opponent of the term, asserting that it "inappropriately divid(es) poor people into moral categories," leaving some people deserving public sympathy and others not deserving support.[10] But Jencks makes distinctions within the broader term of the *underclass* so as to avoid inappropriate generalizations about the behavior of all poor people and to suggest different interventions for those who fall into these distinctive categories.

Although Darlene fits many of Jencks's characterizations of underclass behavior, there is one area in which she differs. Her cultural skills, or her ability to move in middle-class circles and to present herself and her ideas as though she were part of the middle class, are the characteristics that confuse those around her and often cloud her self-identity. One incident she related was very telling:

> This year there's a parent in my son's class who really likes me. She just likes me for some reason and she invited me to dinner. And this is my first outgoing and I was so nervous. I was just—I always kept people, well, these educated people, they're over here and I socialize over here, because I don't know what they do [laughs]. So she invited me to dinner and I had such a wonderful time. And here I was panicked, and I was, you know, I'd say [to myself], "Yeah, I'm having a good time," and I'd panic some more. And you know they listened to me, and I listened to them, and we talked and I came home and I just—you know, these people, they listen and they talk, and you have ideas, and you can socialize this way. And you can get to know people in a totally different way. It was very, very odd. I really enjoy it, but it's living in a different world. It was like going back to school and hanging around people who were intellectual. I could be in a social context with people in a classroom or working on a paper, but just to sit around and talk and have a free flow of ideas going and not relate my conversation to the ball game or to the news or to a card game or to a

party—just to have a flow of ideas is very weird. I mean, you don't know how strange that is for me. It's like being on Mars.

It also, you know, as I go through this process, I recognize that— it's not completed, and I'm not sure that I will complete this process, which is, I really feel, that my class—that I'm going through a class change. And changing your class is like a betrayal of class. It's like you're saying, "That's not good enough for me," or "I want something else." And how do you do that? How do you change something like that? And if I do change my class, who in that class is going to be linked to me, socially, having come from another class? When you start heading in the direction you want to go, 95 percent of the people you know now, you won't know when you get there. It's very scary.

In some ways Darlene does live in two worlds. She can relate to the middle class and take part in their conversations and activities, but not without a significant degree of discomfort. When she is with her family, she shifts her language and demeanor. Darlene is the most reflective member of her family, the one who moves through the two worlds with the greatest ease and the one who is bright enough to notice the duality of her life. Her sister Rochelle, although clearly a member of the underclass by all means of categorization, does not recognize this in herself. Sitting around the living room one afternoon, Darlene was talking about some of her mother's acquaintances:

I wouldn't know them because I'm not part of the black middle class.

Rochelle immediately jumped in, incredulous, "What did you just say!?"

"My family is under the mistaken illusion that I am middle class," Darlene said under her breath to me.

"No," Rochelle responded, "it has just become very apparent to me recently that you're trying as hard as you can to not be middle class. It's not that you are, but you don't want to be. Look, you're not middle class, and we know through no stretch of the imagination that you're upper class, okay. Now, you saw the underclass. They used to live next door. Are you one of them? Who are you? Who are you closest to? Not those people."

Rochelle turns to me, "I think we're middle class and she's crazy."

Darlene explained:

Our family was very poor; our family history was very poor; and one of the ways poor people can cope is by joining the [military] service. And while they're in the service, there are two directions people can take. Quite often they become middle class, or quite often they have more money, but their values and what they do doesn't change. Now the middle class, in my opinion, does certain things that people who are poor, even if they have money, do not do. One thing, they take vacations. Middle-class people take vacations. Our family has never done that. Ever. And they get education for their children. There's a very high priority on education. They pay for it or they invest in it and it's something they're interested in. This group of people has not done that. [They] have money, but they don't have the same values. It was a revelation to me that I wasn't middle class. It was something I had to learn. But all my middle-class friends knew that. They all went to college, and I see the differences between us and I see where they are and I see where I am. I feel very, very distant from this group of people—the black middle class, especially. I feel that we're worlds apart. I don't feel accepted, so I don't feel always at ease with them.

Were they to meet Darlene, many members of the African American middle class would find her bright, compelling, articulate, and entertaining. But Darlene does not believe that. On some level, Darlene knows that if she were to change some of the outward appearances of her life, to get a job, maybe to find a home in a different neighborhood, and to become more involved in her son's school career, she too would move into the African American middle class. But the social expectations that accompany a middle-class lifestyle paralyze Darlene with fear.

William Julius Wilson,[11] a scholar of the problems of the inner city, observes that until the 1960s, African American families lived in the same inner-city communities, whether they were middle class, working class, or lower/underclass. Middle-class values were transferred from one group to another, in part because families used the same public spaces, post offices, and grocery stores, and their children attended the same schools and churches. Yet with the advance of fair housing practices in the 1960s and 1970s, African American middle-class families began to leave the inner cities, leaving lower-class families behind. The middle-class values that had been so powerfully conveyed were no longer readily available for lower-class families to use as models. With the departure of the middle class, the hard-core underclass was left with only a shell of values and expectations for individual behavior that fell far below the norms readily accepted by middle-class Americans.

Darlene is a member of that underclass and knows that there are no generally accepted standards for her behavior. The only expectations she feels are those she places on herself or those she may feel intermittently from society. Since Darlene recently gave up watching television, she no longer has ready access to middle-class values. Since she shops in the stores of the underclass, rides public transit with the underclass, and associates with other underclass families, she is surrounded by standards that are relatively low. Others like her, of the underclass, do not place expectations on her behavior that she will be unable to meet. Therefore, her status, although less than it could be, is safe and comfortable.

Pain and Redemption Through Parenthood

Darlene cares about what other people think about her, and most of the time she meets the simple expectations of those around her. But she also knows that she could join the middle class if circumstances were different. In some ways she leads a dual life, adapting to her immediate surroundings. When she speaks with me, she conveys middle-class attitudes, but when she is with her family, she changes dramatically. Because of her family's early history, she learned to be compliant and flexible. Independence was not encouraged, and throughout her life Darlene had made a conscious effort to be as invisible as possible so that others (especially her father) would not notice her.

Silence about the family secret also made it difficult for her to gain any self-assurance or independence. For example, unable to choose a career path that could be uniquely hers, she followed her mother's patterns of employment. She also, eventually, followed all of her sisters' examples by having a child as a single mother. When she chose not to continue her first three pregnancies, she was actually making a rather bold statement contrasting with her sisters' behavior. One of her sisters became pregnant at age twelve, the next at fifteen, and another at seventeen. Darlene waited a long time before carrying a pregnancy to term, but the fact that she made this choice shows her conformity to her family's values after all.

Today she braves regular conflicts with her family over the way she is raising her son—in this, she has tried to carve out a new path. As the most introspective member of the family, she has become aware of the importance of parenting techniques that other family members mock. In some ways she is trying to be a middle-class parent, with middle-class values regarding consequences and punishment, yet her efforts in this area have met with curiosity and then stern criticism.

> [My parents'] whole perspective on parenting was you get your child to eighteen and get them out. And for most people in my family, I'm afraid, children have not been a very positive thing. Nobody planned any of their pregnancies in my family. Nobody. By and large, I think people got pregnant and they just dealt with it. There's still people in my family who think it's OK to get high in front of your kids and not only to use drugs but that these things are acceptable. I have a large

family, and I'm the only person who doesn't beat their child, so that means that I'm constantly being told what I'm doing wrong.

Darlene is trying to set a new standard, but it is difficult. Her brother was a crack addict until a year ago, and her nephew was killed in a drug-related incident in 1990. The nephew was not an innocent bystander; his drug dealing cost him his life. Despite the waste his death symbolized for everyone in the family, Darlene's sister recently became involved with a man who is a drug dealer himself and who regularly deals in front of her children. Still, Darlene's sisters and brothers do not associate the sadness and anger they felt at the funeral with the influence of their own behavior on the children in the family. Teaching James to avoid the allure of drugs or gangs will be a task of heroic proportions. Darlene knows that this will be a challenge, and it is not clear that she is up to the task.

James is an African American boy heading for turbulent adolescent years. In today's society, young African American men are increasingly found on the margins of our economic, educational, and judicial system. According to Jewelle Taylor Gibbs, young African American males are more likely "to be unemployed, to be addicted to drugs, to be involved in the criminal justice system, to be unwed fathers, and to die from homicide or suicide" than they were thirty years ago. The evidence is startling. The unemployment rate for African American male teenagers is double the rate for all teenagers (34 percent in 1987); more than one out of five young African American men do not have a high school diploma or its equivalent; in 1985, 7 percent of all African American adolescents were arrested; and, most disturbing, the leading cause of death among young African American males is homicide.[12] To counter these powerful trends, equally powerful measures should be taken. Yet Darlene lives each day with only a hope and a prayer that her son will turn out differently. Mostly she denies the odds:

> It's a good thing that I'm not watching TV any more, and I don't buy newspapers. I'm not getting this, "black people are an endangered species; he's going to die on the street" kind of thing. I think I'm aware. You can get to thinking in a rut, thinking there's absolutely nothing that can be done, that black people are doomed and my child is doomed. But I don't want that fear in me. This is not going to be so for him. Children are going to face challenges and you have to talk about them.

Darlene does talk with her son. One of her great strengths is her ability to communicate clearly and effectively—but the messages are intermittent. She shares small pieces of advice as well as long diatribes about good behavior, although it is unclear whether James listens. One morning when I arrived at Darlene's house, she had just come from her son's school. The teacher had called her the day before, warning that James had to improve his behavior or else he would be kicked out of the summer program:

> On the way to school, we started talking about discipline, and I decided that I needed to talk about the people hanging out on the corners in the neighborhood because we walk by them all the time—we never say anything about them—what they're doing or why they're there. It occurred to me that we're being dishonest in not discussing what's going on in the neighborhood, in not saying that this is not OK. On the corner of Jackson and Connecticut Street, there's a liquor store and two doors down there's a crack house with people just milling around and hanging out. A lot of kids, people who are men now, that's where they started off. Their first drinks or their first drugs. And yeah, you can follow that pattern if you want to—being in and out of jail. But there are other alternatives for life!
>
> So I started talking about discipline, and I said these people just have no discipline. This is why you have to have self-discipline. There's the kind of discipline where you do what you have to because someone's standing over you, and then there's self-discipline and you have to have this because this is where you end up when you don't have self-discipline. These are the kinds of problems you have.

But in another couple of years, James will realize the difference between his mother's words and her actions. Darlene is not particularly self-disciplined herself. She tries, certainly, but she has had trouble finishing most of the things that ever meant anything to her. Several times she enrolled in classes at a community college, but she has never been able to complete a series of courses. She also has begun, but never finished, various training programs. Much of the time, Darlene simply gives up on the things around her. So it will be difficult for James to learn self-discipline from his surroundings.

Perhaps James's future is not doomed, but as an eight-year-old, his behavior is very challenging. James is big for his age, not so much tall as very stocky and strong. He has a wide smile that is warm and winning, but his behavior tests Darlene's patience all the time. James also tests his aunts and uncles and his schoolteachers. He is a boy who needs to be the center of attention, who rarely takes directions from his mother, and who regularly causes trouble at school. Darlene does not see James's behavior problems in the same way as his teachers see them. Rather, she explains his behavior by focusing on his strengths and states that she simply has to learn new techniques to deal with his "personality style."

He's got a high level of self. You just can't fight him because you will escalate the violence to get him to back down. Power is everything to James. So with a power child you try to give them the ability to make choices at different times. [Raising] James takes a lot of discipline and a lot of thought.

When Darlene does recognize a problem, she usually frames it in terms of her own shortcomings as a parent. This feeling of inadequacy is not only a regular feature of her personality, but it is also amplified around James. Darlene still has not forgiven herself for not welcoming James into the world as a baby.

One day she told me,

> I was a very poor parent. I went for two years—for two years I ignored him. I didn't abuse him. I was abused, but neglect is a form of abuse. I would sit around and read or watch TV and I would feed him. I fed him like he was a dog. I just gave his physical body things. I didn't talk to him. I just didn't do a lot of things that people would normally do with babies. But then I woke up one day. I think he was eighteen months, or between eighteen months and two years, and he was hitting me. I was sitting and reading a book and I was so engrossed in it, and he was just hitting me on my thigh. And he was hitting me really, really hard. And I finally realized and I thought, "Why is he hitting me?" And it was like, "He's trying to get your attention!". . . click. . . . The light went on. Now I see the progress I've made in parenting but I feel that for those years when I was totally vacant, he suffered.

Darlene replays that period of her life over and over in her mind, trying to make the pieces fit together and hoping that each review will make her understand her life more clearly. Shortly after that epiphany, she enrolled in a parenting class through a local community group and began the process of understanding parenthood from a totally different vantage point. It was at this time that she began to take seriously her responsibilities as a mother. So seriously, in fact, that—like Rebecca—she chose AFDC as a partial means of refocusing her energies, improving her parenting, and improving herself.

AFDC as an Opportunity for Self-Improvement

Darlene explained:

> [After James was born,] a friend of mine started to work at a dialysis clinic, and a job opened up at her clinic. And while I was working for them, after about two years, one of the doctors decided to open up his own clinic. And I had kept trying to go to school, but it was very dif-

ficult. I would start school, but I could never manage to finish a class. I'd buy books and everything, and start out, but I would always drop the classes. I was always doing that. I was working full time, P.M.s. No wonder it didn't work, I know, but I just kept saying, "Well, how come I can't do this?" And what happened to the original clinic was that they didn't have enough patients and they had too many nurses. So I was one of the last ones hired. What they did was they fired a couple of the nurses and they put me on part time. I couldn't afford to work part time. I tried it. I really did. But I had no health insurance. They kept me at eighteen hours so I couldn't get any health insurance at all. Well, you have to have health insurance when you have a child! You know, James was having ear infections back to back, and I was taking him back and forth to the doctor, paying cash, and [the doctor] was giving me samples during this time. It was about six weeks when I tried to manage on halftime. She would give me free samples of medicine because she knew I didn't have any money.

So one day I was walking by a telephone pole and there was a flier about a Section 8 program, a Housing Authority program for low-income people who were full time in school—for single parents who were trying to go to school. I guess this was a Reagan-era program. It had a name, but I can't think of it. Something like, "Pull yourself up by your own bootstraps program."[13] So I said, "Well, I'm not in school, but I can do this." And you know, I told my mom, and she says, "You know, this is a great opportunity. You can go to college." She thought it was great. And that's what I did. I basically just resigned. I went on aid, and I started going to school. As soon as I was registered for twelve units and they saw my verification of enrollment, they gave me a housing certificate. Usually you wait for years for a housing certificate, but I got one as soon as she processed my papers. Just like that.

Darlene had been on AFDC before. She had received six weeks of disability pay when James was first born but did not feel ready to go back to work right away. It was not that she was enjoying her new role as a mother, far from it. Rather, she had slipped into a deep depression and was almost immobilized by her sadness. Darlene went on aid at that time, but after about two months, family members and friends began to worry about her mental health and pushed her back into the world of work, just to keep her occupied.

As she describes it, she handled her work quite well for the next two years, but she ignored her son almost entirely. She also tried to improve herself by going to school, but she was never able to finish a semester. This period of her life explains much about Darlene: She is unable to handle the challenges and complexity that life demands. She can raise her son or work or go to school, but she can hardly do two or more of these major life tasks at once.

Darlene's choice to go on AFDC was a conscious one. She could have looked for a different full-time job, and as a trained nurse she probably could have gotten one. But who would she be disappointing if she went on AFDC? Her mother and all of her sisters had used AFDC at one time or another during their lives. Many of her neighbors—members of the underclass like herself—would not question her decision. Instead, it was the intake worker at the welfare office who let her know that her choice was not a good one, one that society did not value:

> I can appreciate how my intake worker felt. She was appalled that I had quit this job that paid that much money. I could have gone to another job, so I can appreciate how she felt. She probably wanted to know what was wrong with me. "Obviously you're just a lazy person" is what she probably thought.
>
> I feel like I rationalize a lot about being on aid. Because I don't feel like I'm not a productive person. I do feel that because of this I have been a better parent, and I've had more time. I think when I was not on aid, I know clearly that all I was doing was working, sleeping, and I was not giving James any attention at all. I really wasn't. I've had a chance to learn about parenting. Like I said, I've taken those classes. I've taken them twice. I've talked to more people and I've been exposed to more and he's been exposed to more, so it's been beneficial to us that I have been on aid. But I have to remind myself of those benefits. It's just a social message, which you get all the time. People who know I'm on aid will say, "Welfare's the worst thing that could have happened to black people. . . ." It's a very humiliating experience. And the shame is really inside. I don't tell people I'm on aid now. You feel like you're living down to people's expectations and you're a statistic. My father doesn't like it, being on aid. Most people just feel that you're not carrying your load in society. You know, that you're getting away with something. That everybody's taking care of you. That's what you get. It's that you're not doing your part.

Darlene is ambivalent about being on welfare. Although she has internalized society's opprobrium, she is not ready to change her behavior. In one breath, Darlene can say that she needs to leave welfare, that she feels stuck and embarrassed. But then she maintains that welfare has allowed her opportunities for self-discovery and growth that she might not have had otherwise:

> I don't think it's unreasonable for people to look at people who are collecting aid and for them to ask, "What's the focus in your life?" I think it's unfortunate. There's a lot going on, just in parenting, and the fact that you don't put any value on parenting, that you see what

people are doing is just sort of staying at home and parenting and maintaining a household, that it's not valuable. But I don't think it's unreasonable when people are giving money away—and that's basically what they're doing is giving me money—to say, "Well, what's going on here? Are you going to do this forever? What's your focus?" I know people who have been on aid for eighteen years, and when their kid hits eighteen, what do they do with their life? So it's good, I think, to step in at some point in the process. My ideal would be for them to leave me alone, though. You know, don't cut my food stamps when I need food. Just try not to make it more difficult than it already is. I don't know. Maybe their job is just to make it difficult.

I think I lead a really good life. I think I lead a better life than a lot of people. And I think I lead a better life than most people who are working forty hours a week because I have chosen to live with less money so that I can have more time with my kid. I've chosen time for money and I think that's an equal trade. I think that if you choose to trade time for money, it would be nice not to be looked down upon. I have to work very hard not to feel that I am a slovenly person. That I'm just not contributing to society. I think it would be nice if people recognized that everybody here is contributing. That I couldn't be here and not contribute.

Like Rebecca, Darlene sees the trade-off between time and money. This is a familiar refrain for many welfare recipients. A recent study of AFDC mothers showed that many spend a large portion of an average day attending to family matters and household management.[14] It is precisely because they have less money that AFDC women spend more time grocery shopping (often because they rely on public transportation), doing laundry (because they do not have laundry facilities in their homes), and preparing food in the home than the average middle-class American does. With time as their only available commodity, it is put to good use. Applying for AFDC not only takes a great deal of time, but remaining on AFDC also is time-consuming. Women must continually defend their need by providing verification of their income and expenditures.

It takes a lot of organization to keep everything together for these people. This is not an easy job! Not everybody can do this. I think about the amount of time I spend not only keeping my status clear with AFDC, but I have to keep my status current with PG&E [Pacific Gas and Electric], the energy program—they do all this energy conservation stuff to your house. If you're on the food program at school, you have to do that. When I first started school, James was in a state-funded preschool, so I had to do paperwork for that. When I was in [JOBS] I had to do paperwork for their after-school program. There's paperwork everywhere, and then there's your financial aid paperwork; it's like you are constantly filling out papers justifying who you are, what you're doing. It's not a picnic. It does require a certain amount of knowledge. And if you don't do it right, then they're going to deny you, and they're going to send you back the forms, and it's going to take a long time. And they make you wait. It's like AAA insurance—they make you wait to see if you're going to die first.

The rest of my family are not literate people. Getting paperwork done is very difficult for people in my family. Getting things done with deadlines is very difficult, and filling out these forms, and mailing off these forms. For most people it is a monumental task to get the CA-7 done.[15] I know it is. I've not mailed it sometimes. So just getting in the habit of using the mail services. I don't know if it's a class thing, but my family is very oral. They say things, but they don't write them down. So to go to some place and fill out the forms, and you have to follow up. You know, it's like, "I told this to you once, why are you asking me again? Why do I have to write it down?" They don't understand that there's a process. There's a paperwork process, which is a very odd thing for people who don't understand it. If you're on welfare and if you don't read and you don't write, you don't have any idea. I remember when I applied for aid, there was this woman there who could not fill out the forms, and I helped her. She really didn't know what she was doing; this is a person who cannot even apply for help.

Darlene and I talked about her memories of applying for AFDC, and she remembered less about her own experience than she did about the experience of those around her:

There are some people who have no resources; whose families have even less knowledge about society than mine had—which was incredible for me to imagine; that people can live with that kind of poverty and ignorance. There was this one woman who was filling out the form and who asked me, "What does Caucasian mean?" And she was white! She really couldn't read. It was the most incredible thing. There were a couple of other ones that I didn't talk to that I had the same sense about, who needed more services than people could imagine to catch up. They needed a nurturing institution where they could get hugs five times an hour. Besides knowledge, they just needed mothering.

Darlene is not alone in her perceptions of the poor. Michael Harrington, who was credited with bringing the plight of the poor to John F. Kennedy's attention during his presidential campaign, was an ardent defender of the poor.[16] He, too, suggested that many of the poor needed more than money and a job. Many needed personal support in order to cope with the everyday adversities of living in poverty.

Darlene knows that some of these women need help desperately, whereas others exploit the system, giving welfare a bad name and jeopardizing future help for the genuinely disadvantaged. The response she got from her worker, the one that was incredulous and rude, is echoed by welfare recipients across the country. Darlene, however, understands how they feel:

> My worker was not my favorite person. She just had a real attitude. It was OK, she gets to have one, but when I run into a person like that, I was already feeling bad about myself, and then that just makes me feel worse. And then you go home and then you don't want to get up and crawl out of bed and do something.
>
> I think that in order to be an intake worker, you have to be able to handle people, and they get a lot of flak, too. I mean you've got to be able to stand up to people and not take it. It's sort of like the difference between a police officer and a fire fighter. People will fight the police, but they're always happy to see a fire fighter. The police get to carry a gun around and enforce the rules and tell you what to do. You're not going to be so kindly with them. A fire fighter stops you and you'll cooperate. "Can you get out of this building?" "Yeah, I'll go." But as soon as you see a police, a man with a gun, it's a different thing. See, an intake worker is sort of like the person who says who can go and who can stay. It's like when you get on the No. 45 bus line. There are some bus drivers who, they're on some routes and they're very cooperative, and then there are some other routes like the 45 where they've got to have an attitude all the way down because they'll have people giving them a hard time, they'll have people wanting to deal on the bus. They just want to deal and get high. I think that an intake worker does not have an easy job. I think they really encourage people [to work there] who will discourage people. I think it's like, "If you're willing to go through this, then you must really need help."

Disincentives are built into AFDC at almost every step in the process. The system is designed so that it is hard to get aid, and once a woman begins collecting welfare, there are numerous incentives to encourage her to leave as well. Intake workers are notoriously rude and unhelpful. Having witnessed the intake process numerous times, I too can vouch for the "attitude" about which Darlene speaks. The application process is long and cumbersome; the waiting rooms are bleak and cold. Recipients see the locks on the doors that separate the waiting room from their workers' offices, and they see the security guard at the entrance. Although welfare workers may need this protection, as a few recipients are genuinely hostile and dangerous, for the unsuspecting welfare recipient, the needy woman and her child, these barriers are signs of distrust. Low-income women quickly learn that they are not welcome visitors.

Then there is the required documentation that serves to verify eligibility but also serves to suppress frivolous applications. Only the most needy or the most organized would have all of the following documents readily available:

- Birth certificate, driver's license, draft card, alien registration card, or other positive identification for every person in one's household (married women must have identification showing their maiden name).
- Marriage license.
- Divorce papers.
- Death certificates.
- Strike letter, if applicable.
- Student identification card or report card.
- Property tax receipt.
- Notification of assessed property value.
- License fee tags for automobiles, trucks, and the like.
- Wage stubs for this month or for the last month worked.
- Child-care receipts.
- Award letter showing Social Security benefits, disability insurance benefits, unemployment benefits, and the like.
- Rent receipt and landlord's name and address.
- Burial, health, and life insurance policies.
- Account books for any savings, credit union, and/or trust accounts.
- Unemployment benefit registration booklet and work registration booklet.
- Addresses of applicant's children and applicant's parents.
- Social Security cards or request for Social Security numbers for all members of the household (including infants).
- Gas, electric, water, garbage, and telephone bills for the past three months.
- Pregnancy verification.
- Disability statement.[17]

There is no telling how many eligible women never apply for AFDC because they were frightened away by the complexity of the system and the application process. To the more courageous applicants, the barriers are unpleasant but not entirely obstructive. Darlene is a welfare woman who mocks conservative hopes that the disincentives of the AFDC program will be enough to dissuade recipients from applying for aid or from using welfare for a long time. Darlene has now been receiving aid for over six years and has no immediate plans to give it up. She works for her mother under the table, and she does odd jobs babysitting for friends and family, but she is not planning to work again, full time, until something dramatic happens in her life to push her toward this end.

It is unlikely that Darlene will become a lawyer, and she may never finish her courses at the community college. Although she starts taking classes with each new semester, the emotional problems she carries with her daily prevent her from concentrating on her studies. Eventually she always quits, reinforcing her experience of failure and her low self-esteem. She could probably go back to nursing, although her skills might be a little rusty. But at every turn, she uses the excuse of her son and the importance of parenting. Darlene wants to embrace the middle-class ethos of work and self-sufficiency, but she does not trust herself to the task. Certainly working and raising a family are hard, even for two-parent couples,[18] and doubly difficult for single mothers. The challenge for Darlene is great, indeed. James will need her support and her supervision if he is going to survive the odds. Darlene also needs help and would probably benefit from regular therapy for several years. Her life is marked by chaos and depression. She is like a high-jump diver who is afraid of the fall:

> They're going to be looking at what my form is like. It's not only the courage it takes to jump off, but you've got to have form. You've got to flip through the air and do all these somersaults. Whether the experience that I've had, whether I've practiced enough, to be able to land and hit the water and go in perfectly, right in the public eye. . . . And it's not so much the crowds. It's not the fall as much as. . . . Well, I'm saying it's not the crowds and I'm saying it's not the fall . . . what is it then? I guess it may be that I just don't want to do it [chuckles]. Those are the things that I'm afraid of. I think to be a high-jump diver, it must feel really good when you hit the water.

6

Cora: A Portrait of Dependency

I already feel like I'm old. You know, I think by me bein' at home all this time
sort of like got me on the lazy side—sort of ruined me. What slowed me down
was, you know, I was gettin' high and then I didn't go nowhere. I'd just lay
around and get high. Get up in the morning, do the same thing, over and over
again. So the routine just layin' around the house all the time just broke my
spirit, and next thing I'm getting fat and I'm forty-one years old. 'Cause I started
doin' that when I was about twenty-nine. I been doin' it ever since then. Next
thing I know I'm forty years old. I can't get in the spirit like I used to. There
goes fifteen, twenty years of my life doin' nothing.

Cora has been on AFDC all her adult life. She began using AFDC
twenty-four years ago and has continued, without a break, ever since.
In so many respects, her life mirrors our image of the classic welfare
stereotype. She comes from a poor family and will leave her children—
there are six of them[1]—with a legacy of poverty and neglect that they
will not be able to shake. The children have no role model in their
mother of a working, productive member of society. Neither do they
have a model of a law-abiding citizen. Cora never had these role models
either, and for years she has lived in the projects where she is surrounded by poverty, crime, and drug abuse.

Welfare Stereotypes

Welfare stereotypes are powerful. They captivate the American mind and
tell a story that is only a half-truth. The "welfare queen" that President
Ronald Reagan made infamous was real, a woman on welfare who found
a way to cheat the system and bilk taxpayers for thousands of dollars.
Indeed, there are bad, immoral people in the world, and whether they
are poor, middle class, or rich, some of them prey on innocent citizens.

But most Americans do not think about the welfare queen when they think of the average welfare recipient; calculated fraud is not really part of the picture. Ask the average American to tell you who receives welfare, and you will be given a description of a woman who is lazy, has lots of children, does not want to work, does not get up in the morning, is African American, never finished high school, and keeps having more children in order to increase her monthly grant. Like the welfare queen, this image, too, is real. But where we are wrong is in imagining that this woman is typical. She is not. The more typical welfare recipients are Ana, Sandy, and Rebecca, who have temporarily fallen through the cracks and who need some assistance to get back on their feet again, or women like Darlene, whose paths to poverty and whose character and personality are complex, making them difficult to place in a single mold.

Long-term welfare users, or the *persistently poor*,[2] make up about 2.6 percent of the American population, a tiny minority. But Greg Duncan's study (Chapter 2) indicates that a significant proportion of the American population spends at least one, relatively short, period living in poverty. He estimated that between 1967 and 1976, about 22 percent of the U.S. population was poor for at least one of those years.[3] Among these poor Americans, about one-tenth were persistently poor (poor for eight out of the ten years studied).[4] New evidence, however, reveals that patterns of persistent family poverty are less varied, that more families are remaining in poverty for longer periods of time.[5]

The characteristics of families who experience brief episodes of poverty are similar to the characteristics of most American families. As we pointed out in Chapter 2, Duncan's data indicate that many Americans are at risk of falling into poverty, although their spell in poverty does not last long. The characteristics of households that experience long-term poverty are quite different, however, as they are more likely to be headed by a women and to be African American.[6]

Just as there are differences between the short-term poor and the long-term poor, so there are differences among poor single-parent households. Whereas some families use AFDC for a few months or a couple of years, others are persistently poor. Unfortunately, writers on the subject of poor women tend to describe the persistently poor by their personal characteristics rather than by their economic condition. Today, long-term welfare recipients are generally referred to as *welfare dependents*,[7] the *passive poor*,[8] and, in the words of one writer, *pathological*.[9] Some information about who these long-term welfare recipients are may be helpful.

The majority of welfare recipients (about 75 percent) use AFDC for a relatively brief period of time.[10] But according to David Ellwood, a scholar of welfare, "an important minority, at least one quarter, will collect AFDC for ten or more years."[11] If only 25 percent of the welfare population use welfare for a long time, why all the fuss? The sobering fact is that this mere 25 percent of the welfare population consumes about 65 percent of all welfare dollars.[12] Moreover, many of the long-term welfare users have several characteristics in common: Unmarried mothers, high school dropouts, and women of color are far more likely to rely on welfare for longer periods of time.[13]

Cora is an unmarried African American mother. She is a long-term welfare recipient, and her story is important. Several aspects of her past experiences and her present condition, both personal and environmental, are relevant to who she is today. Observers from the left would say that she is a victim of circumstance, that she was never given an opportunity to participate in the American mainstream and so was made a social casualty by her environment, racism, a poor education, and a poor family. Observers from the right, however, would be equally justified in asserting that she is an active participant in her dependency, that she abides by a different set of standards for daily living, and that her life is typified by disorganization and laxity. Both observers would be correct. There are no simple reasons to explain why long-term welfare recipients are poor, just as there are no easy solutions to their poverty. This small group of welfare recipients has an array of complex problems that they bring to the welfare rolls, and their hold on welfare is tenacious once they begin receiving it. Cora is a member of that important minority of welfare recipients who collect aid for several years, but she is not a typical welfare mother. Rather, for Cora and her children, welfare is a way of life. Indeed, Cora will probably live on public aid until she dies.

Welfare as a Way of Life

Cora was raised in Oklahoma, one in a family of nine children. She and her family were among America's rural poor, trying to work to get by but relying most of the time on the church, help from neighbors, and surplus commodities from the government. Her father died when Cora was about twelve. In some ways his death was welcome, as he had regularly battered Cora's mother and abused several of her brothers while he was alive. But after his death, the family's financial condition became desperate:

> The memories, they ain't too good. I mean I had happy moments. If it weren't for my auntie, the one that really raised me, I don't believe I

would have had a happy childhood. If it wasn't for her, I wouldn't know love, or caring, and bein' real sensitive and tender.

'Cause they worked our butts off when we was comin' up. We had to chop cotton. If [my mama] had whooped me and made me go to school and get my education instead of whoopin' me and makin' me go to the fields when I didn't like it—get up at five or six in the morning and work until the end of the day. We'd go to the fields and make like three dollars a day. All that for three dollars. I used to get whooped 'cause I didn't want to go. I hated it. I hated it. And on weekends, [my mama] worked at this motel. I think it had twelve rooms in all, and on weekends we had to go there and help her do the beds and stuff like that. That was durin', when there was no cotton. I never did mind workin' or cleanin' up, but I just never did like the fields.

I asked whether she thought of her family as poor.

Poor? I would pretty much say so. We lived in a big old house. It was a crowded house, a big house. We used a wooden stove, outdoor bathrooms. Compared to some of my friends, though, I see their house and how they was livin', you know, and I was pleased then, you know, to see somebody even worser than me. But then they might not make them go to the fields, though. They went to school. They smart now. We had to work in the fields 'cause they didn't have welfare back then. What they did was they called it, uh, they used to give us free commodities; cheese and that powdered milk and the peanut butter, oatmeal.

Although her family's attitude toward school was lax at the time, Cora saw education as a real asset. She also loved school when she had the opportunity to attend; school was probably one of the best escapes she had from her family.

I taught myself how to read and I taught myself how to spell words. I used to do like that all the time 'cause [Mama would] say, "Go to bed so you can get up and go to the fields in the morning," not "Go to bed so you can get up to go to school in the morning." Never say, "Do your homework" or anything like that. I did it all on my own. And the same thing I'm trying to tell my kids. I say, "My mother hadn't did me like I'm tryin to do ya'll, I want to be 'ppreciated more." Then they always tease me, sayin' "Oh mama, you had to go to special ed." I said, "Well, so what? I still finished school! I still got my diploma. I don't care if I'm not as smart as you want me to be. I still got it." Durin' this time is when, what you call it, exceptional classes started for kids who was slow. Thank God for that, 'cause I loved school. I loved it.

Cora finished school, and that should have provided a buffer between her and her later dependence on welfare, but it is hard to tell what the diploma bought her in terms of skills or preparation. When she graduated from high school, Cora knew how to add and subtract, but she had never learned how to multiply or divide. She knew how to read and spell, but not without a struggle. Her reading, even today, is halting. These criticisms of her education are not to detract from Cora's accomplishment—few of her siblings received a high school diploma—but it calls into question the value we regularly place on a high school education when it signifies little more than the ability to persevere.

Cora stayed in school both because she enjoyed it and because she was encouraged to do so by her mother. For all her faults, Cora's mother did value education more than Cora admits. Cora was in high school when she met Russell, her future husband, but rather than quit school to get married and have children, Cora kept at her studies.

> I was in the tenth, maybe the eleventh grade, I think. I had told [my mama] my intentions, and she said she liked it if I finished school before I did, but otherwise she didn't care. She said, "I want my child to fin-ish school."

It was probably luck more than anything that kept Cora from getting pregnant in high school, as she never used birth control. After high school, however, she did get pregnant, married Russell, and gave birth to Tommy. Right after Tommy's birth, Cora and Russell moved from the Oklahoma countryside to a California city ghetto. There, Cora's world turned around. She was young, she was innocent, she knew nothing of the city or the "system," and Russell became someone she later grew to hate. Sometimes he worked in his father's scrap-metal shop, but most of the time he just got into trouble, drinking, starting fights, and stealing. Russell signed on to welfare, since they had no steady income; he explained to Cora that this was their only option at the time:[14]

> I was eighteen. I was married. Like a country girl in the city, he tried to keep me to that level. He'd go out, stay out, and I didn't know nobody. It was just lonely, weird. I was a long way from home and my family wasn't here, and like I said, when I left home they were real strict. And then when I came out here, my husband, he knew just the right buttons to push. And he knows I'm from the country, so he use me. [The welfare] was comin' in his name, too, 'cause he was the head of the household at that time. He didn't have a job.

So began Cora's welfare experience. She was a young, simple mother with little knowledge of her options. For her, welfare was a stable, important source of income in those early years. She was not expected to work, since she was married and had a small child, but because her husband could not support them either, at least welfare offered a regular income.[15]

A year later their second child, Felicia, was born, and money became even tighter. Cora appealed to relatives and church officials for money and food, but she also started asking around and made some well-placed phone calls. Soon she began to understand how welfare worked, and she started to look for ways to make the system work for her.

> My husband, he started using the money and he wasn't spending it on us. And he was startin' lyin', sayin' he didn't get the check, somebody stole the check, the check is comin' late. And I'm believin' him. I didn't know the welfare system. And he was comin' up with all this partyin', always drinkin' every day. Then when I needed some milk for the baby, he would run out and hustle and get a can of milk.
>
> So I just called the welfare and told her that we ain't get two months' worth of checks. And then she say, "Let me call you back and I'll check on it," and I remember real well and then she say, "You been gettin' your checks." She say, "You checks is signed and you husband signed 'em." I said, "What?" He signed them. Then I was wondering, could I have him prosecuted and they said no because the check is in his name, and they couldn't do nothin' to him. And the checks was cashed and regardless of how they was spent, it was in his name. And I said, "We ain't even got no food and we haven't been getting this and that. . . ." and they said they couldn't help.
>
> So I was real mad with him, but like, you know how it is. He fussin' his way out of it, tryin' to show me and be real good, and he knows he wronged me. So I called again and she said the only way that we can do this so that he's not spendin' the funds properly is they could change the checks over in my name, and I'll be the head of the household with the checks. So that's what they had started doin', and boy did he ever get mad. Boy did he ever get mad. I didn't even tell him what had happened because he was like at home that day. You know how some mens are. Want to be lovely dovey on the first and fifteenth, real sweet to you and all this kind of stuff and he's sittin' there waiting, and I'm knowin' he's gonna get mad, but he still gettin' all sweet and everythin', helpin' me to clean up, bein' nice. Mailman come and I kept lookin' out the window for him. He goes down there and get it and he looks at it like, you know how you look. . . . He says, "What!" I say, "Because you be spendin' the money that we don't never get it!" And he says, "What the hell is goin' on." And I say, "You ain't gonna get it."

Eventually Cora and Russell worked out a compromise. The checks came in her name, and she managed the family bills, but she also gave him an allowance out of each month's check to spend as he wanted.

Once she had some control over the money, she also began to take some control of her life.

> We stayed goin'. We didn't break up at that point, but we used to fight a lot. He was a ruthless man, real ruthless. He was drinkin' a lot of alcohol, became a skid row bum, a wino. He just wanted to be a street bully. He used to beat me, he used to jump on me all the time. Even when I was pregnant. Lucky I survived. Because he used to beat me on my head. I used to go to the doctor a lot, and he always used to x-ray my head. He was crazy, he was just a bully. And he just kept on wantin' to fight me, and I started standin' up for my rights. I started fightin' him back, grabbin' anything I could get a hold of. After a while I fell out completely in love with him. I didn't want him. Not the way he was treatin' me. So I just fell out of love with him. I hated him. I despised him.

Cora and Russell had several turbulent years together even after that. Their relationship grew extremely violent, so much so that when she filed for divorce Russell almost killed her.[16] A judge granted her the divorce and a restraining order, but Russell refused to stay away. Although he was in and out of jail for a couple of years, he always came back to harass her. It was not until the youngsters were around ten years old that he finally left them alone. A couple years later he died from cirrhosis of the liver, and Cora tried not to think about him after that.

Cora looks on that period of her life as pivotal to the events that happened later. Her expectations about love and marriage had not been met, and her hopes for her role in life had been ruined. She often used to talk about her ambitions during high school and how they changed over time:

> When I got out of school in 1968, I wanted to pursue my career because I always wanted to be a cook or a nurse. 'Cause I used to see these nurses with these white hats and I always thought they looked so pretty. And then they say they get benefits, and I thought when I get old and all I got is my Medicare, I can fall back on this. I used to think like that. I wanted to do things and I loved goin' to school, and if I had a man to motivate me and not drive me down like he did I'd probably a went to school. Because bein' with him for so long and not goin' nowhere and I didn't know where to go, or how to start nothin'. And livin' was so hard, and once you get out of school, gettin' back in with all that paperwork to get back in school, I didn't think it was worth it because I had this baby and couldn't find anybody to take care of him because it wasn't safe at home. So I just gave up school. Sometime I think about that, too. I wish I'd met a man who was smarter or a working man who was really motivated and he would have motivated

me a lot too, you know. Because for a long time—see I'll be forty-two next month—and all that time, you know, and I never really thought about doin' anything with my life. It's all dead. It's been killed.

If Cora had married a different man, maybe she would not have grown accustomed to using welfare; certainly her remarks about her early aspirations suggest a longing to be self-sufficient through work and a career. Instead of working, Cora became one of the few women who are completely dependent on public aid. Over time, her ideas about income shifted; her attitude toward work changed; and even her orientation to time was altered.

During my time with Cora I began to see a pattern in her language: Our conversations centered on welfare. Her stories often revolved around events that occurred on the first and the fifteenth, parties and social events in relation to the first and the fifteenth. Often when I went to Cora's house, she was wearing a bathrobe, but on the first and the fifteenth, she usually was dressed and looking smart. The neighborhood was always bustling on the first and the fifteenth, and when we discussed our next meetings or an appointment for herself or one of the children, she fixed the meeting in her mind in relation to the first or the fifteenth. ("Is the sixteenth next Thursday? Let me think. Yes, I should have known, 'cause the first was on a Thursday, and it works like that.") Although Cora did not keep a calendar, she always knew the date.

Her orientation to work changed as well. She never had a very clear picture of what it might mean to work. When she was young she wanted to be a nurse—the appeal lay in the dignity afforded by wearing a "pretty hat." When I first met her and asked what kind of job she might get, she answered, "I want to work in an office where I could wear stockings and be dressed real nice." Cora knew that work was equated with respectability and order, but the details of the day-to-day aspects of work were never very clear. Cora's understanding of the world of work was limited in part because she did not know many other people who were employed.

The Culture of Poverty

There has been a spirited debate in the welfare literature during the past few decades over whether or not a *culture of poverty* exists, whether people who live in poverty for a long time become part of a culture that contributes to their dependence. The term was first used by Oscar Lewis in his account of a poor Mexican family and their struggle to survive.[17] Since that time, writers on the subject have tried to determine whether such a culture exists and its causes and consequences.[18] Many agree that "pockets of poverty" do exist, particularly in the inner cities. These areas, or the groups comprising this underclass, represent a separate sphere geographically, politically, demographically, and behaviorally. As Mickey Kaus observed, the underclass is typified by "out-of-wedlock births, single-parent families, school truancy, crime, and welfare dependency."[19] Other researchers define the underclass by a set of deviant behaviors such as drug addiction or mental illness.[20] Unemployment, according to William Julius Wilson, is an equally strong definer of the American underclass. Although the number of people in the underclass is small relative to the entire population of the United States (some estimates put the underclass at about 1.8 million people; others group the underclass with the "persistently poor" and point out that as few as 2.6 percent of the American population may fit this mold),[21] their problems are perhaps the most intractable.

Naming this a culture of poverty or an underclass may not matter here. After spending a long time with Cora and her family, it became clear to me that they lived in a unique culture in an inner-city ghetto. Everyday life looks different in these neighborhoods; peoples' lives revolve around different activities, goals, and values; and their expectations are different. It is a neighborhood with its own rules for governance and a distinct economy.

Every ghetto has its own characteristics; none of which is pleasant. Cora's neighborhood ranks as one of the worst in the city, with some of the highest rates of AFDC recipiency, unemployment, teen idleness, crime, births to teenagers, low birth-weight babies, and infant deaths.[22]

Cora lives in a neighborhood consisting of twenty square blocks of dense public housing.[23] Although every couple of blocks the look of the housing changes, all of it is owned by the government. The whole neighborhood must have been a frenzy of activity forty or fifty years ago when government officials tried to crowd all the poor people into these newly constructed buildings. After the housing was finished, the construction continued when two freeways were erected, thereby creating a border between the affluent and the poor.[24] A closer look at the buildings makes one wonder what the city officials' intentions were when they had the projects built. Nothing about the buildings gives one a sense of safety or security.

Cora's apartment sits in a cluster of other apartments fashioned into a kind of courtyard. When Cora arrives home, she must enter her apartment away from public view. Although this gives her some privacy, if someone wanted to rob her or hurt her children, she would have to rely on her neighbors to intervene. When visitors come to her home, Cora has no way to identify them; there are no windows next to the front door, and the door is made of solid wood, with no peephole. The apartment has a window in an upstairs bedroom, but the bedroom itself hangs over the front door by about two feet. When I made my first visit to Cora's home, Tommy had to call out of the upstairs bedroom window, "Who that?" The building was very badly designed to protect women and young children.

Cora's children, whose world is circumscribed by their neighborhood, see only the projects. Because Cora has no friends outside this neighborhood, a family outing usually consists of a trip to the local park where the children mingle with the homeless. Other buildings in the neighborhood include the public health clinic, the senior services center, a large public day-care center, and a couple of churches. Van's Mortuary, built in 1919, sits on Washington Street. The irony of this building, standing tall and doing a brisk business in this dying neighborhood, is hard to ignore.

The only other businesses that seem to thrive here are the liquor stores. There are five, one on each block, conveniently located on the street corners. I often see children running in to buy a carton of milk for breakfast. They probably do not notice the iron grates across the front and sides of the store, since these are a regular feature of their environment. But they appear to sense danger as they enter the store. Sometimes they will look furtively at the men milling around outside, but mostly they look straight ahead, remembering their mothers' admonishment to mind their own business. The men usually do not bother them, although sometimes they will make a comment or ask about their big brother or sister. These men mean no harm; they are just bored or drunk and have nothing better to do. The children hurry down the block to reach their home and pass two or three more groups of men who are more menacing. Drugs are exchanged for money; arguments break out between customers and dealers; and children are often enlisted as "runners" to make deliveries.

The children are justified in being scared.[25] The homicide rate in this community is high,[26] and other physical violence is routine. Not only arguments among residents, but also violence against strangers and nonresidents is common.

Like with the mailbox [Cora tells me]. Then our mailbox was in our hallway, we just walk out our door. Now we have to walk way down here—(about a half a block)—the new mailboxes, they just put them out two months ago. I guess it is going to be safe, because the mailman used to get always jumped on if he was late with the checks. People were mad, and jump on him, meet him on the corner. They say you were supposed to be here two hours ago, here it is 5:00, or 4:00. Sometime he run just that late, especially on check days. They beat him up and go through the bag and everybody going through it and looking for they checks. Then he takes off to running and the police have to come. Now the police come with him anyway if he's late. That's why they set [the mailboxes] there so he wouldn't have to go up in the hallway. Now the pizza and the Chinese, they don't deliver here anymore, either. They afraid.

Although children raised in this kind of environment learn to accept violence as routine,[27] they do not necessarily learn that it is wrong, as they have nothing with which to compare it. They also learn a different rhythm and pattern to daily life. The projects are quiet early in the morning. The public buses are running, but there are few residents rushing to their cars or to the buses to get to work. Children walk to school, much as they would in any other neighborhood, and after about 9:00 A.M., the younger children are on the patios, playing and jostling one another. At about 10:00 A.M. the neighborhood begins to wake up. Drug dealers take up their posts on the corners; men begin to cluster in front of the stores; and women move in and out of their apartments, talking to children and neighbors. Unemployment is high in this community, and so many residents have no employers demanding their time or energy.[28]

Cora keeps busy in the mornings. This is her time to clean the apartment, scrub floors, vacuum, and wash dishes. At first I thought Cora cleaned only when I was coming, but after our first meeting together, she was often surprised to see me, and I usually caught her with a broom in her hand. Cora spends hours keeping her home clean. She has a full house, and she always finds herself cleaning up after somebody. Having a clean home is one of the few things she can control in her life, and it is also a symbol of her personal dignity.

Her apartment is compact. With six children, Cora qualifies for a four-bedroom apartment, but every room is small and utilitarian and is also filled with people. Cousins, nephews, nieces, and siblings often visit from Oklahoma, and she always opens her home to them, welcoming the company. One of Cora's most delightful characteristics is her warmth and generosity. Her heart has an enormous capacity for love. Since Cora has little to share in the way of money, she willingly shares her home, food, and time. Her son Tommy (now twenty-three) lives in one of the bedrooms upstairs and shares his room with Cora's brother, Wesley (age twenty-six). Felicia (age twenty) has since moved out and lives with her daughter in another housing project down the street. Darryl (age seventeen) has a room of his own upstairs. He is so argumentative and protective of his things that Cora thought it easier to give him his own room rather than listen to his constant accusations. Sharon, her eight-year-old, stays in the third bedroom with her cousin Janice (age twenty), and Cora has the downstairs bedroom. Raymond (age five) and Joe (age two) store their things in Cora's bedroom, but at night Cora pulls out a pallet for each of them on the living room floor.

Poverty and the Burdens of Poor Health

The stress of living in crowded conditions is exacerbated by the burden of poor health. Cora and many members of her family have a variety of physical ailments that limit their everyday activities. Cora has high blood pressure and has been advised by her doctor to "decrease [her] activity and rest." She comes from a family plagued by cancer and is awaiting the day they find it in her, too. Almost all of the children have one or more serious ailments. Both Tommy and Darryl are hemophiliacs. Although they do not have a problem with the ailment now, as children, Cora often took them to the doctor for checkups. Because their disorder was severe, each had to undergo numerous blood treatments during childhood. Darryl, in particular, had several small accidents that required hospitalization. Making matters worse is the threat of AIDS. Darryl was born in 1976, a few years before the AIDS epidemic was even recognized. And it was not until 1985 that the Food and Drug Administration issued regulations for screening blood. Estimates suggest that of those people receiving blood treatments in the late 1970s and early 1980s, over 50 percent were infected with HIV, the AIDS virus.[29] Today, Darryl and Tommy refuse to be tested for HIV. Neither of them wants to know the bad news. If they do carry the virus, however, there is no telling how many women they may have also infected through sexual contact.

Sharon's health is uncertain. Her teacher has advised Cora to take her to the eye doctor, as she appears to strain and squint when she works in class. Cora has also noticed that Sharon often has tremors or small seizures when she is watching television. Sharon was a crack baby, owing to Cora's drug use. Although her health has improved since birth, there is still some question about possible neurological damage.[30]

Then there are Raymond and Joe. Raymond has the most serious health problems, and if Cora followed through with all his medical appointments, she would be at a doctor's office at least three times a month. Both Raymond and Joe have a disease called *neurofibromatosis*. The problem is genetic, and Cora is a "carrier" (as is Felicia). The problem results in a series of tumors that develop throughout the body. In Raymond's case, a large tumor developed in his brain, causing his head to swell and finally producing a seizure that almost killed him. Several months ago, Cora found him lying unconscious on the living room floor:

> I walked in there and I seen him laying out on the floor with his head turned and I thought he had went to sleep on the floor. And I said, "Raymond, you went to sleep on the floor." And I said, "Raymond, get up," but he was like a rock. So I lift him up and tried to get him up in the bed and he was just limber and I said, "Oh Raymond, you threw up too," and I felt him and he was real cold and I said, "God, Raymond." And I told Tommy to call an ambulance. And I started gettin' worried because his body was so cold. So I was cleanin' him up and I was cryin' cause I thought he was just fit to go.
>
> They said that he had a seizure and they found out that the fluid that's in your brain, that your brain give off fluid and drains, but his wasn't drainin'. I knew he had [the disease] but I didn't know it was buildin' up in his brain, 'cause they always checked him, but we didn't know the tumors was in his brain. And then they went in his head after that and put a shunt in to drain that off.
>
> Then it got infected and he got sick all over again. He had the operation and he still wasn't respondin' right. I told [the doctor] he wasn't right. He wasn't even walking. And he don't have no balance. And when he came home that first week I took him to the doctor every single day 'cause he kept saying, "Mama, my stomach hurts," comin' to me at night and sayin', "Mama, my stomach hurts." And I said, "Oh, you're hot." So I'd put a cold towel on him and give him some aspirin because he has this agonizing cough. So I took him to another doctor, and he gave him a blood count and it was too high, and he said take him on to the hospital. He said they may put him in the hospital. So that same night—this was a week after he got out of the hospital— they put him in that next week and they found out he had a bacteria in the shunt. They took it out and then they cut his head again and they put the shunt on the other side. He spent about three weeks this time. [The shunt] drains the fluid. It's a long tube like a straw going all the way down there and it stops in his stomach. It drains.
>
> They say if it happens again they say he'll die. He would surely a died if they didn't do the operation. They just didn't give me no guarantee, they said we can't guarantee he'll come out of it alive.

The doctor done put it in the record that Raymond's bone structure is changing and he have tumors. They can see all this and his head is growing and the neurofibromatosis is definitely there. The way he talk, he talks like a three-year-old. He should be talking like a five-year-old. Plus he have asthma on top of all that; he's in and out of the hospital all the time.

Raymond is a sweet little boy plagued by a number of serious problems. His speech is slurred, and he will need several years of speech therapy. Nerve damage from the seizure has impaired his use of his hands and feet. He can get by, but he will need intensive physical therapy for a long time before he will have full use of his fingers and toes. He also needs glasses to correct his vision. Then, of course, there is the possibility that the seizure did irreparable brain damage as well. Raymond appears to be developmentally delayed and will need an enriched educational program in order to catch up with his peers.

Joe is in good health so far. Although he has not yet shown any obvious signs of the neurofibromatosis, it is very likely that it will catch up with him in the next year or two. Then Cora will have two young sons with serious medical ailments. Cora used drugs quite heavily when she was pregnant with Sharon, and she did not stop entirely during her pregnancies with Raymond and Joe. Whether the boys may have been affected by the drugs is not known, but the combination of fetal drug exposure and their disease does not suggest a childhood of robust health.

Poverty and the Underground Economy

In Cora's home, the tension that accompanies health problems, combined with poverty and crowded living conditions, can create an explosive environment. Arguments, especially between the adults, are a regular feature of each day. But Cora struggles with the thought of making the older children move out. If she asked them to leave, where would they go? Tommy and Janice work a couple of days a week at local fast-food restaurants, and Wesley picks up odd jobs when he can. None of their incomes is regular or secure, so how could they survive? Although Cora asks them for money to help pay the bills every month, their contributions are spotty at best.[31] Instead, they often barter services as their exchange. Janice babysits a lot, and Tommy runs to McDonalds for pancakes or juice if the little ones have nothing to eat. But the exchange is usually accompanied by an argument, as each tries to position himself or herself for the advantage.

The bartering that goes on inside the apartment reflects the exchange that regularly occurs outside. Part of the alternative culture that exists in the ghetto is a thriving underground economy that is nourished by each person's ability to argue his or her case.

> How do you tell the difference between computers? [Cora asked one day.] I had a guy, he always sells me things. That's how I get my clothes and the stuff I have. He said that he had a computer with the TV part and the keyboard and he say he gonna sell it to me for $300. I say I'll buy it for $100. He say, "No," but he say, "I'll let you know this week." If he can bring it down I may get it. I usually do bring him down. After the third, he knows now nobody gonna have any money around the fifteenth, but he know I always keep a little change or something, so I talk him down.[32]

Neighbors regularly come by Cora's home trying to sell her things. A woman stopped in with a Nintendo one day, trying to make a deal. Having no luck, the woman then started to negotiate with Darryl. A few days later a man came by with dozens of homemade necklaces draped around his neck and arms, selling them for a dollar apiece. On yet another day, one of Cora's neighbors came by in a predicament:

> "I'm fittin' to go move my cousin," he said. "He gonna give me and my brother a hundred dollars to move him and I ain't got no gas to get over there. I got a way to take us over there in the truck, but he ain't have no gas—all he had was $10 in food stamps. I wondered can you give us some gas money?"
>
> Cora answered, "I wish I did, but I ain't got my check either." (It was the first of the month and the mail had not yet arrived.)
>
> "Ain't nobody got no money. Two or three dollars or anything. Three dollars will work to get us out there. But when we get out there, my cousin, she's gonna give us some money."
>
> "I got two or three dollars, but I need it to put in my gas tank."
>
> "Well, how 'bout if I trade you the stamps?
>
> "That ain't gonna put it there."

The man continued to haggle with Cora and then moved on to her son. Finally, Darryl traded $5 in cash for $10 in food stamps. Although food stamps are used in a dollar-for-dollar exchange in a grocery store, they are worth far less on the streets, since they have value only for food and cannot be used to buy other goods or services.

The underground economy works on another level as well, as individual homes are used as outlets to exchange goods. One day when we were talking about work, Cora told me how she used to make tacos. When I asked where she had worked, she said,

At my house. Right out of my house. I used to make them and everybody used to come by and want some. You get like two dozen shells for $1.65. Then you got to cook them. Then I buy one of those big things a ground beef. Then you put the cheese in it, and sour cream if they want it, and peppers. And salsa I make up. I made my own salsa with tomatoes. I put that on there. I sold 'em for a dollar. When I first started out, though, I was saying you getting one free, so they'd buy a lot, especially on the first and fifteenth. I was making almost $100 a day. And then the money started comin' in too good, and I started gettin' paranoid. I used to put a stick behind the window so it would only open that much. I used to leave the window wide open. So I'd leave the crack like that. They'd just put they money through the window. Then my kids play on the patio. 'Cause a girl told me she had got robbed when she was selling cans a stuff at her house, but I never did have no problem. But sometimes they lean into the window and I say, "Get out a my window, get out. If I want you that far in, I wouldn't a put that stick in there." They halfway in. I did real good, especial on the first and fifteenth. Everybody do it. Sell candy, they go to this warehouse and buy a big box of candy and sell them for a dime. Or a little bit of gum. Then they get these soda waters, these big brand soda waters, and sell them for 60 cents. You can buy a case of them, I know they were $2.29 a twelve-pack.

Her entrepreneurial spirit is inspiring. Rather than work in the conventional economy, Cora works out of her home when money is tight. It is not that she has never worked a real job—she has. But the most she was ever paid was just over minimum wage, and even then, she was surprised to find that what she thought would be additional income sharply cut into her welfare grant.

The best pay I ever did get was at Burger Haven. That was the best pay. That was about $4.10 an hour. But I had to send in my pay stub every week. I had to send it in to the welfare, and you know how they make it sound if you're working, you should let us know because you get more from your food stamps? That sure is a lot of baloney. I must have told them, being honest with them, everything I made that week, they cut it out and one month I got $12 in a check from them. I thought it was $102, I wasn't really checkin' it. It hurt me to my heart. I could just be setting up on my butt at home, taking care of my kids. I usually leave my kids by theyselves, you know, and neither one of them over eight or nine at the time, and I could a just stayed at home.

Welfare women are often dismayed to find that their grant is reduced when they work. Cora described her experience as a personal affront, and it was entirely self-defeating. Where was the logic, she wondered, in going to work, risking the health and safety of her children, when she could have done as well financially by staying at home? Working out of her home solved several of her problems. It allowed her to supervise her children, or at least to have them close by without the need or cost of a babysitter. It also permitted her to keep all her earned income in addition to the welfare grant, so that she would not feel the frustration of a smaller welfare payment. Finally, she could be her own boss and establish her own work hours. If she wanted to work on a particular day, she started cooking. If she wanted to rest, she simply sent people away. To her mind, the benefits of working out of her home outweighed the risks. She had held a couple of jobs for which she was paid under the table—some domestic work, some in-home assistance to the elderly, and a couple of other cooking jobs—but the fear of being caught by the welfare department was always on her mind. This way, who would find out? There is probably some bureau in the city government that regulates private businesses, but nobody from that department would bother to make random house calls to apartments in the projects.

Because the activity is not detected, the underground economy of the ghetto thrives. The economy is self-regulating; prices are not fixed but are set by the best negotiator. Verbal skills and quick thinking are absolute necessities. Participants in the economy are vulnerable to abuses, as they have no legal recourse, but each joins knowing there is a risk with every transaction.

Participants in the underground economy would probably resist the imposition of regulations, in part because they would be accompanied by enforcers. Attitudes toward law enforcement officials and rule-enforcing agents are mixed. Police are seen as helpful when gross abuses of personal safety arise, but their general presence is viewed with suspicion when neighborhood residents feel that their innocent activities are under surveillance. Cora sees the police as protection against the "bad boys" in the neighborhood, but she also fears the police, wondering when they may catch Darryl in some kind of illegal activity.

Darryl has had trouble with the police ever since he was a boy. Indeed, he only recently returned home after a year in jail. The trouble began when he was quite young. Cora tried to intervene, but it was not clear what she could do.[33]

> Maybe he was eleven, maybe it was nine or ten, somethin' like that. But it wasn't real bad then, I couldn't foresee it, because Darryl never got in trouble and I never had that kind of problem. Them mild trouble he was getting in, the police used to bring him home and say he was tryin' to break into a machine or we saw him tryin' to take a motor-

cycle or a moped on an elevator and take it up a elevator, try to steal it. I'd get on him about it. I always figured he'd go as far as he wanted to go because he be out there [on the streets]. I don't think he was ever involved with gangs, though. I think I would know that for sure. He just run around with more little bad boys.

Cora calls him one of the "little bad boys," but his behavior is hardly as innocuous as that.

They found drugs on him one time, but he was in jail because he's always getting in trouble. He was supposed to go to court, don't go. They caught him driving one time drinking a beer, driving somebody's car. You name it, you know and they just had a mile-long record on him. Especially when he didn't go to court. Then they sent him to juvenile [hall], and he had caught the chicken pox one time and they wanted him to come home, and they said after the chicken pox clear up [to] bring him back. You think Darryl went back? No he didn't. I kept tellin' him, "Darryl, go back, go back, you got to go back." But I can understand why he wouldn't want to go.

But I worry about Darryl, I worry about him, the one always in the streets calling himself big time and always out late. I told [everybody in the house] that if he comes here late, don't let him in. Because once we go to bed, like 1:00 or 2:00 [A.M.] whatever time we go to bed, don't open that door for Darryl. He had been knocking on the door as late as 2:00 and 3:00 in the morning. What he doin' out there in the street late, I got an idea, but I don't want to think of that. He's seventeen years old, but he don't go to school. He want to run up and down the streets; he sleep all day now and when he gets up he will take a shower, and then in the streets again he is. I don't know what he call himself trying to be big time, out there selling dope and shit, that ain't hitting on nothin'.

When he got out of jail, they asked me if it was OK, would I accept him in the house, can he come back? I said, "Yeah." He said, "Mama, when I get home I'm goin' to go to school, I'm goin' to do good and it ain't about bein' in the streets no more; I want to do right. I'm not doin' nothin' to go to jail no more." He had went to jail many times before, claiming he was going to do right, [but] this time, this was the longest they had kept him, and I'm believin' what he's sayin'. Anyway, he got out, the first he did, out there with his friends.

Darryl causes Cora a great deal of anguish, but Felicia has trouble too; it is as though the two youth live by a different standard of behavior.

I had trouble with her and with him. They the only two I had trouble with. Mostly with Felicia. And whatever he did, it was probably worse than her, but it wasn't every day, all the time. She always have been a habitual liar. Don't care, can't see a lie when she really tellin' it.

Although Cora sees Felicia's problems as more severe, her lying and shoplifting are minor compared with her brother's drug dealing. Cora considers Darryl to be beyond her control. She raised boys and girls differently, so she took more personal responsibility for her girls' behavior and shrugged off the boys' misdeeds.

> Boys is more easy to raise than girls. The reason boys is so much easier is if they get somebody pregnant they don't have to bring the babies home. But girls, I guess they require a little bit more talking to than boys.

Cora generally thinks of boys as raising themselves; that is, whatever the outcome is, their behavior will be regulated by their future girlfriend or wife. But Cora believes that she should have more say over her daughters' upbringing, so Felicia's problems are always on her mind. Cora knows that Felicia lives by a strange set of standards. On the other hand, Cora does not understand how she has contributed to those standards. A story Cora once told illustrates part of the problem:

> One time she [Felicia] called and told me she got caught for shoplifting. I didn't believe her because her daughter was over here. She said, "I'm tellin' you the truth, Mama." I said, "You just lyin, you better come get your baby. I'm gonna call the baby daddy and tell him to come get her," and I hung up in her face. She called back, "Please Mama, please Mama, don't hang up in my face, I'm tellin you the truth." And she really was. As a matter of fact, I hung up in her face twice. Then she called back again and I didn't answer it, I just let it ring and ring. I don't know, somebody else was upstairs, or they was up there smokin' they weed, drinkin' a beer or doin' something. They said, "Mama, are you going to pick up the phone?" Then Janice came down and said that Felicia was at the police station. I said, "I don't care, I done told her about doing that mess. I told her sooner or later she was goin' to get caught and for her to stop, sooner or later she's goin' to get caught because she don't know when to quit." So she was at the police station about twenty miles away, and Janice's boyfriend went and got her, and she told him that she was supposed to give him $3, which ain't nothin' to go twenty miles. He went and got her, and he gonna ask me, am I goin' to vouch for the $3? I said, "No, because I know how my daughter is, I know she's a liar and I don't believe her. I'm not vouchin' for nothin', you go pick her up, you pick her up on your own accord."
>
> So this dude went and picked my daughter up, and she told him, "I got $1," and she would give him the rest of the money later. So she had some stuff she had stolen from another store, right before she got caught in this particular store, and they didn't take these goods, so she

had this big pretty sweater in there and she said she would sell it to
him for $10. Then he said, "Let me give you $7 tomorrow because you
already owe me $3." She say, "No, I need my money now." I said,
"Felicia, you can let that man have that thing for $7 because you al-
ready owe him $3; his word is good; he came and picked you up!" I
say, "That sure is cold," I said, "I have to tell you, honey, this man came
all the way out there to pick you up and you say you goin' to give him
$3 . . . right is right, you know."

Felicia had stolen property; she lied in order to get a ride home; and
she then wanted to turn around and sell the stolen property. Nothing
about what she did was moral, but the part that bothered Cora the
most was not negotiating on the sweater. Cora considered it acceptable to take from those who have more. Shoplifting was serious only
because one might get caught. But taking from a store full of merchan-
dise is not so bad.

Cora's sense of moral behavior is based on relationships.[34] The standards by which she lives are partly determined by the situations in
which she finds herself. Her drug use, for example, is fine as long as
the young children do not know about it and it does not get in the
way of her parenting.

Cora has been using drugs for over ten years now, and many of her
neighbors do as well. She has cut back considerably in the last few years
and feels that it does not compromise her ability to parent, but she hit
rock bottom before she realized that what she was doing was wrong.

> I was using drugs real heavy; I wasn't payin' my bills; I was out in the
> streets. It was real bad, real bad. It was so bad that I didn't pay my
> rent and I was kicked out of my apartment, and I was livin' at the
> bottom of this girl's basement and I just felt so miserable, so bad,
> embarrassed. It's just somethin' I'd like to wipe out of my mind. I used
> to try to conceal it [from the kids], and they'd walk in the kitchen and
> I'd say, "Get out," or I'd walk in the bedroom and shut the door or
> with my friends. And it's just somethin' that I said if I ever get out of
> this, that I promise I'd never do this again.

It all happened when a dealer started using her kitchen to prepare the
crack. He would use the stove, cook the cocaine, distill it, and then
wrap each small package separately. Cora always sat in the other room,
promising herself that she would never try it, but curiosity got the best
of her. One night he offered her a hit, and from that moment on, she
was hooked.

> I curse that nigger the day, 'cause I just tried it once and then it
> was . . . "Oh, that do feel good. That's the way I like it, give me some

more." And he said, "You got some money?" I said, "Yeah, I got some." And he said it's like $30. That's how they get you. I didn't notice, though. And I said, "Ya'll got some, it cost $35?" I can't remember how much I gave them, but I know I must have kept running back in my room, you know, and then I got no more money, and I'm sitting there wishin' for and wantin' some more. And I used to think about it and want some more. And just even dream about it. Dream about hittin' that pipe. Just dreamin'. And so he came over, and ever since then he just comin' over on the first and fifteenth and just got hooked and just got started. But my kids used to hate him, though, 'cause they knew he started me.

Cora lost track of time; she lost track of her money; and she lost track of her children. She knows she neglected her children at the time and feels guilty about the effect her drug use may have had on them. Cora simply checked out. She rarely had food in her home; strange and threatening people were always coming by; and then her eviction from the apartment was very hard for the older children. But the worst moment came when she got pregnant with Sharon and gave birth to a drug-exposed infant.

I was hearing something like when Sharon get older she may have a brain problem or something like that, but they wasn't, they wasn't testing pregnant women at that time for drugs to see, or stopping them, or warning them. I just heard somebody say the baby would be all messed up and they say they mama took drugs. And I used to look at Sharon and she used to have the shakes, and I seen it in her and I say, "Please, God, don't make my baby be like that, retarded when she grows up." And sometimes she looks strange, but I put some of it on me, you know, her attitude and stuff like that, but then what I never did was, I never told the doctor I used heavy drugs when I was carrying her.

So finally I just said, "Damn, I'm tired of all this confusement and I'm not never keepin' no money." And then people's trying to say, "Come and stay with me til you get yourself together." And I said, "No, I'm all right." "Come on, these kids ain't got no business down here, no place like this, with all the rats and stuffs." And I says, "No, 'cause I'm feelin' shame. I'm just cryin', want to get out of it. And [Sharon's] father, he didn't offer. He claimed he did, now, but he didn't. He brought me somethin' to eat, but he didn't offer to put us up in a place or nothin'. And that's when my girlfriend came here [to the public housing office], and she told them about me. She had put my name down, and she told them that I needed some help. And the next three months, they call me and they said they had me a place. I didn't even live down there a year. And they called me, they had me a place, a three bedroom. And we looked at it, me and the kids, and we loved it.

It was clean and nice. It was a luxury. And I mean, I didn't hesitate. We went on and moved in. It was a nice place and I loved it and I said, I'm gonna keep my promise to God. I'm gonna pay my rent every month. It was fabulous, great. My friend said it was a blessin' in disguise. I felt good about myself then. It sure was a blessing. And the kids all loved it and they used to say, "Mama, keep this place, please Mama." So I always pay my rent on time. I was there for eight years, and I didn't miss a lick payin' my rent.

Cora's drug use is symptomatic of a lifestyle and a community in disarray. Her problem is not unique to women on welfare, but it is not the norm either. Studies show that about 28 percent of all adult AFDC recipients abuse drugs or alcohol (about 37 percent among AFDC women aged eighteen to twenty-four). Women on AFDC are twice as likely to abuse drugs or alcohol as are women who do not receive AFDC,[35] and the pattern is the same for alcohol, marijuana, and cocaine.[36]

Some states also have examined the relationship between substance abuse and pregnancy among women on welfare, and again, although the data are not encouraging, they do not point to drug use as a normative experience for most AFDC recipients. One study in California indicated that about 13 percent of pregnant women on AFDC had urine tests positive for drugs or alcohol at the time of birth (with almost 2 percent testing positively for cocaine). What the data do not tell us is whether these women began using drugs before they came to the welfare rolls (and consequently whether the drugs caused them to lose a job or relationship) or whether they began to use drugs after they joined the ranks of the poor.

Certainly the experience of poverty begs for an escape. Cora was raised in poverty, lived in poverty, spent ten years in an abusive relationship, was surrounded by drugs on every street corner, and wanted an escape—if not physical, then at least psychological—from the daily challenges of raising children under impossible circumstances. It is astonishing that Cora's baby escaped the child welfare system and was not placed in foster care. Sharon was born in 1985, about two years before crack came to be recognized as a real epidemic.[37] A year or two later, social workers would have quickly noted the signs of drug exposure and probably taken Sharon from her mother. In any case, it was Sharon's birth and the other children's response to the drugs that made Cora realize that something had to change.

I wanted to stop completely, 'cause I prayed to God but he just don't get the taste outa my mouth. And I wanted to quit and I didn't want to quit, and I enjoyed the high sometimes 'cause when I was sittin' around, not doin' nothin' I just, I guess—it just sounds so bad—I just want somethin'. And a friend came over and he was usin' a roll, like you be doin' a joint or he would roll some in there with the tobaccer. You know, crush it up. So I started smokin'—they call 'em gram joints—so I started doin' that, and ever since then I just haven't smoked a pipe. Even now, to be truthful and frank with you, I do it too, now, ever once in a while, but I can function better now. But still, I just want to stop it all completely. But I got it under control. Sometimes when I go to certain doctors, I tell them when they ask, "Do you use drugs?" I say, "Yeah, but I don't smoke the pipe usually, in terms of using drugs. And I don't go to extremes, and I still can take care of my kids. I still get up in the morning and fix they breakfast and do what I have to do, and I don't let it bother me and get in my way." And one doctor told me, "You mean, you can function?" And I said, "Yeah, that's a good way to put it. I can still function, you know, usin' it and still function." But I don't use it as heavy as I did.

It is hard to understand letting one's children go hungry, losing one's home, and losing one's pride, all because of drugs. If one does not live in or frequent the ghetto, it is hard to imagine the constant exchange of drugs outside one's front door. If one is not living in poverty, it is hard to imagine ever living in a ghetto or the feeling of never doing anything satisfying with one's life. If Cora worked, she would probably get some personal satisfaction for doing a job well, but after a year or two, finding meaning in flipping burgers would probably be difficult. With little entertainment but the television, it becomes easier to see the appeal of a total escape. Cora had dreams of moving up and out: Out of her neighborhood and out of her predicament, but that vision died a long time ago. It is not just that she lost her spirit; she also is practical about the real possibilities for ever getting out.

No Way Out

Cora does not have many alternatives outside welfare. She could work, but then there would be the problem of day care. Although she used to leave Tommy and Felicia home alone when she worked at Burger Haven, she knows that public officials are cracking down on that now and she would probably get in trouble. So if she worked, she would need day care for Sharon, Raymond, and Joe, and that would be difficult, if not impossible, to manage. And what kind of a job could she find? She has never done anything but cook, keep a house, and raise children, so the jobs she would qualify for would probably pay only minimum wage.

I once asked Cora what she would do if the government simply refused to pay her welfare anymore. She looked at me quizzically. She did not respond right away, and when she did, she was pessimistic about her job prospects. Finally her answer focused on another source of government funding:

> I'll play crazy and get on disability. I sure would. Because I don't have the skills, don't nobody want to hire no fiftysome-year-old women, and I can't draw Social Security because I don't think I ever worked long enough. I had various jobs, but I don't think I worked on none of them a year, so I know I can't draw that.

"What if President Clinton let you collect welfare for only two years?" I asked. Again, she looked puzzled, as though the idea had never occurred to her.

> How can he do that? Like my younger kids, he gonna put me on welfare for two years, so otherwise what you sayin' when my baby get five years old I can't get welfare no more? So what am I supposed to do? He got some jobs lined up or something? 'Cause if he got some jobs lined up, and it ain't makin' like two dollars or three somethin' an hour, that'll work. But my baby require my attention. Unless they're gonna pay somebody to take care of him, you know, with the problems we have. And why not pay me? I'm his mother. They're gonna pay somebody else? They're gonna be doin' the same thing I'm doin' you know. I can do it. It seem like they're gonna pay someone else to do the same thing that I been doin'. Babysittin' babies and takin' care of kids.

Cora knows enough math to understand that the economics of work simply do not add up for her. She could manage the day-care costs for Sharon, since she is in school most of the day, but the additional costs of full-time care for Raymond and Joe would be impossible. In her county, the average cost for child care is $3.61 per hour.[38] For two full-time child-care slots and one part-time slot, Cora would be spending about $300 a month for child care. Because of her low income, she could qualify for subsidized child care, but the waiting list in her county is currently three years long.[39]

Then what employer would hire her and allow her the flexibility to come and go for countless doctors' appointments? Families in low-income communities are far more likely to have numerous health problems,[40] and Cora's family is no exception. With all the health problems that her family has, Cora would need a full health-care benefit package if she were working. Partial health insurance in the event of emergencies would not be enough. Cora knows that there are few jobs for which she could qualify that would provide the kind of health coverage she needs, so living on welfare must suffice. It does not provide any comforts, but it does give her the basic coverage she needs to be able to supervise and care for her children. Would education and training make much of a difference in her job prospects? That is not clear. Cora is currently enrolled in the JOBS program, but the personal benefits she gets from participating are probably not those envisioned by the program's founders.

Training and Education to What End?

Cora volunteered for the JOBS program shortly after it began in her county. Three and a half years later she is still in the program. When she first enrolled, her JOBS worker discovered that although she had a high school diploma, Cora could not pass a test of basic skills. Cora needed to brush up on her reading and to learn (or relearn) some math as well. Her worker enrolled her in a local adult education school and started her off with spelling lessons, reading comprehension, and basic math classes. After three months, Cora took a test to determine whether she had learned basic math and reading skills. Had she passed, she would have moved on to a training program. But she did not pass the test in the first three months, or even in the first six months. Three and a half years later, she is still going to the same class, trying to learn the same skills. She cannot graduate into a training program until she passes her test, so every day, five days a week, Cora goes to school for four hours a day. Her attendance is steady, and her enthusiasm for the program is remarkable. She may not be learning what JOBS officials would like her to learn, but Cora is enjoying the program.

"How much longer will you be in school?" I ask.

> After I pass that test. I never pass the test. The only problem I have is I don't know my time tables that well. My teacher, the one that I have now, she's a big help to me. I was so surprised and laughin' at myself when I really learned how to divide long problems. But my only problem is I can't multiply too well. I have to get out the times board or count and she'll be tellin' me that I've run out of time if I'm takin' a test. It's hard to learn those time tables, I don't know why. Because the rest of it come so easy. Spellin', and hard words; I'm learning how to spell the really hard words. I don't know what it is, I'll cry 'cause I can't do certain things. Sometimes I just go to sleep with those numbers in my head, I put them under my pillow, and I just keep studying until I go to sleep. Just keep at it. Just keep at it. It's my times tables. It do get frustratin', it do. It make me so mad at myself. So I say, "Why

can't I just get it?" I don't know why. [My teacher] tellin' me, "You could do it, Cora." I just got to get those time tables. But when I come home and then the babysitter will leave, so then the house is a mess, and I got to get my kids something to eat and I can't study with them in the house, you know. I tell my teacher, I say, by the time they go to bed and sleep, I start studying and next thing I know I'm asleep too. So I don't know how to put my work habits in with my house habits without me going to sleep too. If I don't pass the test, I don't know what's going to happen.

Why must Cora pass a test before she can begin a training program? And what jobs require multiplication? Although these rules might seem unnecessary, for Cora, the JOBS program, designed exactly as it is, works well.

I signed up for it because I wanted to change my life around during that time. Do something. Joe wasn't even born then, and Raymond was just a baby. I just wanted something to do, turn my life around, I got tired of being bored. Now when I come in the house it's just like, well I guess I did something with my life today, I did something today, you know? I feel good about myself, I go in the kitchen and start cookin', fix something to eat, or I sit down and relax. I just feel good about myself when I get out and do something. Sometimes I don't want to go to school. Then sometimes I just do it, and once I get there and get the hang of it I feel good about myself, because time flies past and the next thing I know another day is gone. Start another day. I wanted to do it to keep my mind occupied, because I knew if I sat around the house I would go crazy. When I was sitting around the house, I used to cry and just talk to myself, and I used to say, I'm going crazy, why am I so crazy?

Because of the JOBS program, Cora gets out of the house. It gives her a break from the noise and chaos; it gives her a couple hours of relative quiet; and it gives her a sense of self-esteem. Even her teacher admits that Cora has made great progress in the past three years. "Cora believes in herself, now," she stated. "She's always making progress." Although her progress is slow by conventional standards, Cora is growing and learning, one step at a time.

Going to school also gives Cora a break from her children, helps her relax and keep perspective on all the little things that go wrong at home. Cora's children are a real handful, so the few hours of respite allow her to come home ready to face the noise and confusion of the evening. Like the drugs, JOBS also allows an escape; it takes her out of her house, out of her environment, and away from her everyday worries.

Although Cora enjoys her JOBS program, even she recognizes the absurdity of attending the same class for three years. A couple of years ago she tried to combine her basic education program with a secretarial program also offered at the adult school.

> I was doin' this on my own 'cause [JOBS] wouldn't pay for typing. I was doin' it myself. I was paying $10 a semester. [My worker] said [JOBS] doesn't pay for a typing class, they only pay for science, math, and reading. I can't understand that. That would have gave me five hours in school instead of four. And then after I take typing from 11:00 to 12:00, then I could go to my other class. But they say [JOBS] won't pay for it. They tight. It seem like a more important thing using that computer than those math and science classes.

It is not that Cora resented paying the $10 fee, but she also needed an additional hour or two of child care. After trying it for a semester on her own, Cora gave up. Now she has completely lost track of what her next step in JOBS may be. Her worker told her that there were other steps in the program, but at this point, she cannot imagine what they would be. Indeed, she has completely lost track of the purpose of JOBS. When she began, she knew that it was a job preparation program. Now it is just a pleasant activity that helps her get through the day.

A Grim Future for the Children

Let us imagine that Cora passed her math test and moved on to a job training program. Maybe she would learn how to type or how to use a word processor. When she enrolled in a private business school a couple of years ago (similar to the school that Ana's son attended), she was typing about twenty-five words a minute[41]—maybe she could improve on that. Or maybe she would be placed in a "food preparation" program that would train her to work in a restaurant. When she completed the course, she would probably make about $4.25 an hour, the minimum wage. The good news is that the minimum wage has increased in the past few years. In 1991, federal legislation increased it from $3.35 an hour to $4.25 an hour. But the bad news is that even if Cora worked full time at minimum wage, her income would still be about one-third below the poverty threshold (Darryl will soon turn eighteen and will no longer be her financial responsibility, so she will have to provide "only" for Sharon, Raymond, Joe, and herself). Cora would need to make about $7.00 an hour just to reach the poverty line of $14,381 for a family of four. When the most she has ever made at a job was $4.10 an hour, the prospect of finding work paying nearly double that is very unlikely.[42]

Let us further assume that Cora does get a job. If the job did pay enough to get her off welfare, the state would pay for child care for her three youngest children for one full year. But at the end of that year, Cora would be harnessed with a significant child-care bill. Cora's estimation of the situation is quite accurate: Why pay someone else several hundred dollars a month to care for her three small children when she can do it for the price of a welfare grant? The difference in dollars and cents is not that much.

Perhaps rather than asking whether we want to pay Cora and women like her to raise their own children or whether we want these children in publicly supported day care, we should ask whether Cora's care—by itself—is enough. Cora's children are her life—they are the one thing that gives her life meaning. She does not abuse them. Sometimes she disciplines them with a spanking or threatens them with a belt, but most of the time she relies on a "time-out" to take care of the little ones ("Go sit on the steps!" is the usual demand). The children are always simply, but appropriately, dressed, and they are always fed (although mealtimes are not a scheduled event).

Nonetheless, Cora often lapses in the care of her children and inadvertently allows them to suffer from medical and educational neglect. Cora therefore needs occasional help with her parenting. She needs reminders about school homework and medical appointments. Her children need someone who will make sure that they are receiving all of the services to which they are entitled.

When I visited Cora, I often found that she had forgotten another doctor's appointment for Raymond or Joe or an eye doctor's appointment for Sharon. And although she was supposed to enroll Raymond in kindergarten in September, she still had not done so in April because she had missed all his appointments for special screening and assessment. (The fact that the school is located one block from her home makes her inattention to his needs all the more frustrating.) Finally, a team of school officials, including the school psychologist, a resource specialist, the speech pathologist, and a physical therapist, all descended on Cora's home one morning in May to test Raymond for kindergarten placement.

Then there was the frightening morning when Cora could not find Sharon. Darryl had taken Sharon and Cora's granddaughter, Malika, to the fair the night before. When they returned home at about 9:30 P.M. in the evening, Sharon had walked Malika home. Although Malika and Felicia live only two blocks away, the thought of sending two small girls—aged eight and five—through the projects at that time of the night attests to the complacency that can result from growing up in a dangerous environment.[43] Cora came home from a friend's house a couple of hours later and went to bed, never checking on her sleeping children. The next morning when I arrived and asked about Sharon, Cora had to stop for a minute to remember where she was:

> I think she's at [Felicia's]. Matter of fact, she went to her sister's yesterday, to the fair, and she went with her yesterday and I went out somewhere . . . when I came back home . . . I think she spend the night there. [Cora dialed Felicia's telephone number.] Sharon spend the night with you? . . . Girl, don't be lying to me . . . hold on a minute . . . Janice!! Janice!! [she called upstairs] . . . Is Sharon upstairs?! Felicia say Sharon supposed to came home last night, were you here when Sharon took Malika home? Were you, Darryl? Well, Felicia say Sharon's not at her house, that Sharon came home last night!

Cora flew into a panic and sent Darryl out onto the street to look for Sharon. She also put a coat over her bathrobe and went calling down the sidewalk. In the meantime, Felicia called back and told Janice that she had played a trick on her mother. When Cora returned, crying and shaking, Janice told her, "She say she playin' a trick, she at Felicia's house."

> Man, that's real stupid, huh? Somebody playin' a fuckin' trick like that?
>   "That's stupid, Mama," Darryl chimed in, always trying to get a dig at his sister. "Felicia stupid, Mama."

Cora called Felicia again and began screaming into the phone,

> Why in hell did you tell me that? Don't you know I'd be worrying about my baby, and I went all down the neighborhood looking for her? . . . Well, what the hell you thought I was goin' to do if I thought she wasn't at your house? What the fuck! Don't you play no games like that with me no goddamn more!! Ignorant! I been thinkin' all sorts of things, that my baby could a been layin' in one of those fucking garbage cans and somebody might a had her there dead and raped!

Cora slammed down the phone and began talking, not to anyone in particular, but to anyone who might listen:

> I just thinkin' the worst, 'cause it dark and she lives, well, two blocks down, she got to go through the village, you know, and I was thinkin' one of these old dirty boys probably snatched her somewhere, you know, and took her to one of these deserted houses. That girl's always have been a habitual liar. Can't see a lie when she really tellin' it.

That night and others as well, Cora did not know where her children slept; that night and others, an eight-year-old escorted a five-year-old through the projects at night. Although there is no way out of the projects for Cora, they will have an enormous impact on her daily life and, more tragically, on the way she raises her children.[44]

Take Felicia, for example. At age fourteen, Felicia got pregnant. Rather than watch her daughter carefully and caution her about the consequences of sex, Cora had paid some but not much attention to her daughter's comings and goings. Cora had a very close relationship with Sharon's father at the time. Unfortunately, what Cora did not recognize was that while she was involved with Sharon's father, Felicia was also involved with a young man.

> I told her, I said, "You ain't old enough to cope," 'cause she was just fourteen. "You ain't old enough to cope and see I'm not lettin' you see no boys."
>
> "Mama, I ain't talking about no boyfriend. Girlfriend, boyfriend. He just a friend. He can come talk to me."
>
> She explained it to me just like I'm talkin' to you. And I tried to see her point. And I said, "Well, OK then, it's OK, he can come over and talk. But no goin' up in the bedrooms.
>
> She was fourteen. I think he was like sixteen or seventeen. And he came over. They used to sit down in the living room and talk for a while. Then one thing led to another and my company come over and we'll be in my bedroom talking and one thing led to another. And then I know I'm two months pregnant, three months pregnant, and then I'm noticing Felicia ain't havin' her period. So when I'm downstairs makin' it out, she's upstairs doin' the same thing with her boyfriend!
>
> And I takes her to the doctor and they wouldn't tell me at the time 'cause the doctor had came out, and I said, "Is she having sex?" And he told me, "No," straight up, you know? So I'm knowin' she ain't pregnant. So Felicia never did tell me. She just let it go on. And then this nurse call me, and she say I should come into the office so that we can have a talk. So then they told me. And I just looked at her, not so much surprised because I done already suspected it. It's a matter of just disappointment and sadness 'cause it is true and hoping that it wasn't. We talked and I was mad, and I was tellin' 'em, why couldn't they have told me? And I said, "I don't think she should have any kids 'cause she too young. I'm against abortions, but she too young to be havin' a baby and I said I'm pregnant myself. I got my own baby comin' to think about." And she was sayin' she wanted to have it. She can handle it. 'Cause she so in love with this boy. I said, "Felicia, do you know that you and him ain't guaranteed to be together for life?" You know I'm trying to explain to her, she young and he ain't gonna be with her all her life. But "we love each other" is what she say.

Cora tried to talk Felicia into an abortion, but Felicia refused. She carried the baby to term and had Malika just four months after Raymond was born. Felicia stayed in her mother's house for the next three years, collecting AFDC for her and her daughter, but by age seventeen, Felicia was ready to be on her own, and so she and Malika moved into another public housing apartment a couple of blocks away.

Although we might characterize Cora as "welfare dependent," her daughter's use of welfare was not predetermined. Many believe that children raised in AFDC homes are likely to become dependent on AFDC themselves when they grow up, yet as we noted in Chapter 1, this also is a myth that the available evidence has disputed. In most cases, children raised in welfare-dependent households are not more likely to become dependent on welfare themselves.[45] Nonetheless, Felicia defies the statistics. She and her daughter have been on AFDC for five years now, and the most likely route off aid would probably be marriage, as her earning capacity is very low.

Until last year, Cora was proud of her daughter's parenting.

> Well, she did do good up until now that they broke up and she want a life for herself. And she'll tell me now, "Mama, I love my daughter, but I just don't want her no more. I don't want to take care of her no more." She not givin' her no attention. She always runnin' out havin' fun now. She's runnin' around partyin'. She stays out late and she's really not givin' her daughter anything. Because the teacher send letters home sayin' that she gonna have to repeat the kindergarten again because she don't know her letters, she don't know her colors, she can't write her name, she's always late for school. And she's a smart little girl if her mother would work with her.
>
> She just don't want to be a mama now and she say, "I see what you're talkin' about, Mama." She's young and now she got that freedom and she just gone crazy, went all berserk. And she just take it out, she just get angry, you know, because she can't do certain things. Sometimes she just hit her baby, too.

Cora's neglect of her children led to Felicia's neglect of Malika. Cora's neglect of Raymond has left him a year behind in school. Early treatment for his speech and his disability might have helped, but now it will take months or even years to correct the damage done by his seizures. Frequently missed doctor's appointments for Joe mean that he, too, could develop a brain tumor without Cora's even being aware of it.[46] It is not clear whether Raymond and Joe will even survive to adulthood, for in some cases their disease can be fatal. Sharon's falling behind in her schoolwork and her bad eyesight is probably part of the problem. The long-term effects of Sharon's exposure to drugs while Cora was pregnant with her will probably become more apparent over time as well. Tommy and Darryl may be HIV positive, passing the AIDS virus around the neighborhood and beyond, and Darryl's drug dealing will either result in jail or death at an early age. None of the three older children ever finished high school. Tommy dropped out at age sixteen; Felicia dropped out after she had her baby; and Darryl has essentially dropped out, although he still tells his mama that he may return to school.[47] None of these children has a bright future.[48] Without a high school diploma, they will likely be unemployed, on welfare, and impoverished.[49] And the fact that Cora uses drugs to distract her from the extreme and insurmountable difficulties of her life means that she cannot be a fully responsible parent. Her heart may be in the right place, but Cora and her children are not. The projects are no place to raise a family. Cora says,

> Every time I look at my babies when they sleep at night, I cry. I pray to God that he let me, so Raymond won't have to take care of themself, you know. I don't want nothing bad to happen to him. It worries me to think it might. I ask God to let me live long enough to see them old enough to take care of themselves.

But it is unlikely that any of them will be able to take care of themselves. Cora and her children and perhaps her grandchildren will probably be cared for by the state for most of the years of all of their lives.

7

Finding a Better Way

Ana, Sandy, Rebecca, Darlene, and Cora—five American women raising children without fathers and trying to survive. All these women relied on welfare, which helped stave off absolute destitution.

Ana might have foreseen the financial problems associated with her restaurant, but how could she have prepared for her injury? If we were in similar circumstances, we might also hope for assistance once our family resources were exhausted. Ana is a good example of Greg Duncan's conclusion (see Chapter 2), that most welfare recipients have the same characteristics as average Americans.[1] Each year, hundreds of thousands of families rise above poverty, and others slip into it. They are the hapless instruments of an economic system that provides little insurance against hard times.

Sandy turned to welfare because it was impossible to work. Recall that Sandy's problem was not welfare per se but the attendant problems such as health care, child care, and work disincentives. Changes in welfare policy alone would have little effect on women such as Sandy, because their needs go far beyond the welfare system. Had there been a better strategy for recouping child-support payments or for obtaining health care, Sandy would not have needed welfare at all.

But Sandy did sign on to welfare because it was an option that made sense. Welfare recipients are rational actors in the economic market; they do whatever is necessary to maximize the health and well-being of their children. If they have no health insurance or if they believe that they will be somewhat better off on welfare, they will apply for it. Welfare recipients are a diverse group of women, but they have common American values. Like most other Americans, welfare recipients usually put the needs of their children first.

Rebecca initially used welfare as an agent of maturity. Later she used it as a source of financial aid while she attended college. When she finishes her degree, her service as a teacher will be a fair exchange for the aid she was given in her younger years.

Darlene represents the complexity of the welfare population. A woman of intelligence and insight, she nevertheless is greatly challenged by the daily requirements of providing for her family without some government support. She might be viewed as a member of the "residual" welfare population.[2] They include women with physical or mental handicaps, women who are geographically isolated from jobs and transportation, and women with such severe family problems that they cannot fulfill the daily requirements of employment. As is a very small proportion of the AFDC population, Darlene is emotionally unstable. Perhaps she suffers from mental illness. Although compared with the severely emotionally disturbed, her problems are mild, they do interfere with her ability to function productively. For women such as Darlene and those with more serious problems, AFDC acts much like a disability insurance program. But without its associated mental health and case management services, AFDC does little to ameliorate many of these women's problems. At the least, it ensures that they have housing, heat, and food.[3]

Finally, Cora exemplifies the difficulty of solving the welfare problem. Although she made some mistakes, perhaps they could not have been easily avoided. Cora has limited intelligence and is a victim of an inadequate educational system. She was raised in a poor rural, abusive family, and marriage only brought more assault and battery—hardly an endorsement for family stability. Cora knows that she has very limited job prospects and also no guarantee of child care. If she had fewer children, she would have fewer problems, but as the other case studies in this book illustrate, the size of one's family is not a determinant of welfare use. Rebecca, with one child, was as needy as Cora with six. Nonetheless, Cora's large family makes the likelihood of leaving welfare much more remote.

None of the women depicted here wanted to be on welfare, and few of them expected to use it for a long time. Cora is realistic about her skills and the labor market. Given the medical needs of her family and the high cost of child care, her prediction that she will have to continue on welfare is accurate. Cora and her family give insight into the lives of many of the persistently poor. The outlook for Cora's children also highlights the urgency of confronting family poverty.

The Many Faces of Poverty

Despite their differences—these women's paths to welfare, their various experiences with education and training programs, and their readiness for work—all are similar, having raised their children for a time in poverty. Some children, like Kim, may live in poverty only briefly, but others, like Raymond and Joe, may live in poverty throughout their lifetime. Social scientists and welfare experts may disagree about the relative merits of various welfare reform proposals and the advantages and disadvantages of different economic incentives, but most agree on one fundamental aspect of the welfare program in the United States: It impoverishes children. Women turn to AFDC because they are poor, and they remain poor while on welfare. Although some may escape poverty once they leave the welfare rolls, many do not. Sadly, while these women are living in poverty, the opportunities for their children to grasp the American dream diminish considerably.

Beyond these similarities, however, the differences among women on AFDC are pronounced. As this book has shown and as large national studies confirm, women on welfare are a diverse group and only infrequently fit the common welfare stereotype. It is precisely this diversity, however, that makes it difficult to address welfare. Policymakers are reluctant to tackle such multifaceted problems because the likely solutions themselves are complex. But if women on welfare have diverse needs, policies and programs should provide diverse services.

Not all women need employment and training programs, for instance. Women such as Ana already have very strong job skills and simply need welfare to tide them over until their economic fortunes change. Other large sectors of the poverty population need few services other than an economic safety net and a supportive environment. Women with recent job experience and those with a strong educational background may request training in interviewing or preparing résumés, but they may not need the more intensive services offered by programs such as JOBS.

At the other end of the spectrum are those women with many and great needs. Owing to a combination of personal characteristics and environmental conditions, some women may require individualized services to help them become self-sufficient. They may also require close case management to ensure their children's healthy development. To ignore these distinctive needs when considering the welfare population is to fall into the trap of simplicity that has plagued the welfare debate for so long.

What percentage of the population lies on each end of the continuum? How many are in the middle?[4] What characteristics—personal and environmental—determine these differences? Research is beginning to tease out the qualities that predict short- and long-term stays on welfare. We now know, for example, that women with stronger educational backgrounds, with recent work experience, and with children over six years old are more likely to leave the welfare rolls rapidly.[5] Although these findings are not definitive, they point to an emerging technology that, over time, may be able to guide policymakers and program managers. Whether we target certain services to women on AFDC because of the particular characteristics they present when entering welfare or offer services based on their identified needs once they are collecting welfare is a political problem. Nevertheless, our point should be clear: If women on welfare are diverse, reforms that are universal in their coverage yet singular in their approach are destined to fail. Instead, as the public image of welfare is expanded to accommodate the heterogeneity of the population, the welfare debate should shift to encompass the multidimensional needs of women and children.

The current debate surrounding welfare reform does not highlight the diversity among mothers on AFDC, nor does it focus on ending poverty for children. Instead, welfare reform is being addressed this year just as it was in 1988 and will be again in five or ten years. Welfare will never be removed from the public agenda as long as we continue to tinker with it only at the edges and ignore the real issues of inadequate job prospects, poor education, low wages, and all of poverty's attendant problems.

Reforming Welfare: Current State and Federal Initiatives

A look at the debate surrounding welfare reveals the political capital of the issue. Playing on the public's fears and misconceptions about welfare stereotypes, the discussion in recent years has centered on women's inadequacies as workers, parents, and contributors to society and on a system out of balance with mainstream values. Most people know that welfare does not support and protect children. The system makes liars out of their mothers who must cheat the welfare system in order to make ends meet. The system relegates children to long-term hardship because it creates impossible obstacles for mothers to surmount in order to rise above the poverty line. And the system does not allow children to receive the support of an absent parent who is economically able to help. Because welfare is widely disparaged, demands for its reform come from all across the political spectrum.

The tenacity of the problem and the political divisiveness of the issue has generally kept the federal government out of the business of welfare reform. Recently, however, many reforms have been initiated at the state and local levels. Consequently, although the core welfare program remains intact, innovations are being introduced throughout the country.[6] Some are meant to assist poor families, whereas others are more mean-spirited in their design. The following describes some of these reforms and how they are likely to affect women and children.

Reform 1: The Two-Year Time Limit

Starting in 1995, Wisconsin's "Work Not Welfare" program will put a two-year cap on cash aid for about 1,000 recipients in two counties. . . . Recipients [will] be barred from reapplying for benefits for three years.[7]

The most recent national debate on welfare reform was initiated by President Bill Clinton when he claimed in his first State of the Union address that he would "end welfare as we know it. . . . We have to end welfare as a way of life," he told the nation, "and make it a path to independence and dignity." Throughout his campaign, Clinton stated that he wanted to

> provide people with the education, training, job placement assistance, and child care they need for two years—so that they can break the cycle of dependency. After two years, those who can work will be required to go to work, either in the private sector or in meaningful community-service jobs.[8]

Although the two-year policy indicates a willingness to support women and children, albeit for a limited time, at the end of two years the cash benefits would end. Why two years rather than three, four, or five? Looking back on the research conducted by Bane and Ellwood (Chapter 1), we see that the majority of women leave welfare within two years.[9] Those who remain on welfare for more than two years are considerably more likely to remain on it for a very long time. But the two-year limit also reflects Americans' discomfort with the notion of welfare "dependency" and the assumption that most welfare women fit the classic stereotype.

Conservative policymakers generally favor the two-year limit because it emphasizes women's responsibility to work. Women's employment is seen not only as an appropriate exchange for cash assistance, but it is also considered equitable, as more and more women from all economic groups are joining the labor force.

But does this approach appeal to the American public? A national poll found that "while voters approach issues of poverty and welfare with a conservative *diagnosis*, they are not eager to embrace conservative *prescriptions* for reforming the welfare system."[10] In fact, one of the least popular reforms suggested by pollsters was the two-year time limit: 88 percent of the respondents noted that the two-year time limit would hurt innocent children.

The time limit may indeed harm welfare children. Research conducted since the original Bane and Ellwood study indicates that two years is not the cutoff point for most welfare users.[11] As the structure of the American economy continues to change,[12] women are finding it increasingly difficult to leave welfare for work. Women like Ana, who bring job skills, a work history, or a solid educational background to the program, may leave welfare relatively quickly and so will not be affected by a policy such as this. But research informs us that because some women are more likely to rely on welfare for a very long time, the two-year limit may penalize certain groups of aid recipients.[13] Because these women require additional services and support, a policy that cuts them off will only push them farther from the economic mainstream rather than closer to it.

Critics of the welfare system such as Charles Murray contend that such a drastic policy would force otherwise reluctant women into the labor market.[14] Yet we can see on any city street the effects of our retreat from assisting the poor. Women and children are the fastest-growing group of homeless people.[15] These women already have been forced to become resourceful, and many are working. But homelessness—the most obvious sign of desperate poverty—shames the American public. Policies such as the two-year limit will only exacerbate poverty and ultimately deplete the American spirit.

Reform 2: Expanded Education and Training Opportunities

The report [Washington] found that vocational education and training, when analyzed in combination with all other variables, had a statistically significant effect upon employment.[16]

In connection with the two-year limit, the current thinking on welfare reform centers on supplying education and training services to help AFDC recipients improve their marketable skills (similar to the

JOBS program). Many proposals are highly restrictive, offering women short-term assistance in finding a job, whereas others are broader in their scope, encouraging women to enhance their skills to the greatest extent possible.[17] Many short-term proposals are founded on the common assumption that women on welfare are able but unwilling to work outside the home. As we already pointed out, however, many women on welfare are prevented from working because of problems with child and health care, transportation difficulties, and a welfare system that penalizes their efforts. Their attempts are also discouraged by their lack of education and skills.

An opportunity-based approach would help large numbers of women who need a limited amount of education or training in order to catch up to their competitors in the labor market. But even two years of services should not be seen as a panacea. If only two years of services had been available to Rebecca, she might not be on welfare today, but the prospects for her long-term independence would probably also not be bright. After two years of the JOBS program, Rebecca probably could have taken a position as a teacher's aide in a local elementary school. The job would have paid the minimum wage, enough to remove her from welfare but not enough to lift her and Tanya above the poverty line. Rebecca would therefore have continued to live on the margin, only a month or two away from economic disaster.

The question we must ask about women such as Rebecca is whether the government should maximize human potential or minimize welfare receipt. If we want only to shorten the welfare rolls, then services that cost little and are aimed toward the bottom rungs of the job market will work moderately well. But if we want to lift families out of poverty and to provide long-lasting support, then we will need a more intensive human-capital approach. Two years will not buy a college degree, and it will not land a job paying $20,000 or $30,000. Two years may offer enough to some to escape welfare, but rarely will it be enough to avoid poverty.[18]

As more and more families slip into poverty, fundamental questions arise about the structure of the American economy. A recent Census Bureau report states that the percentage of Americans working full time yet still living in poverty increased 50 percent in the past thirteen years. Young workers and workers without a college degree (these would include most young women eligible for AFDC) were the hardest hit.[19] When almost one-quarter of the population of all full-time working women cannot support themselves and their families, the economic prospects for women on AFDC—who are marginalized both educationally and socially—are grim.

Reform 3: Work Requirements

Long-term welfare recipients would be required to perform 20 hours of community service work or have their grants cut . . . [Massachusetts].[20]

Although the stereotype of the long-term welfare recipient persists, most women who use AFDC voluntarily leave the welfare rolls quickly, particularly if they are given health insurance, child care, child support, assistance with housing, and the opportunity to gain work skills through training or education. Some women, however—though a small minority—never return to work. Some of them are mentally unstable, like Darlene. Others refuse to work because of fear; a lack of self-esteem, skills, and/or education; personal disorganization; family problems; or simply lethargy. After a limited time on AFDC and after help finding a job, the new reforms may require these women to work as a condition for receiving aid.

This emphasis on work has its roots in American attitudes toward employment and cultural values of reciprocity. That is, Americans believe if they receive a gift from someone, there is an implicit assumption in the exchange that the gift will be reciprocated. The debt owed may be financial, material, or emotional, but on some level, most Americans feel strongly that it is not appropriate or fair to obtain something for nothing. Accordingly, the debt incurred by long-term welfare recipients is not just financial. Owing to the cultural shift that has taken place in the United States and the value placed on women's work outside the home, it is no longer equitable for women on welfare not to work. Therefore, our insistence on reciprocity demands that women on welfare do something in exchange for their financial assistance. Yet if work is made a requirement, we should consider the work patterns of other working mothers. That is, even though most mothers work, few do so full time.[21] For women such as Cora, whose children require much of her attention and who also suffers from a chronic problem with disorganization and indolence, a forty-hour workweek would be impossible; indeed, most women with small children find it very difficult to maintain a forty-hour work schedule.[22]

Work requirements that are meant to punish women for their AFDC use may help the American public come to terms with the welfare problem but ultimately will be counterproductive for the women and children who need public assistance. If work reforms take into account the varying capabilities of persons on welfare and do not make demands on women that they cannot meet, a number of significant goals may be achieved. Public fears about welfare dependency may be assuaged as welfare comes to be associated with new expectations and activities. Public misconceptions about the welfare population also may be clarified when welfare mothers become more visible in the public sphere through their work outside the home. If the work is meaningful—to the women and to the neighborhoods in which they work—the public will recognize that welfare recipients are making a contribution to their communities. Most important, work opportunities for women on welfare may help them open doors to the market economy that otherwise might be closed.

Reform 4: Welfare Cuts

Nine [states] reduced grants in 1991 more sharply than at any time in the past 10 years, according to a new report.[23]

In state after state across the country, welfare cuts have been introduced as an important element of welfare reform. In some cases, the cuts have represented a small but steady erosion in family benefits. In others, the cuts have been more drastic.[24] Behind these efforts to scale back cash benefits has been the implicit assumption that women on welfare receive enough to survive. But the case studies of the women described in this book show that the money women receive from AFDC rarely even covers all of their basic expenses. It requires a fair amount of ingenuity to stretch welfare dollars, and not all women are as able or resourceful as Ana is in multiplying the purchasing power of their AFDC checks and food stamps. Moreover, efforts to reform welfare by cutting welfare benefits harm children the most. They also impede women's efforts to raise children in healthy, positive environments. Research indicates that as women's incomes rise, the quality of the home environment they provide for their children improves as well.[25] Public policy that alleviates rather than perpetuates poverty for children may be especially beneficial to their well-being.

Reform 5: The Family Cap

Governor William Donald Schaefer (D-Maryland) has asked the General Assembly to abolish an $80 increase in aid to welfare recipients who have additional children.[26]

Many states are experimenting with the notion of a "family cap," a policy based on the myth discussed in Chapter 1, that once women start collecting welfare, they continue to have children simply to increase the amount of their check.[27] The policy also bolsters common misconceptions about the average size of the welfare family: Although the public imagines it to be rather large, the evidence shows that the size of AFDC families has grown smaller over time. According to one government report, large families (women with four or more children) are almost half as likely to be found among the welfare population than they were fifteen years ago.[28] Furthermore, women who receive welfare are not only more careful about using contraception than are women in the general public, but the receipt of AFDC actually has a dampening effect on women's fertility.[29] A study by Mark Rank shows that the odds of conceiving a child decrease notably with each additional year that a woman receives welfare.[30]

Rather than designing policy based on fact, a "family cap" policy would only exacerbate public fears regarding welfare recipients and confirm an already exaggerated image. Furthermore, such a policy would not affect most welfare families. The unlucky women who did become pregnant, however, would become even more marginalized economically and so would have to work even harder at stretching their dollars. Consequently, these women and their children would fall even deeper into poverty.

Reform 6: Interstate Disincentives

Newcomers to the state [Iowa] . . . would be limited to welfare payments equal to what they received in their home state for one year.[31]

One of the more prominent misconceptions regarding welfare, as described in Chapter 1, is the extent to which states with higher welfare benefits act as "magnets" for welfare recipients. Even though policies now being enacted across the country prey on people's fears about this magnet effect, they are not based on sound research regarding the actual mobility patterns of AFDC families. Poor families, like other families, usually move in search of opportunity. Rather than portraying welfare recipients as ordinary people, policymakers vilify AFDC families through policies such as these, categorizing them as "other" in their rhetoric.

The unfortunate families who cannot find employment when they move will be penalized by these measures for their well-meaning efforts to provide a better life for their children. Although the majority of welfare recipients—those who do not move—will not be affected financially by these reforms, their impact on welfare families more generally will be significant. Policies that capitalize on public fears play a symbolic role in shaping the policy debate and the public's understanding of family poverty.

Reform 7: Economic Inducements to Regulate Behavior

The measure [Nevada] . . . would fine welfare parents who don't work with school counselors to make sure their children go to school regularly.[32]

Welfare charges the American psyche. It does so in part because there is great disagreement about the extent to which women create their own misfortune or whether they are merely victims of a poorly designed system. This book has tried to lay out both sides of the controversy. No one can win this debate because everyone is right—sometimes. But reforms that provide economic incentives within the welfare system play into the assumption that women must be constantly cajoled into behaving responsibly. Absent from the discussion is the notion that the typical welfare recipient indeed lives by common American standards.

Several initiatives have emerged that threaten to cut women's income unless they abide by certain practices. "LearnFare" is an excellent example of such an approach. Several states now penalize AFDC families whose children do not attend school regularly. The reasoning is that low-income children are less likely to complete high school and to have worse attendance rates than do children from higher-income families.

Completing school is indeed a problem in low-income communities. Children from families with an annual income of less than $10,000 are twice as likely to drop out of school than are those from families whose annual income is between $10,000 and $20,000.[33] But is the problem of not attending school worse among welfare children? A study conducted in Wisconsin showed that attendance records for AFDC and non-AFDC children were very similar.[34] In this study, AFDC children lost about three more days of school during an elementary school year than non-AFDC children did, a difference that is not statistically significant.

One of the only evaluations of the effects of economic sanctions for LearnFare families indicates that the program does not improve school attendance among targeted adolescents.[35] More important, the study shows that penalized children had the highest dropout rates. That is, rather than encouraging children to finish high school, the program may unintentionally drive children away from school.

Similar to the economic penalties associated with attending school, "ImmunoFare" efforts are aimed at encouraging women on welfare to obtain immunizations for their young children. The effort is based on the assumption that low-income women are not aware of the importance of vaccinations and that they are not concerned about the health of their children.

Immunization rates have declined considerably in recent years. A study by the Centers for Disease Control indicates that vaccination rates among poor, inner-city preschoolers have plummeted.[36] A study by George also suggests that less than half of all two-year-old children in the United States are fully immunized and that poor children are the least likely to receive immunizations.[37] Yet further evidence shows that the reasons for these problems may be found as much in the health-care system as in individual failings. That is, although many parents understand the importance of immunizations, problems with transportation, clinic hours, shortages of vaccines, and too few Medicaid providers may be exacerbating the problem.[38] Moreover, even though the problem is particularly serious in poor communities, there is no evidence that women on welfare are more likely than are other poor or near-poor families to fail to have their children vaccinated.[39]

Policies such as ImmunoFare illustrate the one-sided approach to welfare reform—fixating on the problem of parental behavior and ignoring the related problems in the larger environment. The unintended consequences of these policies are also ironic and painful. Although legislators may be trying to ensure the health and safety of young children by having them vaccinated, instead their health may be compromised further if their basic needs cannot be met by the most meager family income. Any efforts to penalize families by reducing their monthly income may unwittingly push children further into poverty, thus exacerbating already untenable living conditions.

Economic disincentives for irresponsible behavior are usually coupled with positive financial incentives to reward socially acceptable conduct. For example, students who complete high school while receiving AFDC may receive a "bonus" check for their responsible behavior. In addition, through the use of economic incentives, many states now encourage women to control their fertility. For example, as early as 1991, Wisconsin's governor, Tommy Thompson, was advocating a $500 bonus for recipients who agreed to receive a Norplant implantation. (Norplant is a relatively new form of birth control in which small, hormone-releasing rods are surgically implanted into a woman's upper arm, preventing pregnancy for five years.)[40] Other states have followed suit in introducing Norplant legislation as well.[41] Norplant implants have not found much favor with the public, however, in part because they restrict women to only one form of birth control. Norplant incentives are also seen as a form of coercive bribery in which states should not be involved.

A closer examination of policies such as the Norplant reforms suggests that policymakers may themselves be hiding behind the myth of the welfare problem rather than trying to find effective solutions to poverty. (As shown in Chapter 1 and earlier in this chapter, women on welfare take significant measures to control the size of their families.) Policies that offer positive and negative incentives for women's behavior only increase the public's misgivings about welfare and can be dangerous to the women and children identified as welfare recipients.

Reform 8: Increased Asset Allowances

The governor's plan [New Jersey] will allow welfare parents to save up to $5,000 to buy a home or pay for college. They may also own a car worth less than $15,000 without it counting against their benefits.[42]

Under current law, women are allowed $1,500 in assets and a car worth $1,500 in order to qualify for welfare. There is some logic to this approach. It would be unfair for women with large sums of money in savings to turn to welfare. But the current policy allows such meager assets that its negative effects are beginning to be revealed. That is, accumulating assets is the only means by which women can move out of poverty. Because of the ceiling on assets, Rebecca was forced to use an old and very unreliable car for her transportation. On some days she missed her college classes, not because she was irresponsible and needed encouragement to attend, but because her car had broken down on the way. Sandy, who refused the precarious and unsafe conditions of owning an old car, made special arrangements for her mother to buy a used car, for which she paid her monthly. Although the welfare office never knew about it, the decision was a wise one for Sandy and her daughter.

Although it might have been better to adjust the asset ceiling for Sandy and Rebecca, not all women should have unrestricted asset ceilings. Some women might benefit from a savings account, with their accessibility to it determined by a case manager.

In some cases, a savings account is all that poor people have to rely on during financial crises. Reforms that allow women the flexibility to create a nest egg that will tide them over difficult times or that can be used to invest in their future would be a significant step toward positive reform.

Reform 9: Revised Income Disregards

A new four year demonstration program [Illinois] will allow welfare workers to disregard two-thirds of the income earned by working welfare recipients when figuring monthly benefits.[43]

There is no question that Americans subscribe to the Protestant work ethic. As early as the 1830s, Alexis de Tocqueville commented on Americans' intense drive for work. Based on his observations of American life he wrote, "To work is the necessary, natural, and honest condition. . . . Not only is no dishonor associated with work, but among such peoples it is regarded as positively honorable; the prejudice is for, not against, it."[44] One of the defining characteristics of American society, which makes it unique among other Western societies is the emphasis on—indeed, the reverence for—work.

Work is considered valuable because it is generally believed that people prosper when they work. The more people work, the more money they will make. Like most Americans, Sandy subscribes to these values, but because she got caught in a web of welfare receipt, she quickly found that different rules applied to her and her daughter.

Under current welfare policy, women's AFDC grants are quickly reduced once they move into the taxed economy. The effect is unfortunate. Some women, like Cora, are discouraged from working because even if they find a full-time job, they will not improve their financial situation. They also know that working takes more effort than remaining on AFDC. That is, transportation and child care must be arranged; meals require greater preparation and care; and time with children is markedly reduced.[45] Women like Rebecca who want to get ahead financially are forced to lie to the government if they work. Furthermore, if they work in the underground economy, although their wages are not taxed, they become welfare cheats, both an unsavory and a financially precarious predicament.

In order to encourage working in the taxed economy, policymakers are looking at changes in income disregards so that women will find it easier to combine work with welfare. The current law disregards the first $30 of income for four months, in addition to one-third of earned income for an additional eight months.[46] A higher initial disregard and/or a slowly increasing marginal tax on earnings might allow more families to gradually move off the AFDC rolls instead of suffering the sharp cut in benefits that occurs under prevailing regulations.[47]

Changes in earnings disregards will do little for women such as Ana who move into well-paying jobs after welfare. But for many women, the transition to work is slow. Many jobs do not pay well and many women are unable to work full time, so they often try to combine work with a partial welfare grant, at least initially. As with the other reforms noted, changes in the equation for earnings disregards will affect only some women. The diversity of the welfare population dictates that changes in welfare policy must be multidimensional and flexible to meet the needs of all AFDC recipients.

Reform 10: Requirements for Adolescent Parents

The law [Georgia] also requires unwed teens who receive welfare and who are either pregnant or parents of a dependent child to live with a parent or guardian in order to collect benefits.[48]

Services and standards that are targeted to the special needs of welfare recipients will move the welfare policy debate considerably further toward an equitable and rational system. New policy considerations that are aimed at adolescent parents may be a first step toward recognizing this group's specific interests and the obstacles to their self-sufficiency.

There is ample evidence that the United States leads all other countries in the number of unplanned (and often unwanted) pregnancies and births to teenagers. In this country, it is not simply a matter of access to birth control. Many teenagers are aware that they could become pregnant and they know about the birth control devices available to them. But ensuring that they are used—correctly—continues to be a problem for family-planning workers and policymakers. Some evidence suggests that income and education play a role in the likelihood of becoming pregnant as a teen. Whereas a college-educated woman has about an 8 percent chance of unintentionally becoming pregnant, a woman without a high school diploma stands a 33 percent chance.[49]

Once an unmarried teenage girl has a child, the likelihood of bringing years of poverty to her children is almost inevitable. Teenage pregnancy is one of the fastest avenues to poverty for children, and so efforts to discourage teenage pregnancy should be pursued wherever possible.[50] But as long as children are growing up in pockets of extreme poverty, where they are reminded each day that they have little to look forward to, some girls will continue to choose early pregnancy and parenthood. In a world that regularly denies these girls participation in the mainstream and in which the system itself is not concerned about how they turn out, a baby is regarded as an opportunity for self-expression.

Some efforts toward reform emphasize preventing teenage pregnancy.[51] Other policies are less focused on prevention and are more concerned with intervening once the baby has been born. Reforms that require adolescent mothers to live with their parents and guardians, for example, may reflect more the helplessness that policymakers feel about the problem of preventing teenage pregnancy than a solution to the problem of welfare use among adolescents. Such reforms may have some effect on girls who are close to their caregivers and who are open to advice and assistance from their parents. But girls who have less congenial relationships with their parents or who have been abused will likely use desperate measures to flee their parents' influence. Furthermore, the evidence concerning the role of grandmothers in improving the parenting skills of teenage parents is mixed.[52] Therefore it is unlikely that requirements regarding teenagers' living arrangements will do much to resolve the issues associated with teenage childbearing and welfare use.

Although we demand that children reach a certain age before they can legally drive a car, drink alcoholic beverages, or elect our national leaders, we set no age at which they can become a parent. Once a young girl has selected this option, our most common response is to give her a monthly check to pay for her expenses. Now some states are also experimenting with requirements regarding teenage parents' living arrangements. But these solutions address only a short-term problem. A more constructive approach to working with the target population of teenage parents might include substantial prevention efforts in addition to an array of services once a newborn arrives. Efforts to target teenage parents on AFDC are commendable, but restricted programs that ignore the multiple needs and problems associated with teenage childbearing may fall short of their goals.

Beyond Welfare: Affirming Children and Families

The reforms just cited may be helpful for some families in poverty, but other women and children will not be affected or may even be harmed. Welfare reform should not impose new standards and obligations on all women, nor should it offer the same collection of services to all. Real reform will tackle the individual needs of women, offering them opportunities to raise their children well.

It is easy to conclude that welfare is the crux of the poverty problem, but this is only a ruse that the public should ignore. Welfare is only part of the dilemma. If we change only its rules, we will not end "welfare as we know it." Welfare reform will do little to reduce the absolute size of the AFDC caseload unless a series of complementary measures are instituted that support families in general and poor families in particular. Because the problem of welfare is only one rather limited obstacle to creating lasting support for poor families, the following several reforms are suggested to provide context and breadth to the issue:

- Expanding health coverage for all families.[53]
- Providing child care that is safe and affordable.[54]
- Encouraging fathers to participate in the care and upbringing of their children.[55]
- Further expanding the Earned Income Tax Credit.[56]
- Raising the minimum wage.[57]
- Making more concerted efforts to prevent teenage pregnancy.
- Making housing more affordable.[58]
- Providing jobs to raise people's standard of living.[59]

The details of the programs in each of these areas are beyond the scope of this book. But welfare reform without attention to family and economic policy reform will merely perpetuate the "welfare problem" into the twenty-first century.

The lessons we learned from previous administrations may be instructive. Shortly after the Family Support Act was passed in 1988, President Ronald Reagan noted that the bill would "lead to lasting emancipation [for those on the public benefit rolls]."[60] More than once, efforts at welfare reform have been sold to the public as the answer to the welfare dilemma. Yet according to the primary evaluator for the JOBS program in California, a more modest assessment of welfare reform is probably in order. James Riccio noted:

> The income gains [from JOBS] are not so dramatic as to think the program is getting many people out of poverty. The fact that there are positive effects on earnings and the trend is upward is very encouraging, suggesting it has a role to play in reforming welfare, but it is not a program to end poverty or welfare.[61]

As with other welfare-reform efforts, the costs of any new welfare plan may demand that politicians initially oversell the outcomes of such programs. In the ensuing media campaign, welfare recipients will be admonished to take advantage of the generosity of these public officials' efforts. Yet when mothers on AFDC remain on the welfare rolls because of structural barriers in the American economy and the absence of a family policy, they will be blamed for the program's only modest success. Unless there are other supports offered to these women and their children, the gains from welfare reform cannot be great.

The welfare dilemma can be approached from several angles, but any attempt at reform that does not markedly improve the economic well-being of children will be inadequate at best and intentionally cruel at worst. The economic plight of children has steadily worsened in recent years so that today one-fifth of all children live in poverty—double the rate for adults. For African American children, the statistics are startling: One in two are poor.[62] More and more children in the United States are living in poverty, and the effects are tragic.

For children such as Kim, James, Tanya, or Raymond, there must be a better answer than the legacy of poverty that their parents and our social institutions have willed to them. We are a country rich in economic, intellectual, and creative resources, and we are humane and compassionate in our collective social will. Now we face a choice, one that will have a great impact on not only these children but all children in America.

APPENDIX

Study Methods

The study reported here began several years ago. The School of Social Welfare at the University of California at Berkeley was granted funding from the Smith Richardson Foundation and the Walter S. Johnson Foundation to examine the social implications of welfare reform for families. Neil Gilbert, Marcia Meyers, and I looked at the experiences of more than four hundred women and and their children in the GAIN program in California and also at child-care patterns and changes in family life.[1]

Our study consisted of three structured telephone interviews with AFDC mothers. We spoke with them before they began the GAIN program, three months into the program, and a full year after our original interview. Each interview lasted between forty-five minutes and an hour. We probed for information about the women's experience in the GAIN program, and in the process, they told us about their poverty and their experience with AFDC. One of the challenges in conducting this quantitative study was in finding patterns of similar responses, because these women's experiences with poverty were very different.

The later study undertaken for this book analyzed these women's different experiences of living on AFDC. Unlike the earlier study, this project relied solely on qualitative data. I used secondary data from large-scale national studies to clarify the aggregate experience of welfare.

Sample Selection

Unlike quantitative studies whose sample of participants is statistically representative of the population at large, the samples for qualitative studies are selected somewhat differently. The sample of participants that I selected for this book was fairly limited in scope and size. I looked for AFDC recipients that were typical of the various types of women on welfare. Some of the characteristics that I looked for were differences in education, race, marital status, and work history.[2]

Other factors may be, of course, relevant to selecting the participants in a qualitative study. Some researchers look for respondents who are somewhat "trustworthy, observant, reflective, articulate, and good storytellers."[3] Bernard observed that the selection of a sample is based on "luck, intuition, and hard work by both parties to achieve a working relationship based on trust."[4] The respondents in my study contained some or all of these qualities.

Four of the five women selected for this project had participated in the earlier GAIN study. In accordance with the design of the earlier study, I excluded short-term AFDC recipients. (Women who use AFDC for a short period of time are not likely to enter the GAIN program.) Therefore, Ana had not participated in the original study. In order to find an appropriate respondent to illustrate the experience of the short-term user, I interviewed fifty-four women by telephone or in person, and I asked the staff at local AFDC offices to identify short-term users. In addition, I placed ads for study candidates in newspapers. I interviewed eleven women in depth at least twice before I finally selected Ana.

Besides the other four study participants, additional respondents initially participated in the study. But because of family crises, some of the women dropped out of the study for a time and then reentered later. Three women who participated at the beginning of the study had to drop out entirely; one, for example, moved several hundred miles away when her son was seriously injured in an accident, and she understandably found time and distance to be insurmountable obstacles to continuing to participate.

All the names and identifying information of the women have been changed, but all of the women are real; none is a composite. Women on welfare live in constant fear of being "found out" by welfare officials, and therefore I felt obligated to hide their identities.

Methods

I conducted this study using qualitative field strategies including in-depth interviews, informal participant observation, and key informants.[5] By means of these methods, a researcher can obtain direct knowledge of experiences, events, and the emotions they elicit in real-life settings.[6]

These women welcomed me into their homes and allowed me to sit back and unobtrusively observe their family life. At other times I actively participated in family activities. In addition to these informal gatherings, some of our meetings were unstructured interviews, usually focusing on a specific theme.[7] Central to the interviewing process was the development of an oral history for each woman as she reexamined and told her life story. Wiener and Rosenwald noted that individual life stories often take place as a series of episodes, some of which the respondents remember more clearly than others.[8] Therefore, part of my analysis of the notes I took when eliciting these life stories was find their meaning to their teller.[9] Accordingly, I hope that I have been true to these women's understanding of their lives as I tried to capture their perspective in each chapter.

Each meeting with the women and their families lasted between two and six hours. I collected data for between three and eighteen months, intending to approximate an informal conversation between friends whenever possible.[10] In some cases, our relationship developed into a friendship, making it difficult for me to make a completely unbiased analysis.[11] Other factors also were relevant to my data. My own personal characteristics, such as my race, class, and age, were influential at first in gaining my respondents' trust. In some cases, we needed to talk through their perceptions of who I was or, more important, the institutions I represented.[12] For example, some of Cora's family members initially responded to me with some skepticism, if not hostility, as a "researcher." Their responses are not unusual.[13] But one way to overcome fear or hostility is to become a familiar person in the family landscape. When I brought birthday gifts for the children or helped run errands with Cora, her children began to see me as a friendly visitor and eventually welcomed me into their home.

Analyzing the Data

I audiotaped all my meetings with the women and their families, and at the end of each meeting I also took notes about any tone or manner that might not be discernible on the tape. I then had each tape fully transcribed.

My data analysis included identifying and labeling those themes that were consistently repeated in each meeting.[14] I also found patterns in the women's oral histories that related back to the initial themes, and I was able to tie some of my initial analyses to my interviews.[15] Those issues and themes that needed further exploration I often discussed with the respondents at a later meeting, either informally or in an unstructured interview. Before beginning my final analysis and writing, I had to put some distance between myself and the families, in order to regain my objectivity.[16] I communicated the data by means of two methods: *narrations* and *augmentations*.[17] The narrations are those portions of each chapter provided directly by the respondents, and the augmentations are my descriptions of or notations regarding striking events or experiences. Throughout the book I attempted to tie the women's and children's individual life experiences to aggregate experiences of welfare use, gleaned from large-scale national studies.

All the women discussed in this book reside in California, a state with relatively high welfare benefits, an extremely high cost of living, and a recession that has lasted far longer than have those in other states. These women's experiences should not be seen as "average." Indeed, a sample of five women cannot be generalized to the larger population; they and their experiences are offered only as a complement to existing quantitative studies and are meant as an illustration of the effects on women and children of living in poverty.

Notes

Introduction

1. Andrea is one of the women who took part in our study, although that is not her real name. All the names of all the women and children discussed in this book have been changed, and any information that might indicate any of their identities was changed to protect them. All these people, however, are real, and none is a composite. For more details about my study methods, please see the Appendix.

2. Two authors developed this argument: Mickey Kaus contends that because of the increasing separation of the poor from the nonpoor, public sympathies for the poor have waned. That is, whereas in the past the mixing of classes had a moderating effect on the American culture—producing a mainstream mentality that many, regardless of class, adopted—today, with their separate facilities, activities, and entertainment, two distinctive classes of people have been created that are ignorant and less tolerant of each other. See M. Kaus, *The End of Equality* (New York: Basic Books, 1992). Other writers supporting this view are T. D. Cook and T. R. Curtin, "The Mainstream and the Underclass: Why Are the Differences So Salient and the Similarities So Unobtrusive?" in J. C. Masters and W. P. Smith, eds., *Social Comparison, Social Justice, and Relative Deprivation* (Hillsdale, NJ: Erlbaum, 1987), pp. 217–64.

3. Fox Butterfield, "Record Number in U.S. Relying on Food Stamps," *New York Times*, October 31, 1991, p. 9; Gina Boubion, "More Children Than Ever Are Poor, State Study Says," *San Jose Mercury News*, June 21, 1991, p. 16; E. McCormick, "Welfare Rolls Rise 6% in a Year; Wilson Wants System Changed," *San Francisco Examiner*, June 19, 1993, p. A-8.

What Is Welfare?

1. See H. Heclo, "The Political Foundations of Anti-poverty Policy," in S. Danziger and D. Weinberg, eds., *Fighting Poverty: What Works and What Doesn't* (Cambridge, MA: Harvard University Press, 1986), pp. 312–40; I. A. Lewis and W. Schneider, "Hard Times: The Public on Poverty," *Public Opinion* 8 (1985): 2–8, 60; A. Lewis and W. Schneider, "Opinion Roundup: Poverty in America," *Public Opinion* 7 (1985): 27; "Poverty in America," *Public Opinion*

8 (1985): 25–31. One poll indicated that Americans ranked the welfare system below the educational, tax, and health-care systems. Their criticisms were broad based: No socioeconomic, spatial, or ethnic group accepted the current system. See G. G. Molyneux, and L. DiVall, "Public Attitudes Toward Welfare Reform: A Summary of Key Research Findings," unpublished manuscript (Washington, DC: Peter D. Hart Research Associates, 1994).

2. James Leiby asserts that at the height of the WPA (1938), more than 3.3 million people were served, at a cost of $11.4 billion. See J. Leiby, *A History of Social Welfare and Social Work in the United States* (New York: Columbia University Press, 1978).

3. The original program was actually called ADC (Aid to Dependent Children), reflecting the program's emphasis on children's needs. Payments were made directly to mothers for their children, but the mothers were not included in the calculation of monthly grants. In 1962, the program's name was changed to AFDC (Aid to Families with Dependent Children), reflecting a renewed focus on the program's "family" aspects.

4. The precursor to the ADC program was the "mother's pension." These state-operated programs were not available in all states, and the standards for eligibility varied considerably. ADC was initiated in part to provide federal assistance to states in implementing their pension programs.

5. In 1934, on the eve of the transition from mothers' pensions to ADC, Abramovitz notes that there were 110,000 families on aid and an additional 358,000 female-headed households on federal emergency relief rolls. See M. Abramovitz, *Regulating the Lives of Women: Social Welfare Policy from Colonial Times to the Present* (Boston: South End Press, 1988).

6. See E. D. Berkowitz, *America's Welfare State: From Roosevelt to Reagan* (Baltimore: Johns Hopkins University Press, 1991).

7. AFDC payments were minimal, initially set at $18 per month for the first child and $12 per month for each additional child. See Abramovitz, *Regulating the Lives of Women.*

8. R. A. Cloward and F. F. Piven, *Regulating the Poor: The Functions of Public Welfare* (New York: Pantheon Books, 1971).

9. Indeed, in 1939 a major amendment to the Social Security Act (Survivor's Insurance, or SI) provided a type of life insurance plan for families whose primary earner—the father—had died. Based on the assumption that many of the women claiming AFDC were widows, it was expected that these families would soon transfer to SI status and that AFDC would eventually wither away.

10. In 1960, about three million women and children were collecting AFDC, but by the end of the decade, that number had increased threefold. Viewed in a somewhat different light, in 1960, AFDC recipients accounted for 2 percent of the entire population, but by 1969, this percentage had doubled. The number of families on aid should not be confused with the number of individual persons on aid. By 1970 approximately 7.4 million recipients and 1.9 million families were collecting AFDC. See the U.S. government's *Green Book* for data on AFDC participation rates, and for a description of the caseload, see S. A. Levitan, M. Rein, and D. Marwick, *Work and Welfare Go Together* (Bal-

timore: Johns Hopkins University Press, 1972); M. Rein, *Dilemmas of Welfare Policy: Why Work Strategies Haven't Worked* (New York: Praeger, 1982).

11. During the 1970s, the number of caseloads continued to grow. By the end of the decade, 3.6 million families were collecting aid. See U.S. House Committee on Ways and Means, *1992 U.S. Government Green Book: Overview of Programs* (Washington, DC: U.S. Government Printing Office, 1992).

12. Information on caseload size is provided by the American Public Welfare Association (APWA). Although caseload size grew slowly during the 1980s, it expanded rapidly again in the late 1980s and early 1990s. Estimates from the American Public Welfare Association suggest that caseloads increased 33.7 percent from July 1989 to March 1993.

Figures in the text are provided for March 1993. The caseload size finally topped the five million mark in March and was duly noted by the press. See ibid.

13. Berkowitz provides a good description of the history of AFDC and the adjustments in the program over the past several decades. See Berkowitz, *America's Welfare State*. For a vivid description of the "suitable home" criteria used by various states, see Abramovitz, *Regulating the Lives of Women*. Abramovitz discusses dating patterns, friends and associates, parenting, and household management as criteria for turning away AFDC applicants. Race was also used as a factor to deny applicants.

14. D. T. Ellwood and L. H. Summers, "Is Welfare Really the Problem?" *Public Interest* 83 (1986): 57–78.

15. The implications of this figure are remarkable, as current estimates suggest that well over half of all children of color spend some portion of their lives in a single-parent family.

16. The remaining 28 percent of children live with grandparents, other relatives, or foster parents. Vanessa Atkins, "Murphy Brown They're Not: Single Parents Plentiful, Poor," *San Francisco Examiner*, July 20, 1994, p. A1.

17. D. J. Besharov and A. J. Quin, "Not All Female-Headed Families Are Created Equal," *Public Interest* 89 (1987): 48–56.

18. Rein, *Dilemmas of Welfare Policy*.

19. See ibid. for a full discussion of the changing composition of the AFDC caseload. A study conducted by the General Accounting Office (GAO) also confirms that more than 50 percent of all women receiving AFDC in 1992 never had been married. General Accounting Office, *Families on Welfare: Sharp Rise in Never-Married Women Reflects Societal Trend* (Washington, DC: General Accounting Office, 1994).

20. See Berkowitz, *America's Welfare State*. For details on the characteristics of today's caseload, see U.S. Department of Health and Human Services, *Characteristics and Financial Circumstances of AFDC Recipients* (Washington, DC: Administration for Children and Families, 1991).

21. Participation in the AFDC program is not federally mandated. Although all states now participate, some were slow to join, many because of their interest in excluding certain women from the program. For example, during the 1940s and 1950s, the state of Nevada had no AFDC program so that it did not have to provide benefits to Native Americans. Similarly, the state of Missis-

sippi put a 10 percent ceiling on the number of participants on AFDC, as it was widely recognized that the majority of women who would need assistance were African American. For many years, Texas also purposely excluded Hispanics from AFDC. See L. Leighninger, *Social Work: Search for Identity* (Westport, CT: Greenwood Press, 1987).

22. J. F. Handler and Y. Hasenfeld, *The Moral Construction of Poverty* (Newbury Park, CA: Sage, 1991).

23. D. T. Ellwood, *Poor Support: Poverty in the American Family* (New York: Basic Books, 1988).

24. Another 20 percent chose not to work at all because of family obligations; about 10 percent of women did not work because of illness or disability; and about 4 percent were unable to find work. Also, as recently as 1991, 57.3 percent of all women in the United States were participating on some level in the labor force. See U.S. Bureau of the Census, *Statistical Abstract of the United States*, 12th ed. (Washington, DC: U.S. Department of Commerce, 1992).

25. The Work Incentive Program (WIN), enacted in 1967, called for AFDC clients to register with their state employment department, to take part in job search activities, and to accept a job if one were offered. Although by 1971, AFDC recipients had to register for WIN, few did so because funding was often inadequate. Financial incentives to work were written into the law in 1967. AFDC recipients who had found work before 1967 had essentially been penalized by an equal reduction in their welfare grant for every dollar earned. The former policy did little to encourage recipients to work, but the new regulations allowed AFDC recipients to keep a partial grant. What came to be called the *thirty plus one-third disregard* allowed working AFDC recipients to keep $30 plus an additional one-third of their gross earnings before calculating their welfare benefit. This amendment was particularly beneficial for families who were trying to work their way out of poverty.

Other welfare reform packages were introduced in the 1970s. President Richard M. Nixon's proposal for a guaranteed income under the Family Assistance Plan (FAP) included work incentives and some funding for day care. The FAP was perhaps the most ambitious reform of the welfare system ever attempted. Essentially, a negative income tax (NIT) would have provided a guaranteed income floor for all individuals. If a person chose not to work, he or she would at least have received the NIT on a monthly basis, putting his or her income at about the poverty level. If a person did choose to work, however, his or her NIT would be only moderately taxed, thus encouraging that person to remain in the workforce. Because one of the common concerns regarding welfare is the disincentive to work, the NIT had a built-in incentive to work: The more that a person worked, the more money he or she would make.

Some of the largest-scale social experiments in the United States were devoted to studying the effects of the NIT. Experimental studies were carried out in several states and cities, including New Jersey, Pennsylvania, Denver, and Seattle. These studies found several different outcomes, making it difficult to describe all of them briefly. The results also were complex and sometimes contradictory. However, some of them led policymakers at the time to question the practicality of the approach. Specifically, one of the studies found that although the NIT did not affect men's working hours, married women (particularly Caucasian women) did work fewer hours when they were guaranteed a minimum income. Other effects on the work effort were found, and this dampening effect, although modest, was deemed considerable enough to question the long-term impact of the NIT on the American economy and productivity. After considerable debate, the FAP was never fully implemented.

A few years later, under the Carter administration, reform was tried again. President Jimmy Carter proposed the Program for Better Jobs and Income, but Congress failed to pass it. For a number of reasons, including political considerations, and cost—the projected costs for adequate day care were especially high—Carter's reform was never accepted.

The most recent attempt at welfare reform is the Family Support Act (FSA) passed in October 1988. The FSA's principal attempt to strengthen the family was its expansion of benefits to unemployed fathers in all states and the enforcement of child-support payments. But the FSA also contains an education and training component—the Job Opportunities and Basic Skills Training Program (JOBS)—that includes supportive services for participating families. Indeed, participation in the JOBS program is mandatory for all women whose children are aged three or older, although the program is targeted to those women whose children are sixteen or older (because these women will shortly be moving off welfare) and to teenage mothers who have not completed high school. An array of services are offered to JOBS clients, including short-term "job club," job search activities, basic education, vocational training, and on-the-job training. See V. J. Burke and V. Burke, *Nixon's Good Deed: Welfare Reform* (New York: Columbia University Press, 1974); R. K. Caputo, "Limits of Welfare Reform," *Social Casework* 70 (1989): 85–95; D. P. Moynihan, *The Politics of a Guaranteed Income: The Nixon Administration and the Family Assistance Plan* (New York: Random House, 1973); P. H. Rossi and K. Lyall, *Reforming Public Welfare: A Critique of the Negative Income Tax Experiment* (New York: Russell Sage, 1976); E. Zigler and E. W. Gordon, eds., *Day Care: Scientific and Social Policy Issues* (Boston: Auburn House, 1982).

26. Headlines noted in the *Washington Post* and the *Los Angeles Times*, respectively, quoted by P. L. Szanton, "The Remarkable `Quango': Knowledge, Politics and Welfare Reform," *Journal of Policy Analysis and Management* 10 (1991): 590–602.

27. Handler and Hasenfeld, *The Moral Construction of Poverty*.

28. "Data File," *Welfare to Work*, February 1, 1993, p. 3.

29. "Backing off Proposal to Sell Organs," *New York Newsday*, July 20, 1990, p. 8.

30. The proposal called for an immediate 10 percent cut in all welfare benefits and a further reduction of 15 percent if welfare recipients remained on the rolls after six months.

31. Gloria Bristo-Brown, "Letter to the Editor," *Oakland Tribune*, February 18, 1991.

32. General Accounting Office, *Families on Welfare*. This rate has doubled since the 1970s.

Notes

33. I. Lav, E. Lazere, R. Greenstein, and S. D. Gold, *The States and the Poor* (Washington, DC: Center on Budget and Policy Priorities, 1992).

34. Many writing about welfare argue that the benefits are indeed generous when they are considered in combination with a package of in-kind benefits such as food stamps, Medicaid, and housing vouchers. However, public housing subsidies are available to only about 18 percent of the welfare population. Food stamps bring a sizable proportion of the welfare population close to the poverty line but hardly guarantee a comfortable existence. And the value of Medicaid is very difficult to gauge, because some families have extensive medical needs, whereas others need medical services only rarely. See L. Mead, *The New Politics of Poverty* (New York: Basic Books, 1992); C. Murray, *Losing Ground: American Social Policy 1950–1980* (New York: Basic Books, 1984).

35. AFDC is financed jointly by the federal and state governments (counties may also contribute a share of costs). Generally, federal funds pay for between 50 and 80 percent of the costs (the average is about 54 percent); the percentage depends on each state's per capita income. Those states with a low per capita income (e.g., Mississippi) receive a higher share from the federal government, with the richer states paying more of the cost themselves.

Each state sets its own AFDC benefit level. The state first sets a "needs standard," which is the amount determined essential to purchase basic necessities such as food, clothing, and shelter. Families whose income and assets fall below this level are eligible for AFDC assistance. Each state then decides the maximum amount it will provide to eligible families as a percentage of the "needs standard." The benefit that each family receives is based on the maximum allowable grant minus earned income (disregarding child-care expenses at $175 per child per month, transportation and work-related expenses of $75 per month, $30 of earned income for four months, and an additional one-third of earned income for twelve months).

36. Alaska has always had especially high welfare payments, owing to the high cost of living in that state and a fairly generous attitude toward welfare recipients. In 1994, the average welfare payment for a family of three was $923 per month. For several years, California and New York were the second and third highest in welfare payments, although recent cutbacks in each of these states have made them far less generous, now at $607 and $703, respectively. (New York City has a different rate, $577.) See U.S. House Committee on Ways and Means, *1994 Green Book: Overview of Programs* (Washington, DC: U.S. Government Printing Office, 1994).

37. The median across states is $366; see ibid.

38. M. J. Bane and D. T. Ellwood, *Welfare Realities: From Rhetoric to Reform* (Cambridge, MA: Harvard University Press, 1994).

39. Although rents may be somewhat lower, physically deficient housing is far more prevalent in the South. One study shows that this is true for residents in both the cities and the rural areas of the South. See E. B. Lazere, C. N. Dolbeare, P. A. Leonard, and B. Zigas, *A Place to Call Home: The Low Income Housing Crisis Continues* (Washington, DC: Center on Budget and Policy Priorities, December 1991).

40. Note also that although food stamps may increase the total family income in kind, they cannot be used to buy housing.

41. P. A. Leonard and E. B. Lazere, *A Place to Call Home: The Low Income Housing Crisis in 44 Major Metropolitan Areas* (Washington, DC: Center on Budget and Policy Priorities, November 1992).

42. Proponents of the disparity in welfare benefits across states point out that food stamps make up the difference between low welfare benefits and the cost of living. However, analyses by Peterson and Rom show that combined AFDC and food stamp benefits vary twice as much as does the cost of living across all states. They also note that although the cost of living differs by only about 10 percent from the national average across states, welfare benefits vary by 40 percent. See P. E. Peterson and M. C. Rom, *Welfare Magnets* (Washington, DC: Brookings Institution, 1990).

43. Although this issue has been the point of considerable debate in recent years, well-documented studies either proving or disproving the "magnet" theory are difficult to find. Whereas earlier studies by Clark (1992) and Gramlich and Laren (1984) were somewhat inconclusive, recent evidence from Hanson and Hartman (1994) indicates that there is little to the welfare magnet theory and that so few poor people move between states as to be insignificant for policy consideration. See R. Clark, "Do They Leave the Safety Net: The Effect of Level of State Welfare Payments on the Outmigration of Low-Income Mothers," paper presented at the annual meeting of the Population Association of America, Denver, 1992; E. M. Gramlich and D. S. Laren, "Migration and Income Distribution Responsibilities," *Journal of Human Resources* 19 (1984): 489–511; R. L. Hanson and J. T. Hartman, *Do Welfare Magnets Attract?* (Madison, WI: Institute for Research on Poverty, 1994).

44. Nevada's welfare benefit for a family of three is equivalent to $262, and the increase in its caseload size between 1989 and 1993 was 74.3 percent. The figures for welfare rates are 1994 figures. See House Ways and Means Committee, *U.S. Government Green Book*, 1994.

45. Michael Wald also believes that welfare families commonly move to be near family. He notes, "This is hardly surprising; a poor family is unlikely to move a great distance without the support system provided by family or a job." See M. Wald, *Welfare Reform and Children's Well-being* (Stanford, CA: Stanford Center for the Study of Families, Children, and Youth, 1992), p. 30.

46. Bane and Ellwood, *Welfare Realities*.

47. The remaining 10 percent of AFDC entries fall into "other" categories.

48. L. J. Weitzman, *The Divorce Revolution* (New York: Free Press, 1985). Weitzman also observes that the fathers' income usually rises by as much as 42 percent. Other writers on the topic have found somewhat less dramatic effects. Duncan and Hoffman found a 33 percent decrease in women's income one year following divorce. See G. J. Duncan and S. D. Hoffman, "A Reconsideration of the Economic Consequences of Marital Dissolution," *Demography* 22 (1985): 485–98.

49. I. Garfinkel and S. S. McLanahan, *Single Mothers and Their Children: A New American Dilemma* (Washington, DC: Urban Institute Press, 1986), p. 24.

50. Owing to the demands of caring for young children, women often work part time or for part of the year. Women are also more likely than men to take an extended leave of absence from work after the birth of a child. Due to sociological factors connected with tracking from an early age, women are

also more likely to work in service or clerical fields, areas that generally pay less than do jobs in administrative or technical fields. For a discussion of some of the issues associated with women's work patterns, see H. R. Rodgers, *Poor Women, Poor Families* (Armonk, NY: M. E. Sharpe); F. N. Schwartz, "Management Women and the New Facts of Life," *Harvard Business Review*, January–February 1989, pp. 65–76.

51. This proportion has held somewhat steady over the years. Moore and Burt made this claim in 1975, and Zill, Moore, Nord, and Stief made a similar assessment in 1991. See K. A. Moore and M. R. Burt, *Private Crisis, Public Cost: Policy Perspectives on Teenage Childbearing* (Washington, DC: Urban Institute, 1982); N. Zill, K. A. Moore, C. W. Nord, and T. Stief, *Welfare Mothers as Potential Employees: A Statistical Profile Based on National Survey Data* (Washington, DC: Child Trends, 1991).

52. M. J. Bane and D. T. Ellwood, "The Dynamics of Dependence: Routes to Self-Sufficiency," unpublished manuscript (Cambridge, MA: Urban Systems Research and Engineering, 1983).

53. The most prominent welfare critic in this camp is Charles Murray, who helped circulate the idea that welfare caused greater family dysfunction, more marital breakups, and the formation of single-parent families. See Murray, *Losing Ground*.

54. D. T. Ellwood and L. H. Summers, "Poverty in America: Is Welfare the Answer or the Problem?" in S. H. Danziger and D. H. Weinberg, eds., *Fighting Poverty: What Works and What Doesn't?* (Cambridge, MA: Harvard University Press, 1986), p. 94.

55. William Julius Wilson's thesis regarding single parenthood stresses the role of joblessness in the inner city, particularly among African American youths. He suggests that high rates of unemployment have reduced the marriageable "pool" of African American youth, thus making single motherhood a more attractive alternative for many young women. See W. J. Wilson, *The Truly Disadvantaged: The Inner City, the Underclass, and Public Policy* (Chicago: University of Chicago Press, 1987); W. J. Wilson and K. M. Neckerman, "Poverty and Family Structure: The Widening Gap Between Evidence and Public Policy Issues," in S. H. Danziger and D.H. Weinberg, eds., *Fighting Poverty: What Works and What Doesn't?* (Cambridge, MA: Harvard University Press, 1986), pp. 232–59.

56. Although these data are taken from 1991, the evidence regarding family size has not changed significantly in several years. See U.S. Department of Health and Human Services, *Characteristics and Financial Circumstances of AFDC Recipients*.

57. M. R. Rank, "The Blending of Qualitative and Quantitative Methods in Understanding Childbearing Among Welfare Recipients," in J. F. Gilgun, K. Daly, and G. Handel, eds., *Qualitative Methods in Family Research* (Newbury Park, CA: Sage, 1992), pp. 281–300.

58. P. J. Placek and G. E. Hendershot, "Public Welfare and Family Planning: An Empirical Study of the "Brood Sow" Myth," *Social Problems* 21 (1974): 660–73.

59. H. B. Presser and L. S. Salsberg, "Public Assistance and Early Family Formation: Is There a Pronatalist Effect?" *Social Problems* 23 (1975): 226–41.

60. The average difference between a two-person family and a three-person family is $72.71 (including the District of Columbia and excluding the U.S. territories). The range is great, however. In Mississippi the increase in income for each additional child is $24.00, whereas in Hawaii the increase is $135.00. See House Ways and Means Committee, *1992 U.S. Government Green Book*.

61. U.S. Department of Health and Human Services, *Characteristics and Financial Circumstances of AFDC Recipients*.

62. U.S. Bureau of the Census, *Statistical Abstract*.

63. U.S. Department of Health and Human Services, *Characteristics and Financial Circumstances of AFDC Recipients*.

64. K. Edin and C. Jencks, "Reforming Welfare," in C. Jencks, *Rethinking Social Policy: Race, Poverty, and the Underclass* (Cambridge, MA: Harvard University Press, 1992), pp. 204–36.

65. N. Gilbert, J. D. Berrick, and M. K. Meyers, *GAIN Family Life and Child Care Study* (Berkeley, CA: Family Welfare Research Group, 1992).

66. One of the most influential writings on the topic of welfare is by Bane and Ellwood, a remarkably well documented paper on the dynamics of welfare use. Although their analysis of AFDC data was not based on a series of snapshots of the welfare caseload, it accounted for movement on and off the welfare rolls. Although their first work was in an unpublished manuscript, it was later incorporated into articles and books. Details regarding welfare entrances and exits can be found in Bane and Ellwood, "The Dynamics of Dependence."

A more recent overview of welfare studies indicates that more than two-thirds of periods on welfare are less than two years and over half last for twelve months or less. See M. Greenberg, *Beyond Stereotypes: What State AFDC Studies on Length of Stay Tell Us About Welfare as a "Way of Life"* (Washington, DC: Center for Law and Social Policy, 1993).

The length of women's welfare spells is perhaps the most contentious issue among academics and public officials who follow the welfare debate. Well-respected liberal welfare scholars are quick to point out the transitory nature of welfare and women's brief episodes in the program, and equally well informed conservative scholars emphasize the size of the long-term welfare population. Their arguments are confusing to those less familiar with the debate, especially because both sides of the argument are correct. A now frequently used example from Mary Jo Bane and David Ellwood may explain the complexity of the issue in terms somewhat easier to grasp.

The example comes from a hospital analogy and goes something like this: Assume that a hospital serves patients with acute needs who are admitted and released over a period of a few days or a week. This same hospital also serves patients with chronic conditions whose stays in the hospital often last for a period of several months. If you examine the records of all people admitted into the hospital over the period of one year, you will notice a far higher number of acute patients (with short-term stays) than chronic patients (with long-term stays), as every acute patient who quickly leaves the hospital makes room for another acute patient to take his or her place.

This view of the hospital suggests that it is more likely to admit short-term patients than long-term patients. It also indicates a highly dynamic population, with great movement into (entrances) and out of (exits) the hospital. An observer would thus be correct to say that the majority of patients beginning a stay in the hospital and the majority of those who ever stay in the hospital are those with acute needs who stay for a short period of time.

Now we take a snapshot view of the hospital's current clientele and find that most of the patients occupying hospital beds are those with chronic conditions. Although fewer chronic than acute patients were admitted to the hospital, because they stay for longer periods of time, we are more likely to see them occupying the current hospital beds. Observers who viewed the hospital from only this perspective would therefore be correct in stating that the total "caseload" of patients was overrepresented by long-term chronic patients.

This hospital analogy should clarify the dynamics of the welfare population: Most of the women who "enter" welfare stay on it for less than four years. But when you look at the caseload at one point in time, those who stay on welfare for eight years or longer represent more than half of all the women on welfare.

67. Again, according to Bane and Ellwood, of the women who remain on AFDC for at least two years, 60 percent stay for six years and 30 percent stay for more than eight years.

68. G. J. Duncan, M. S. Hill, and S. D. Hoffman, "Welfare Dependence Within and Across Generations," *Science* 239 (1988): 467–71; D. Ellwood, "Targeting the Would-be Long-Term Recipients of AFDC: Who Should Be Served?" unpublished manuscript (Princeton, NJ: Mathematica Policy Research, January 1986).

It is interesting to note that race as a single factor (i.e., holding all else constant) is not a strong predictor of the length of stay on welfare. But because African-American women are more likely to have had less education, to never have been married, and to have more children, these factors combine to account for much longer stays on welfare. See Bane and Ellwood, *Welfare Realities*.

69. Corbett provides an excellent example of targeted services for various groups in the welfare population. See his "Child Poverty and Welfare Reform: Progress or Paralysis?" *Focus* 15 (1993): 1–17.

70. Duncan, Hill, and Hoffman, "Welfare Dependence Within and Across Generations."

71. In this study, the authors examine a period of ten years in the lives of these welfare mothers. They define "high" welfare use as having used welfare for three out of three years. "Some" welfare use means one or two years out of three, and "no" welfare use is no use of AFDC during the three-year period.

72. G. J. Duncan and S. D. Hoffman, "Welfare Dynamics and the Nature of Need," *Cato Journal* 6 (1986): 31–54; Duncan, Hill, and Hoffman, "Welfare Dependence Within and Across Generations"; M. S. Hill and M. Ponza, "Does Welfare Dependency Beget Dependency?" unpublished manuscript, University of Michigan, Institute for Social Research, 1984.

73. L. Pavetti, "The Dynamics of Welfare and Work: Exploring the Process

by Which Women Work Their Way off Welfare" (Ph.D. diss., Harvard University, 1993).

74. The 1 percent figure is an estimate based on Burtless's figures for 1985 and includes only the costs of the AFDC program. (When the costs of Medicaid are included, they are estimated to be approximately $36 billion.) The 1985 figure is likely still accurate, as cash assistance has not increased since that time. In comparison, the cost of all social insurance programs in the United States (including Social Security, Medicare, and unemployment insurance) was more than ten times the amount spent on AFDC, or more than $250 billion. As another recent example, the victims of a major flood in 1993 were given $5.7 billion. The public's sympathy for these victims of natural disaster was extremely generous. Our efforts to help the most unfortunate among us are equally noble.

For a full description of the costs of all cash and in-kind assistance programs, see G. Burtless, "Public Spending for the Poor: Trends, Prospects, and Economic Limits," in S. H. Danziger and D. H. Weinberg, eds., *Fighting Poverty: What Works and What Doesn't* (Cambridge, MA: Harvard University Press, 1986), pp. 18–49. See also House Ways and Means Committee, *1994 U.S. Government Green Book: Overview of Programs* (Washington, DC: U.S. Government Printing Office, 1994).

75. Burtless, "Public Spending for the Poor."

76. Noted in M. W. Edelman, *The Measure of Our Success* (Washington, DC: Children's Defense Fund, 1992).

77. Low birth weight, which is often associated with the mother's poor nutrition, lack of prenatal care, prenatal stress, extreme youth, insufficient weight gain, and smoking, is closely connected to poverty. Low birth weight is also significantly related to infant mortality and later health and developmental problems. See P. A. Margolis, R. A. Greenberg, and L. L. Keyes, "Lower Respiratory Illness in Infants and Low Socioeconomic Status," *American Journal of Public Health* 82 (1992): 1119–26; S. Parker, S. Greer, and B. Zuckerman, "Double Jeopardy: The Impact of Poverty on Early Childhood Development," *Pediatric Clinics of North America* 35 (1988): 1227–40; S. Singh, A. Torres, and J. D. Forrest, "The Need for Prenatal Care in the United States: Evidence from the 1980 National Natality Survey," *Family Planning Perspectives* 17 (1985): 122–23.

78. Infant mortality rates in the United States are remarkably high. Our current rate of ten deaths per one thousand live births makes the United States comparable to many Third World nations in infant mortality. See United Nations, *World Population* (New York: Population Division Department of Economic and Social Development, 1992).

In addition, according to the Children's Defense Fund, "poor children are about three times as likely to die during childhood as their non-poor peers"; Children's Defense Fund, *CDF Reports* (Washington, DC: Children's Defense Fund, July 1993). p. 8. See also C. W. Spurlock, M. W. Hinds, J. W. Skaggs, and C. E. Hernandez, "Infant Death Rates Among the Poor and Nonpoor in Kentucky, 1982 to 1983," *Pediatrics* 80 (1987): 262–69.

79. Anemia and growth retardation are far more common among poor

Notes

children than among nonpoor children. See National Center for Children in Poverty, *Five Million Children: A Statistical Profile of Our Poorest Young Children* (New York: National Center for Children in Poverty, 1990).

80. L. McBarnette, "Women and Poverty: The Effects on Reproductive Status," in C. A. Perales and L. S. Young, eds., *Women, Health, and Poverty* (New York: Haworth, 1988), pp. 55–81.

81. Children from poor families are more likely to be exposed to lead poisoning, as lead is most often found in old paint, which is most often found in older, substandard housing and is more likely to flake off walls and be eaten by young children. Lead poisoning also has been directly linked to the development of learning disabilities among young children. See H. L. Needleman, A. Schell, D. Bellinger, A. Leviton, and E. N. Allred, "The Long-Term Effects of Exposure to Low Doses of Lead in Childhood," *New England Journal of Medicine* 322 (1990): 83–88.

82. Data from the National Incidence Study indicate that families with incomes below $15,000 had incidents of child mistreatment seven times higher than rates for higher-income families. Pelton pointed out, however, that reports of maltreatment (especially child neglect) are biased toward low-income families because of their constant surveillance by public authorities. Although his theory probably contains some truth, he also states that the attendant stress of living in poverty may contribute as well to higher absolute rates of child maltreatment. See L. H. Pelton, *For Reasons of Poverty* (New York: Praeger, 1989); U.S. Department of Health and Human Services, *Study of the National Incidence and Prevalence of Child Abuse and Neglect* (Washington, DC: U.S. Department of Health and Human Services, 1988).

83. The cost of living in dangerous housing and dangerous neighborhoods, often with less than adequate supervision, is unimaginable. See F. P. Rivara and B. A. Mueller, "The Epidemiology and Causes of Childhood Injuries," *Journal of Social Issues* 43 (1987): 13–32; R. D. Mare, "Socioeconomic Effects on Child Mortality in the United States," *American Journal of Public Health* 72 (1982): 539–47; W. W. Nersesian, "Childhood Death and Poverty: A Study of All Childhood Deaths in Maine, 1976–1980," *Pediatrics* 75 (1985): 41–50; K. Zinsmeister, "Growing up Scared," *Atlantic Monthly*, June 1990, pp. 49–66.

84. According to the Children's Defense Fund, "Every year that children live in poverty significantly increases their risk of falling behind in school by ages 16 to 18. Poor children are more likely to fall behind in school even after accounting for such differences as race, gender, region, family composition, mother's education, and parents' involvement in the child's schooling." Children's Defense Fund, *CDF Reports*, July 1993, p. 8. See also N. Baydar and J. Brooks-Gunn, "Effects of Maternal Employment and Child-Care Arrangements in Infancy on Preschoolers' Cognitive and Behavioral Outcomes: Evidence from the Children of the NLSY," *Developmental Psychology* 27 (1991): 932–45; G. J. Duncan, J. Brooks-Gunn, and P. K. Klebanov, "Economic Deprivation and Early Childhood Development," *Child Development* 65 (1994): 296–318; R. Haveman, B. Wolfe, and J. Spaulding, "Childhood Events and Circumstances Influencing High School Completion," *Demography* 28 (1991): 133–57.

85. L. B. Schorr and D. Schorr, *Within Our Reach: Breaking the Cycle of Disadvantage* (Garden City, NY: Doubleday, 1988).

86. P. Garrett, N. Ng'andu, and J. Ferron, "Poverty Experiences of Young Children and the Quality of Their Home Environments," *Child Development* 65 (1994): 331–45.

87. For a review of some of the issues associated with ethnicity and poverty, see G. J. Duncan and W. L. Rodgers, "Longitudinal Aspects of Poverty," *Journal of Marriage and the Family* 50 (1988): 1007–21.

88. Duncan, Brooks-Gunn, and Klebanov, "Economic Deprivation and Early Childhood Development," pp. 303–4 and 311. Data for this study were derived from the Panel Study of Income Dynamics (PSID).

89. In 1990, AFDC payments for a family of three were frozen at their 1989 levels in twenty-six states and territories and reduced in the state of Kansas. When calculating the higher cost of living between 1989 and 1990, all AFDC recipients in these states were net losers during fiscal year 1990. In 1991, benefits were frozen in twenty-nine states. For information regarding AFDC rates, see House Ways and Means Committee, *1991 U.S. Government Green Book: Overview of Programs* (Washington, DC: U.S. Government Printing Office, 1991).

90. Center on Budget and Policy Priorities, *The States and the Poor: Budget Decisions Hurt Low Income People in 1992* (Washington, DC: Center on Budget and Policy Priorities, 1992).

91. Ellwood and Summers, "Poverty in America."

92. When the War on Poverty was launched, approximately 27 percent of children under the age of eighteen were living in poverty. By the end of the 1960s, only 14 percent of this group still lived in poverty. This figure rose again in the 1970s, to about 20 percent, and has remained at or around that level since that time. See A. C. Huston, V. C. McLoyd, and C. G. Coll, "Children and Poverty: Issues in Contemporary Research," *Child Development* 65 (1994): 275–82.

Ana: Caught in Circumstances Beyond Her Control

1. California housing prices rose about 11 percent each year during the 1970s and 1980s. In 1991, the median price of a home in Los Angeles was $195,600, whereas the median price in the rest of the country at that time was $93,100. See Tom Furlong, "The New Reality in Real Estate," *Los Angeles Times*, February 24, 1991, p. D44.

2. Although California's housing market is beyond the reach of many people, buying a house has also become more difficult across the country. From the 1930s to the 1960s the proportion of families owning their own homes grew at a healthy rate, from about 48 percent of the population to about 62 percent. However, since the 1960s, home ownership has stagnated, in part because of rising home prices and level incomes (and for many years, increasing interest rates). In 1985, about 64 percent of American households owned a home—a 2 percent increase from the rate twenty-five years earlier. By 1992, the median price of a house was $100,900. In Ana's community, the median

Notes

price of homes in 1990 was $259,300. See S. Levitan, R. S. Belous, and F. Gallo, *What's Happening to the American Family?* (Baltimore: Johns Hopkins University Press, 1988); Mark S. Hoffman, ed., *The World Almanac, Book of Facts* (New York: Pharos Books, 1993), p. 714.

3. According to the Small Business Administration, an average of 57,107 businesses failed in the United States between 1985 and 1990, and an average of 644,992 new business corporations have failed each year since 1981. See Office of Advocacy, *1992 State of Small Business* (Washington, DC: Office of Advocacy, 1992).

4. In 1990, more than 190,000 people filed insurance claims with the Worker's Compensation Insurance Rating Bureau of California, amounting to more than $4 billion in incurred losses. About 15 percent of all injuries were the result of falls. Personal communication, David Bellusci, Worker's Compensation Insurance Rating Bureau, San Francisco.

5. Ana's employer did not want to approve the worker's comp. The DMV was short of staff at the time and needed her to work on the trucks. It also was suspicious about the severity of her ailment, as she had returned to her job for a few weeks without any immediate negative consequences.

6. D. Ellwood, *Poor Support: Poverty in the American Family* (New York: Basic Books, 1986), p. 4.

7. A recent study by Hagen and Davis confirms this view and reveals the social distancing of women on welfare toward others in like circumstances. See J. L. Hagen and L. V. Davis, *Another Perspective on Welfare Reform: Conversations with Mothers on Welfare* (Albany, NY: Nelson Rockefeller Institute of Government, 1994).

8. About 16 percent of the welfare population has three children. See U.S. Department of Health and Human Services, *Characteristics and Financial Circumstances of AFDC Recipients* (Washington, DC: U.S. Department of Health and Human Services, 1991).

9. M. J. Bane and D. T. Ellwood, "The Dynamics of Dependence: Routes to Self-Sufficiency," unpublished manuscript (Cambridge, MA: Urban Systems Research and Engineering, 1983).

10. G. J. Duncan, *Years of Poverty, Years of Plenty* (Ann Arbor, MI: Survey Research Center, 1984), pp. 14, 10.

11. Ibid., p. 10.

12. I. Shapiro and R. Greenstein, *Holes in the Safety Nets: National Overview* (Washington, DC: Center on Budget and Policy Priorities, 1988).

13. During the Clinton–Bush campaign of 1992, much public debate surrounded the expansion of unemployment benefits from twenty-six to fifty-two weeks. In 1991 the Unemployment Insurance Reform Act was passed and signed by President George Bush in an effort to highlight the "deserving" nature of unemployed wage earners, in addition to recognizing the sometimes bad effects of the market on laborers. For a brief discussion of some of the issues surrounding this law, see W. J. Eaton, "Congress Passes Jobless Aid and Bush Says He Will Sign," *Los Angeles Times*, July 3, 1992, p. A16.

Other examples can be found, of course. For instance, according to Piven and Cloward, during the 1973/74 recession, the twenty-six-week period of

180

coverage was extended to sixty-five weeks. See F. F. Piven and R. A. Cloward, "The Historical Sources of the Contemporary Relief Debate," in F. Block, R. A. Cloward, B. Ehrenreich, and F. F. Piven, eds., *The Mean Season: The Attack on the Welfare State* (New York: Pantheon Books, 1987), pp. 3–44.

14. Mimi Abramovitz provides an interesting discussion about the role of government in buffering the effects of the market on workers: *Regulating the Lives of Women* (Boston: South End Press, 1988).

15. Michael Katz characterizes these differences in terms of the "deserving" and the "undeserving" poor. Although this characterization has been used before, Katz describes the differences between these two groups. See M. B. Katz, *The Undeserving Poor* (New York: Pantheon Books, 1989).

16. Lee Rainwater argues in favor of a more equitable distribution of income in his book *Behind Ghetto Walls: Black Families in a Federal Slum* (Chicago: Aldine, 1970). He made his argument at a time when federal legislators were considering a guaranteed income for all Americans, based on a negative income tax. Although a guaranteed income is rarely considered today, some policymakers have proposed something like a "child allowance" as a means of raising family income. See I. Garfinkel and S. McLanahan, *Single Mothers and Their Children: A New American Dilemma* (Washington, DC: Urban Institute Press, 1986).

17. Today, the top 4 percent of Americans have as much income as does the bottom 51 percent. For details regarding the changes in income distribution wrought by recent policies, see D. L. Bartlett and J. B. Steele, *America: What Went Wrong?* (Kansas City, MO: Andrews and McMeel Press, 1992); K. Phillips, *The Politics of Rich and Poor: Wealth and the American Electorate in the Reagan Aftermath* (New York: Harper Perennial, 1990).

18. Center on Budget and Policy Priorities, *Real Life Poverty in America: Where the American Public Would Set the Poverty Line* (Washington, DC: Center on Budget and Policy Priorities, July 1990).

19. Several private business colleges prey on low-income communities, promising well-paying jobs at graduation. The programs usually offer the same array of classes that are available in an inexpensive community college, but the marketing strategy used by these private schools is quite compelling. The tuition at these schools can be very high. Most of the schools with which I am familiar cost between $5,000 and $6,000 per year. Often low-income people are lured into the program with promises of low-interest loans. Although some leave the programs once they realize how few skills are provided, their contract usually stipulates that they must pay the full amount of their tuition. Other people complete their program and begin their search for work with no guarantee of employment. Some default on their loans, either because the cost is too high or, in some cases, because they feel the agreement was not ethical. The default, however, is listed in their credit file, and so such persons have a difficult time obtaining future loans until they pay it off.

20. Roberto and his girlfriend plan to get married. He has joined the army and will move around the country with his wife this summer. They have talked about the importance of waiting to have children until they are financially secure.

21. In addition, Ana was fortunate to have established an account in her

local bank, and when she went on welfare she continued to do business with her bank. Because she lived in a working-class neighborhood near a shopping district, she also had easy access to her bank. Many welfare recipients are not so lucky. Banks generally do not locate in inner-city, low-income neighborhoods, and so most welfare recipients must rely on check-cashing outlets to conduct their financial business. These outlets often charge higher prices for financial services, further penalizing poor people for their financial plight. For a discussion of financial services for the poor in New York City, see M. Green, "The Poor Pay More . . . For Less," unpublished manuscript, April 1994.

22. Ana's idea is not so far fetched. I recently had a phone call from a local for-profit organization that wanted to set up a system designating each week the "best buys" for each store in a neighborhood. Welfare recipients would pay a nominal fee each week to obtain the listing and then they could shop according to their updated lists.

23. One estimate notes that for every ten thousand employed workers in 1918, for example, seven were killed. Accidents were most common in the railway business, building, and agriculture. Employment in mining was (and still is) hazardous as well. See W. L. Chenery, *Industry and Human Welfare* (New York: Macmillan, 1922); H. M. Somers and A. R. Somers, *Workmen's Compensation: Prevention, Insurance and Rehabilitation of Occupational Disability* (New York: Wiley, 1954).

24. Piven and Cloward's theory states that the development of the modern welfare state was primarily in response to the mass demonstrations of the 1930s and 1960s. Because of the large-scale displacement and instability, people organized and demanded greater protection from the market. The welfare state was designed and later expanded in an effort to quell such disturbances. Piven and Cloward describe a political compromise between industry and the government that resulted in an essentially conservative approach to relief, in which benefits would be low enough that workers would not be tempted to retreat from the market. When unemployment rates dipped and the economy stabilized, eligibility requirements were tightened. See F. F. Piven and R. A. Cloward, *Regulating the Poor: The Functions of Public Welfare* (New York: Pantheon Books, 1971).

25. Bane and Ellwood, "The Dynamics of Dependence."

26. Efforts were made under the Carter administration to provide government-sponsored jobs to welfare recipients, but the plan never moved forward.

27. In four California counties (Imperial, San Benito, Sutter, Tulare), unemployment rates reached well over 17 percent in 1991. See *California Statistical Abstract* (Sacramento: Department of Finance, 1992).

28. Figures from 1991 show that the rates of unemployment for African Americans in the United States were double the rate (12.4 percent) of Caucasians (6.0 percent). Latinos had a rate of unemployment somewhat above that for Caucasians but lower than the rate for African Americans (9.0 percent). See U.S. Bureau of the Census, *Statistical Abstract of the United States*, 12th ed. (Washington, DC: U.S. Department of Commerce, 1992). For a more detailed description of the role of race and joblessness in the inner city, see W. J. Wil-

son, *The Truly Disadvantaged: The Inner City, the Underclass, and Public Policy* (Chicago: University of Chicago Press, 1987).

29. From July 1989 to March 1993, California's caseload grew by a phenomenal 42.5 percent. Although this is a rapid growth rate, it paled in comparison with those of other states. Of fifty-four states and territories, California ranked nineteenth in caseload growth. New Hampshire's caseload increased by 109 percent and Florida's by 108 percent. See U.S. House Ways and Means Committee, U.S. Government Green Book, 1993.

Sandy: Working but Poor

1. Many of the data on the dynamics of women's welfare patterns were studied by David Ellwood and Mary Jo Bane, "The Dynamics of Dependence: The Routes to Self-Sufficiency," unpublished manuscript (Cambridge, MA: Urban Systems Research and Engineering, 1983). Their earlier estimates were recently updated and suggest the following reasons for entering and leaving the welfare system: The reasons for entering AFDC were divorce or separation, 42 percent; giving birth while unmarried, 39 percent; drop in income, 7 percent; and other, 12 percent. The reasons for leaving AFDC were marriage, 29 percent; earnings, 25 percent; increase in transfer income other than AFDC, 12 percent; no longer having eligible children, 11 percent; and other, 23 percent. See M. J. Bane and D. T. Ellwood, *Welfare Realities: From Rhetoric to Reform* (Cambridge, MA: Harvard University Press, 1994).

2. Kim is five years old. At the time that her mother received AFDC she was between the ages of one and three, like about 30 percent of all youngest children on aid. Kim and Sandy also are Caucasian, similar to more than one-third of the AFDC population (38.1 percent of AFDC mothers are Caucasian, and 33.5 percent of AFDC children are Caucasian). See U.S. Department of Health and Human Services, *Characteristics and Financial Circumstances of AFDC Recipients* (Washington, DC: U.S. Department of Health and Human Services, 1991).

3. D. J. Besharov, "Targeting Long-Term Welfare Recipients," in P. H. Cottingham and D. T. Ellwood, eds., *Welfare Policy for the 1990s* (Cambridge, MA: Harvard University Press, 1989), pp. 146–64. See also Chapter 1, Myth 2.

4. In addition, studies have found that between 41 percent and 58 percent of teenage girls do not use any form of contraception at first intercourse and continue not to do so for at least one year. See Center for Population Options, *Adolescent Sexuality, Pregnancy and Parenthood* (Washington, DC: Center for Population Options, 1993); C. D. Hayes, ed., *Risking the Future: Adolescent Sexuality, Pregnancy and Childbearing* (Washington, DC: National Academy Press, 1987); W. D. Mosher and J. W. McNally, "Contraceptive Use at First Premarital Intercourse: United States, 1965—1988," *Family Planning Perspectives*, May—June 1991, p 111; L. S. Zabin, J. F. Kantner, and M. Zelnik, "The Risk of Adolescent Pregnancy in the First Months of Intercourse," in F. F. Furstenberg Jr., R. Lincoln, and J. Menkin, eds., *Teenage Sexuality, Pregnancy,*

and Childbearing (Philadelphia: University of Pennsylvania Press, 1981), pp. 136–48.

5. Although it is not clear how frequently women turn to welfare because they have no health insurance, some studies show that women's exit from AFDC is often confounded by the availability and accessibility of health-care coverage through private providers or Medicaid. See D. T. Ellwood and E. K. Adams, "Medicaid Mysteries: Transitional Benefits, Medicaid Coverage, and Welfare Exits," *Health Care Financing Review,* December 1990, pp. 119–31; S. C. Shuptrine, V. C. Grant, and G. G. McKenzie, *A Study of the Relationship of Health Coverage to Welfare Dependency* (Columbia, SC: Southern Institute on Children and Families, 1994); R. Moffitt and B. Wolfe, "The Effects of Medicaid on Welfare Dependency and Work," report prepared for U.S. Department of Health and Human Services (Cambridge, MA: National Bureau of Economic Research, 1989); A. Winkler, "The Incentive Effects of Medicaid on Women's Labor Supply," *Journal of Human Resources* 26 (1991): 308–27.

6. Between 1977 and 1987, employer-provided health insurance for these families dropped by 25 percent. See Children's Defense Fund, *The State of America's Children: 1992* (Washington, DC: Children's Defense Fund, 1992).

7. The system of health care described here may change at some point in the future, as the Congress is continuing to review health care reform legislation.

8. Omnibus Budget Reconciliation Act of 1987, P.L. 100-203, Section 4101, re Medicaid benefits for poor children and pregnant women.

9. Omnibus Budget Reconciliation Act of 1989, P.L. 101-239, Section 6401, re mandatory coverage of certain low-income pregnant women and children.

10. National Center for Children in Poverty, *Five Million Children* (New York: Columbia University Press, 1990).

11. C. Murray, *Losing Ground: American Social Policy 1950–1980* (New York: Basic Books, 1984).

12. Estimates vary slightly. According to Ruggles, about 6 percent of the AFDC population worked in 1983 (down from 15 percent in 1973). P. Ruggles, "Changes in Assistance Programs over Time: Are Income Support Programs Losing Their Sensitivity to Changes in Economic Circumstances?" unpublished manuscript (Washington, DC: Urban Institute, 1985).

13. Federal funding is provided to supplement state spending (excluding child care) at a matching rate that varies from 50 to 90 percent, depending on the state. States can lose federal funding above 50 percent if they do not have enough participants in their JOBS program (less than 15 percent of eligible adults in 1994), if they have not spent enough of their JOBS dollars on eligible target groups (target groups include adults whose older children will soon "age out" of the system, and young parents), or if they have not included enough eligible AFDC-UP families in the program (40 percent in 1994). General Accounting Office, *Welfare to Work: JOBS Automated Systems Do Not Focus on Program's Employment Objective* (Washington, DC: General Accounting Office, June 1994).

14. JOBS clients receive a total of $200 during their time in the program and also a monthly bus pass for transportation. Child-care expenses are paid up to 75 percent of the mean rate for the community in which the client lives.

15. For a more thorough description of public sympathies as they are tied to welfare use, see J. F. Handler and Y. Hasenfeld, *The Moral Construction of Poverty: Welfare Reform in America* (Beverly Hills, CA: Sage, 1991).

16. W. D. Wandersee, *Women's Work and Family Values: 1920–1940* (Cambridge, MA: Harvard University Press, 1981).

17. F. D. Blau and M. A. Ferber, *The Economics of Women, Men and Work* (Englewood Cliffs, NJ: Prentice-Hall, 1986).

18. U.S. Department of Labor, Office of the Secretary, Women's Bureau, "Facts on Women Workers," fact sheet no. 86-1, 1986.

19. L. W. Hoffman, "Effects of Maternal Employment in the Two-Parent Family," *American Psychologist* 44 (1989): 283–92.

20. H. Hayghe, "Rise in Mothers' Labor Force Activity Includes Those with Infants," *Monthly Labor Review* 109 (1986): 43–45.

21. Sandy is referring to Section 8 certificates (also called *vouchers*), which act as subsidies for low-income families to use toward their monthly rent. In principle, Section 8 vouchers can be used in any county and any neighborhood, as long as the landlord is willing to honor them. In practice, however, Sandy is referring to the fact that many of the landlords willing to take these certificates are located in very dangerous neighborhoods.

22. For a review of the many welfare-to-work initiatives that have been attempted in recent years, see J. M. Gueron and E. Pauly, *From Welfare to Work* (New York: Russell Sage Foundation, 1991).

23. Estimates are taken from S. A. Levitan, F. Gallo, and I. Shapiro, *Working but Poor: America's Contradiction* (Baltimore: Johns Hopkins University Press, 1993). The poverty rate for other family sizes is as follows: A family with just one member, $7,320; two members, $9,467; three members, $11,216; four members, $14,381; five members, $17,000; six members, $19,204; and seven members, $21,790.

24. Ibid.

25. N. Gilbert, J. D. Berrick, and M. Meyers, *GAIN Family Life and Child Care Study* (Berkeley, CA: Family Welfare Research Group, 1992).

26. K. Hartman, "The Cliffs of Self-Sufficiency," unpublished manuscript (Golden, CO: Jeffco Self-Sufficiency Council, October 1992), p. 1.

27. A number of studies reviewed by Polit and O'Hara show that child care is an important factor in women's entering the workforce. See D. Polit and J. O'Hara, "Support Services," in P. Cottingham and D. T. Ellwood, eds., *Welfare Policy for the 1990s* (Cambridge, MA: Harvard University Press, 1989), pp. 165–98.

28. Gueron and Pauly provide a detailed analysis, in their *From Welfare to Work*, of the trade-off between high-cost and low-cost programs for welfare departments and recipients.

29. California Department of Finance, *California Statistical Abstract* (Sacramento: California Department of Finance, 1992).

30. Sandy's expenses are as follows: rent, $550; day care, $116; car payment, $100; car insurance, $41; food, $200; gas and electric, $20; telephone, $25; cable TV, $40; entertainment, $40; gas, $25; credit cards, $40; and incidentals, $50; for a total of $1,247.

Sandy's monthly income is about $1,352. She is also entitled to child support up to $300, but she does not always receive the full amount.

31. Details regarding the mechanics of the EITC for 1992 can be found in "Tax Credit Plan Reopens Debate on Aid to the Working Poor," *Welfare to Work*, November 23, 1992, pp. 4–5. The EITC was expanded considerably under the new Clinton budget bill. The details of the expansion, which take effect in 1994, are described in Chapter 7. For more information regarding the credit, see "WashingtonGram," *Welfare to Work*, August 16, 1993, p. 8.

32. Horror stories among women trying to collect child support from absent fathers are commonplace. Many women also have few kind words for the local district attorney's office. In their defense, DAs have an impossible job. Caseload sizes are incredibly high (one local county has regular caseload sizes of approximately three hundred child-support requests per worker); paternity determinations are cumbersome; and obtaining accurate assessments of income are time-consuming and rife with problems. With the new regulations intended for implementation in fall 1993, the DA's office will also be responsible for reviewing and modifying existing child-support orders every three years, which will increase the workload considerably.

33. Statistics on the incidence of sexual abuse of children vary greatly by study. The main reason for these differences is in the definition the researcher has used to determine whether or not sexual abuse has occurred (from acts that include penetration to acts that include exhibitionism). Most studies show that the majority of perpetrators are family members, extended family members, or friends of the family. Abuse by strangers is less common. See J. J. Hauggard and N. D. Reppucci, *The Sexual Abuse of Children: A Comprehensive Guide to Current Knowledge and Intervention Strategies* (San Francisco: Jossey-Bass, 1988).

34. Garfinkel and McLanahan, *Single Mothers and Their Children: A New American Dilemma*.

35. When women are collecting AFDC, any child-support payments that may come from the father (minus $50) go directly to the state to offset the costs of the AFDC benefit. Women then receive their regular AFDC check, with an additional $50 bonus. The bonus acts as an incentive to encourage women to supply information about the father's whereabouts to the AFDC office.

36. Charles Murray (*Losing Ground*) has been a proponent of marriage for welfare recipients. The state of Wisconsin has been the most involved of the states in reforming welfare by offering women a "bonus" if they marry. An article from the *New York Times* stated: "Gov. Tommy G. Thompson, who has made a national reputation with his aggressive proposals to overhaul Wisconsin's welfare system, offered another one this month. He wants to reward teen-age mothers who marry and penalize those who do not. As part of the budget he presented to the legislature on Thursday, the Republican Governor unveiled a pilot program to cap welfare payments to unwed teen-age mothers regardless of how many children they have, and to pay larger grants to those who marry. . . . Those who married would get nearly $80 a month extra." Isabel Wilkerson, "Wisconsin Welfare Plan: To Reward the Married," *New York Times*, February 12, 1991, p. A16.

37. Most of the data on the income loss associated with single parenthood

come from studies of women following a divorce. Although Sandy and Ben were never married, the point here is that most two-parent households are better off financially than single-parent households are. For example, one year following a divorce or separation, women find that their income is about 67 percent of what it was a year previously. In general, rates of poverty for female-headed households are roughly three times higher than poverty rates for two-parent households. See Garfinkel and McLanahan, *Single Mothers and Their Children*; H. R. Rodgers Jr., *Poor Women, Poor Families: The Economic Plight of America's Female-Headed Households* (Armonk, NY: M. E. Sharpe, 1990).

38. Like many women who use or have used welfare, Sandy has somewhat traditional views about the role of women. In studies asking AFDC mothers about their views of working or parenting, the majority often state that their role is primarily that of a parent and secondarily a provider. One study conducted by Zill and associates indicated that about one-third of AFDC mothers had negative attitudes toward women employed outside the home and an additional third had views that "leaned toward the traditional orientation." See N. Zill, K. A. Moore, C. W. Nord, and T. Stief, *Welfare Mothers as Potential Employees: A Statistical Profile Based on National Survey Data* (Washington, DC: Child Trends, 1991), p. 20.

39. This estimate comes from S. Coontz, *The Way We Never Were: American Families and the Nostalgia Trap* (New York: Basic Books, 1992). She also notes that this rate dropped significantly in the last two decades. In 1975, 44 percent of families were "traditional." Sar Levitan, Richard Belous, and Frank Gallo give even more dramatic estimates, indicating that only 10 percent of families are "traditional." "In 1987, divorced, separated, widowed, and never-married persons headed . . . one in every five [families]. Four of five of these families were headed by women. Six percent of all women expect never to have children, while about 5 to 10 percent of the American population will never marry, and about 12 percent of all adults live alone." S. A. Levitan, R. S. Belous, and F. Gallo, *What's Happening to the American Family?* (Baltimore: Johns Hopkins University Press, 1988), p. 8.

Rebecca: Motivation and a Fighting Spirit

1. Like about 30 percent of the AFDC population, both Sandy and Rebecca are Caucasian.

2. National Center for Health Statistics, quoted in Children's Defense Fund, *The State of America's Children, 1992* (Washington, DC: Children's Defense Fund, 1992).

3. R. A. Weatherley, "Teenage Parenthood and Poverty," in H. R. Rodgers Jr., ed., *Beyond Welfare* (Armonk, NY: M. E. Sharpe, 1988), pp. 114–34.

4. J. B. Hardy, A. K. Duggan, K. Masnyk, and C. Pearson, "Fathers of Children Born to Young Urban Mothers," *Family Planning Perspectives* 21 (1989): 159–63, 187; W. Marsiglio, "Adolescent Fathers in the United States: Their Initial Living Arrangements, Marital Experience, and Educational Outcomes," *Family Planning Perspectives* 19 (1987): 240–51.

Notes

5. A. Hacker, *Two Nations: Black and White, Separate, Hostile, Unequal* (New York: Ballantine Books, 1992).

6. Barbara Ehrenreich postulates that the United States is experiencing a cultural phenomenon in which men are fleeing from their responsibilities to their families. Ruth Sidel also indicates that the problem is not only cultural but economic as well. As men realize their limited ability to contribute to their families, their shame draws them away from active involvement. Other researchers show that fathers' involvement is greater when the child is very young but wanes with age and that their involvement is enhanced if they are well employed. See S. K. Danziger and N. Radin, "Absent Does Not Equal Uninvolved: Predictors of Fathering in Teen Mother Families," *Journal of Marriage and the Family* 52 (1990): 636–42; B. Ehrenreich, *The Hearts of Men: American Dreams and the Flight from Commitment* (Garden City, NY: Doubleday, 1983); R. Sidel, *Women and Children Last: The Plight of Poor Women in Affluent America* (New York: Penguin Books, 1986).

7. Ozawa and Wang note that the more children a woman bears (particularly Caucasian women), the less she will earn during her lifetime. See M. Ozawa and Y. Wang, "The Effects of Children and Education on Women's Earnings History," *Social Work Research and Abstracts* 29 (1993): 17–27. This theory is also postulated by Victor Fuchs, in "Sex Differences in Economic Well-being," *Science* 232 (1986): 459–64.

8. There also are differences by race: 85 percent of African American teen mothers receive AFDC at some time during their lives, and 40 percent of white teen mothers do. See N. Rudd, P. McKenty, and M. Nah, "Welfare Receipt Among Black and White Adolescent Mothers: A Longitudinal Perspective," *Journal of Family Issues* 11 (1990): 334–52.

9. Many of these statistics are taken from L. B. Schorr and D. Schorr, *Within Our Reach: Breaking the Cycle of Disadvantage* (Garden City, NY: Doubleday, 1989). They get their numbers from the following sources: U.S. Department of Education, *The Condition of Education* (Washington, DC: U.S. Government Printing Office, 1986); F. L. Mott and W. Marsiglio, "Early Childbearing and Completion of High School," *Family Planning Perspectives* 17 (1985): 234–37; K. A. Moore and M. R. Burt, *Private Crises, Public Cost: Policy Perspectives on Teenage Childbearing* (Washington, DC: Urban Institute Press, 1982); M. J. Bane and D. T. Ellwood, *Slipping into and out of Poverty: The Dynamics of Spells* (Cambridge, MA: National Bureau of Economic Research, 1983).

10. Like Rebecca, increasing numbers of women are coming to the welfare rolls better educated than the women who preceded them on welfare twenty years ago. A GAO report shows that the educational levels of women receiving AFDC have increased over time. "In 1976, 38 percent had at least a high school diploma. By 1992, 55 percent of women receiving AFDC had at least a high school diploma." Similarly, the percentage of women with some college rose as well, from about 6 to about 17 percent. These figures are much lower, however, than the rates of high school completion and college education for all single mothers. General Accounting Office, *Families on Welfare: Sharp Rise in Never-Married Women Reflects Societal Trend* (Washington, DC: General Accounting Office, 1994).

11. For example, J. P. Robinson, *How Americans Use Time* (New York: Praeger, 1977), found that working women have about sixty-six fewer minutes of leisure activities per day than do nonworking women. D. R. Hill and R. Stafford, "Parental Care of Children: Time Diary Estimates of Quantity, Predictability, and Variety, *Journal of Human Resources* 15 (1980): 217–39, also found that women give up about a half hour of sleep each night when they move into the workforce. In my own study of welfare recipients, I found that when AFDC mothers began a work or training program such as GAIN, they got about twenty minutes less sleep each night. See N. Gilbert, J. D. Berrick, and M. Meyers, *GAIN Family Life and Child Care Study* (Berkeley, CA: Family Welfare Research Group, 1992).

12. One researcher found that professional or managerial mothers give a higher priority to work than to family. These women may have the flexibility to attend to family matters when they arise because of the type of work they are engaged in. In contrast, working-class women (married or single) give their families the highest priority and find that family issues often intrude on their role as a worker. Because their jobs are the most structurally inflexible, they have fewer opportunities to negotiate and balance the divergent roles of mother and worker. See B. H. Burris, "Employed Mothers: The Impact of Class and Marital Status on the Prioritizing of Family and Work," *Social Science Quarterly* 72 (1991): 50–66.

13. Background material and data on programs under the jurisdiction of the House Committee on Ways and Means, 1989. Quoted in C. Jencks, *Rethinking Social Policy: Race, Poverty and the Underclass* (Cambridge, MA: Harvard University Press, 1992), p. 564.

14. California ranks fiftieth among all the states in the percentage of subsidized housing available to its families. See House Committee on Ways and Means, *Data and Materials Related to Welfare Programs for Families and Children* (also known as the *Green Book*) (Washington, DC: U.S. Government Printing Office, 1992).

15. California may actually be tied for first place with Massachusetts. See E. Lazere, *The Costs of Decent Housing for Low Income Families in California* (Washington, DC: Center on Budget and Policy Priorities, 1992).

16. The average rent for a two-bedroom apartment in California is a little less at $750, about $220 more than the national average. See M. K. Meyers and S. Brown, *Beyond Rhetoric: The Facts About Poverty and Welfare in California* (Berkeley and Los Angeles: University of California Press, 1992).

17. The Thrifty Food Plan (TFP) is calculated by the U.S. Department of Agriculture and is used to determine food stamp benefits. For more details, see D. M. DiNitto, *Social Welfare Politics and Public Policy* (Englewood Cliffs, NJ: Prentice-Hall, 1991).

18. Brown and Pizer studied hunger in the United States and concluded that a 25 percent increase in food stamp benefits was modest in comparison with the real need but was a necessary first step in food stamp reform. See J. L. Brown and H. F. Pizer, *Living Hungry in America* (New York: Mentor Books, 1987). A 25 percent increase would result in an allowance of approximately $213 per month for a mother with one child.

Notes

19. Oakland Unified School District, *School District Information Summary* (Oakland, CA: Department of Research and Evaluation, Oakland Unified School District, 1991/92).

20. Rebecca has a twenty-year-old car that has terrible gas mileage. Each day she drives about sixty miles to get to Tanya's school, her classes at the community college, back to Tanya's school, and then home. She estimates that gas costs between $8 and $10 per weekday.

21. Irwin Garfinkel and Sara McLanahan estimate that about 40 percent of absent Anglo fathers and 19 percent of absent African American fathers pay child support. And when they do pay, the amount is small. They calculate that Anglo mothers receive about $3,129 per year and that African American mothers receive about $1,698. I. Garfinkel and S. S. McLanahan, *Single Mothers and Their Children* (Washington, DC: Urban Institute Press, 1986). For women living below the poverty level, Rodgers estimates that in 1985 about 40 percent had been awarded child support but that only about 21 percent received payments from the absent father. H. R. Rodgers, *Poor Women, Poor Families* (Armonk, NY: M. E. Sharpe, 1990).

22. Recent political events have revealed the extent to which the wealthy also rely on child care and cleaning help. Zoe Baird withdrew her nomination for Attorney General during the Clinton administration because she had failed to pay the "nanny taxes" required for her employment of a child-care worker in her home.

23. For a discussion of the Social Security system, see C. P. Chelf, *Controversial Issues in Social Welfare Policy* (Newbury Park, CA: Sage, 1992).

24. K. Edin and C. Jencks, "Reforming Welfare," in C. Jencks, ed., *Rethinking Social Policy: Race, Poverty, and the Underclass* (Cambridge, MA: Harvard University Press, 1992), pp. 204–36.

25. This is commonly called the *30 and a third rule*.

26. The 8 percent estimates are from 1990. In 1979, official estimates were closer to 13 percent of women working while collecting aid. See S. A. Levitan, F. Gallo, and I. Shapiro, *Working but Poor: America's Contradiction* (Baltimore: Johns Hopkins University Press, 1993). Some suggest that this downward trend may reflect changes in policy in the 1980s that have altered the incentives associated with work, so that women are now less inclined to work while receiving AFDC. This may be the case, although other alternatives are also possible. Common knowledge about the acceptability of committing welfare fraud may have expanded in the ensuing years, with women more likely to take the chance of working without reporting income to welfare authorities. The economic circumstances may have also grown more precarious as women spend larger portions of their AFDC checks on housing; therefore the need for outside work may have become greater. When women compare the economic benefits of disclosing their work to the welfare office with the possible risk of being found out, they may decide that the economic advantage to them and their children is worth the associated dangers.

27. See, for example, C. Murray, *Losing Ground: American Social Policy 1950–1980* (New York: Basic Books, 1984).

28. Rebecca got caught in the JOBS program before funding cuts severely

limited the number of women who could participate. Currently, AFDC recipients with children over age sixteen, and teenage recipients, are the primary targets for the JOBS program.

29. Personal communication, Maria Hernandez, GAIN Bureau, California Department of Social Services. This figure is based on data from fiscal year 1991/92. Average wages in other states can be expected to be much lower, as California's minimum wage is higher than that in most other states.

30. In other words, women exiting the GAIN program generally make poverty wages (for a family of three).

Darlene: Complex People, Complex Problems

1. In 1991, the median age of female welfare recipients in the United States was 28.9 years. For details regarding the AFDC population, see U.S. Department of Health and Human Services, *Characteristics and Financial Circumstances of AFDC Recipients* (Washington, DC: Administration for Children and Families, 1991).

2. About 30.4 percent of the welfare population is drawn to AFDC when they become a female head of household with a child.

3. One survey, conducted by the Roper Organization, found that an astounding 93 percent of women under age thirty believed that marriage would give them satisfaction and pleasure and was the preferred lifestyle. See S. A. Levitan, R. S. Belous, and F. Gallo, *What's Happening to the American Family?* (Baltimore: Johns Hopkins University Press, 1988) p. 79.

4. Estimates vary, depending on the socioeconomic status of the parents, the region of the country in which a family raises a child, and the goods and services that an individual family deems "necessary" to care for a child. T. J. Espenshade, *Investing in Children* (Washington, DC: Urban Institute, 1984) estimates costs ranging from about $70,000 to $170,000 from birth to age eighteen (not including college expenses). Lino also estimates a cost of about $100,110 in constant 1989 dollars. M. Lino, "Expenditures on a Child by Husband–Wife Families," *Family Economics Review* 3 (1990): 2–18. The U.S. Department of Agriculture estimates that the typical middle-class family spends between $12,000 and $15,000 annually.

We can make our own calculations as well. Assume that a mother raising two children on AFDC receives an average payment of $349 per month. (This rate is an average based on the maximum AFDC benefit in all fifty states, minus the District of Columbia, for 1992, provided by the American Public Welfare Association). Assuming (liberally) that two-thirds of this income goes directly to the care and feeding of one child, this adds up to $49,753 over eighteen years. (This amount also suggests the relative poverty of children living on AFDC.)

5. H. Hayghe, "Rise in Mothers' Labor Force Activity Includes Those with Infants," *Monthly Labor Review* 109 (1986): 43–45; L. W. Hoffman, "Effects of Maternal Employment in the Two-Parent Family," *American Psychologist* 44 (1989): 283–92.

Notes

6. According to two studies, the adult children of alcoholics (ACOAs) have a tendency to marry alcoholics. They also have a number of recognizable characteristics that may define them as "different" from other adults. For example, some studies suggest that ACOs have difficulty separating emotionally from family members, deny their inner feelings, have poor communication skills, avoid intimacy, and lack trust in others. One study also found a higher rate of physical and sexual abuse in alcoholic families. See C. Black, S. F. Bucky, and S. Wilder-Padilla, "The Interpersonal and Emotional Consequences of Being an Adult Child of an Alcoholic," *International Journal of the Addictions* 21 (1986): 213–31; J. E. James and M. Goldman, "Behavior Trends of Wives of Alcoholics," *Quarterly Journal of the Study of Alcohol* 32 (1971): 373–81; J. Nici, "Wives of Alcoholics as 'Repeaters'," *Journal of the Study of Alcohol* 40 (1979): 677–82.

7. D. Finkelhor, *A Sourcebook on Child Sexual Abuse* (Beverly Hills, CA: Sage, 1986); J. J. Haugaard and N. D. Reppucci, *The Sexual Abuse of Children* (San Francisco: Jossey-Bass, 1988).

8. C. Jencks, *Rethinking Social Policy: Race, Poverty, and the Underclass* (Cambridge, MA: Harvard University Press, 1992).

9. M. B. Katz, "The Urban Underclass as a Metaphor of Social Transformation," in M. B. Katz, ed., *The Underclass Debate: Views from History* (Princeton, NJ: Princeton University Press, 1993).

10. Michael Katz frames the issues succinctly in the introduction to his edited volume, *The Underclass Debate*. For a more detailed description of the historical roots of the term *underclass* and a further understanding of the usefulness of this term, see Katz, ed., *The Underclass Debate*, pp. 4–5.

11. W. J. Wilson, *The Truly Disadvantaged: The Inner City, the Underclass, and Public Policy* (Chicago: University of Chicago Press, 1987).

12. J. T. Gibbs, *Young, Black and Male in America: An Endangered Species* (New York: Auburn House, 1986) p. 5.

13. After much discussion, I never found out the name of the program Darlene was referring to. Although she later participated in the GAIN program, the program she refers to here was specifically sponsored by HUD.

14. N. Gilbert, J. D. Berrick, and M. Meyers, "GAIN Family Life and Child Care Study: Final Report," unpublished manuscript (Berkeley: Family Welfare Research Group, University of California at Berkeley, 1992).

15. The CA-7 is the monthly reporting form for welfare recipients to explain their income and expenditures. It is due on the eighth of every month and guarantees continued welfare payments based on eligibility. If the form is late or completed incorrectly, the recipient may have her welfare benefits terminated until the problem can be cleared.

16. See M. Harrington, *The Other America: Poverty in the United States* (New York: Penguin Books, 1962); M. Harrington, *The New American Poverty* (New York: Penguin Books, 1984).

17. This is the applicant checklist given to all applicants in one California county.

18. See A. Hochschild, *The Second Shift: Working Parents and the Revolution at Home* (New York: Viking, 1989).

Cora: A Portrait of Dependency

1. Cora's family size is not representative of the average welfare recipient's. With six children, she represents only 1.4 percent of the AFDC population, and as an African American woman, she represents 38.8 percent of all AFDC recipients.

2. This is the term that Greg Duncan uses in his book *Years of Poverty, Years of Plenty* (Ann Arbor, MI: Survey Research Center, 1984).

3. In regard to these data, Tom Joe and Cheryl Rogers commented that the percentage of ever-poor American families was probably much higher during the economically turbulent 1980s. For a discussion, see T. Joe and C. Rogers, *By the Few, for the Few: The Reagan Welfare Legacy* (Lexington, MA: Lexington Books, 1985).

4. Duncan, *Years of Poverty*, p. 42.

5. J. Garbarino, "The Meaning of Poverty in the World of Children," *American Behavioral Scientist* 35 (1992): 220–37.

6. Duncan, *Years of Poverty*, p. 48.

7. Lawrence Mead and Charles Murray have been the greatest proponents of the term and have used it to refer not only to long-term AFDC recipients but also to any recipient of public aid. See L. Mead, *Beyond Entitlement: The Social Obligations of Citizenship* (New York: Free Press, 1986); C. Murray, *Losing Ground: American Social Policy 1950–1980* (New York: Basic Books, 1984).

8. Ken Auletta wrote a book entitled *The Underclass* (New York: Vintage Books, 1982). Although in the introduction, he distinguishes among welfare recipients, hostile street criminals, hustlers, and traumatized drunks, these distinctions are lost when one turns to the first chapter and beyond.

9. E. C. Banfield, *The Unheavenly City: The Nature and Future of Our Urban Crisis* (Boston: Little, Brown, 1968).

10. About 50 percent move off the welfare roles within two years, and another 25 percent receive AFDC for eight years or less. For more details, see D. T. Ellwood and L. H. Summers, "Poverty in America: Is Welfare the Answer or the Problem?" in S. H. Danziger and D. H. Weinberg, eds., *Fighting Poverty: What Works and What Doesn't?* (Cambridge, MA: Harvard University Press, 1986), pp. 78–105.

11. D. T. Ellwood, *Poor Support: Poverty in the American Family* (New York: Basic Books, 1988).

12. Michael Kaus provides a second look at the Ellwood and Bane data, cautioning the reader that among young women (women who begin collecting AFDC before the age of twenty-five), the vast majority (over 90 percent) receive AFDC for eight years or longer. M. Kaus, *The End of Equality* (New York: Basic Books, 1992).

13. Douglas Besharov points out that marital status may be the single most powerful predictor of long-term welfare recipiency. He examined data from several welfare scholars and found that differences by race all but disappear in regard to the marital status of the mother at the time of the first child's birth. And as Adams writes: "Being unmarried at the time of the first birth is most consistently associated with both an increased likelihood of entering the

welfare system within a few years of giving birth, and a decreased probability of leaving it within the first few years of welfare receipt." See D. J. Besharov, "Targeting Long-Term Recipients," in P. H. Cottingham and D. T. Ellwood, eds., *Welfare Policy for the 1990s* (Cambridge, MA: Harvard University Press, 1989), pp. 146—64; G. Adams, *The Dynamics of Welfare Recipiency Among Adolescent Mothers* (Washington, DC: Congressional Budget Office, 1987).

14. Cora is talking about ADC–UP, otherwise known as Aid to Dependent Children–Unemployed Parent. The original AFDC program's name reflected its focus on aid to children (rather than aid to families). When it was first established, families could collect aid only if they were headed by a single parent. In 1961, Congress allowed the states the option of establishing programs for two-parent families. These UP options were exercised by twenty-two states, including California. Then, in the late 1970s and 1980s, cries were heard from across the political spectrum to expand AFDC–UP coverage to all states, as the program's original focus on single parents encouraged women to break up their marriages. Eligibility for the program was strictly limited, and in most states, coverage was for the short term until the unemployed father found work. (The expectation that the father would be the primary breadwinner in the family was still strong in the 1960s and 1970s.)

Although AFDC–UP was required in all fifty states with the enactment of the Family Support Act, its use is still quite limited. In all, about 5 percent of the national caseload is represented by two-parent families using AFDC–UP. See Ellwood and Summers, "Poverty in America."

15. As of 1991, about 7 percent of the total AFDC caseload consisted of two-parent families under AFDC–UP. U.S. Department of Health and Human Services, *Characteristics and Financial Circumstances of AFDC Recipients* (Washington, DC: U.S. Department of Health and Human Services, 1991).

16. Straus and Gelles show a rate of 116 per 1,000 couples experiencing husband-to-wife violence. The rates are especially high for lower socioeconomic couples, with assaults by husbands on wives 368 percent higher when the annual family income is below $9,000 (1985 data). In addition, abuse appears to escalate significantly when alcohol is involved. Although the data are disturbing, the reader should also bear in mind that women are also responsible for much spousal abuse in the family. M. A. Straus and R. J. Gelles, eds., *Physical Violence in American Families: Risk Factors and Adaptations to Violence in 8,145 Families* (New Brunswick, NJ: Transaction Publishers, 1990). K. Dunn, "Truth Abuse," *New Republic*, August 1, 1994, pp. 16–18.

17. O. Lewis, *The Children of Sanchez* (New York: Vintage Books, 1963). The concept of a culture of poverty was also made famous in the so-called Moynihan Report of the mid-1960s. Moynihan's study of the black American family focused on the disintegration of family structure and values, which brought fierce criticism and debate by liberals of the time. The report, however, brought the concept of the culture of poverty out of the Mexican ghetto into the American inner city, and the term was widely used throughout the remainder of the 1960s and 1970s. See D. P. Moynihan, *The Negro Family: The Case for National Action* (Washington, DC: U.S. Department of Labor, Office of Policy Planning and Research, 1965).

18. In the 1960s, much of the debate on poverty focused on the notion of a culture of poverty. In recent years, this terminology has been replaced with the term *underclass*. Noted writers on the topic of the underclass include Auletta, *The Underclass*; C. Jencks and P. E. Peterson, eds., *The Urban Underclass* (Washington, DC: Brookings Institution, 1991); Kaus, *The End of Equality*; Murray, *Losing Ground*; W. J. Wilson, *The Truly Disadvantaged: The Inner City, the Underclass, and Public Policy* (Chicago: University of Chicago Press, 1987).

19. Kaus, *The End of Equality*, p. 105.

20. See M. Corcoran et al., "Myth and Reality: The Causes and Persistence of Poverty," *Journal of Policy Analysis and Management* 4 (1985): 516–37.

21. Estimates vary, but these figures are taken from Kaus, *The End of Equality*. Duncan notes, however, that the "persistently poor" are more likely to reside outside major urban areas and also to include a sizable elderly population. This may mean that the 2.6 percent rate is inflated and that the real underclass is represented by an even smaller percentage of the American population. See G. J. Duncan and S. D. Hoffman, "Welfare Dynamics and the Nature of Need," *Cato Journal* 6 (1986): 31–54.

22. Urban Strategies Council, *A Chance for Every Child* (Oakland, CA: Urban Strategies Council, 1988). The infant mortality rate for her neighborhood is estimated at eighteen per one thousand live births, double the rate for the rest of the county in which she lives. See Chauncey Bailey, "Program Helps Pregnant Teens Bear Healthy Babies," *Oakland Tribune*, July 16, 1993, p. A13.

23. The city of Oakland has 9,247 individual public housing residents (or 3,214 families). Of these, the vast majority (79 percent) are African American. Of the more than 3,000 families, about half live in this one area of town. Several more apartment units and houses in the area accept Section 8 vouchers. A large housing project is included in the estimates of the families given here. This housing project is not administered by the Oakland Housing Authority but is managed by the U.S. Department of Housing and Urban Development (HUD). Several years ago, the project was developed and managed by a private developer. However, after years of mismanagement and bad press, the federal government took it over. Today, after an estimated $9 million facelift, the project is regularly patrolled by security guards, at a cost of more than $3 million per year. Security has indeed improved, although not so much that these projects could be considered a desirable place to live. (Information regarding public housing comes from Bob Williams, Oakland district coordinator of neighborhood planning, and Tom Woo, management analyst, at the Oakland Housing Authority office.)

24. Bartelt provides an interesting analysis of the segregation of the poor in the inner city, first with the flight of heavy industry to the suburbs and then with the intentional development of public housing in central-city areas. See D. Bartelt, "Housing the 'Underclass,'" in M. Katz, ed., *The Underclass Debate* (Princeton, NJ: Princeton University Press, 1993), pp. 118–60.

25. Living in neighborhoods such as these pose "environmental risks" to children. The combination of poverty, isolation, poor education, and few job opportunities have led to concentrated areas of poverty that research has shown to be unhealthy for children. See C. J. Coulton and S. Pandey, "Geo-

Notes

graphic Concentration of Poverty and Risk to Children in Urban Neighborhoods," *American Behavioral Scientist* 35 (1992): 238–57.

26. From January 1993 through May 1993, the city of Oakland had 67 homicides. In 1992, the total was 176.

27. For a review of the effects of chronic violence on children, see J. D. Osofsky, S. Wewers, D. M. Hann, and A. C. Fick, "Chronic Community Violence: What Is Happening to Our Children?" *Psychiatry* (February 1993), pp. 36–45.

28. In May 1992, the unemployment rate for the entire city of Oakland was 10.1 percent, but a year later, that rate had dropped somewhat, to 9.9 percent (California State Employment Development Department, Labor Market Information, Guides and Economic Research, Sacramento). Other studies examining pockets of poverty suggest that unemployment rates in the more depressed sections of the city are often double the average for a whole community. William J. Wilson provides an excellent account of unemployment and poverty rates in the ghetto, in *The Truly Disadvantaged*.

29. These figures are taken from B. Riske, "Special Initiatives for Hemophilia: Pediatric AIDS and Title V: Notes from Maternal and Child Health Bureau, Health Resources and Services Administration, U.S. Department of Health and Human Services," *Children with AIDS* 5 (1993): 4–5. Robert Searles Walker also provides an excellent account of the development of AIDS. He notes that in 1982, the Food and Drug Administration (FDA) issued recommendations to clean up the U.S. blood supply but that blood screening was not made mandatory until 1985. In 1990, Congress passed the Ryan White Comprehensive AIDS Act which requires states to develop public information campaigns. Those persons who received blood transfusions between January 1, 1978, and April 1, 1985, are targeted for special information about the risks of infection. See R. S. Walker, *AIDS, Today, Tomorrow: An Introduction to the HIV Epidemic in America* (Atlantic Highlands, NJ: Humanities Press. 1992).

30. In addition to her exposure to drugs, Sharon was born at low birth weight. Although there is some evidence that low birth weight by itself may not lead to cognitive deficits or other adverse developmental outcomes for children (Escalona, 1982; Sameroff, 1983), new studies indicate that the combination of low birth weight with poverty may result in serious negative outcomes. Furthermore, when poor parents are able to provide a protective environment for their child (defined in one study as having a male parent figure, living in stable and low-density housing, having a safe environment for play, having available a variety of learning materials for the child, and having an accepting and responsive mother figure) (Bradley et al., 1994), they may be able to ameliorate some of the otherwise negative effects, but the vast majority of poor, low birth-weight children may suffer from cognitive, behavioral, and physical problems. See R. H. Bradley, L. Whiteside, D. H. Mundfrom, P. H. Casey, K. J. Kelleher, and S. K. Pope, "Early Indications of Resilience and Their Relation to Experiences in the Home Environments of Low Birthweight, Premature Children Living in Poverty," *Child Development* 65 (1994): 346–60; S. K. Escalona, "Babies at Double Hazard: Early Development of Infants at Biologic and Social Risk," *Pediatrics* 70 (1982): 670–76; A. Sameroff,

"Developmental Systems: Context and Evolution," in W. Kessen, ed., *Handbook of Child Psychology*, vol. 1 (New York: Wiley, 1983), pp. 237–94.

31. Cora's income fluctuates every month, because the contribution from the older children and from Wesley and Janice is never the same. Her income is also complicated. She does not get the basic AFDC rate for a family of five because Darryl gets Social Security—for his late father—and Cora receives SSI for Raymond's disability. When the income from these sources is taken into account, the welfare office gives Cora $624 for herself, Sharon, and Joe. Darryl's Social Security is available as long as he is a minor and he is enrolled in school. The following is an account of her regular income: $624, AFDC; $232, Social Security for Darryl; $400, SSI for Raymond's disability; and $115, food stamps, for a total of $1,371. Cora's expenses are hard to measure. Some weeks she pays for all of her children's food, and other weeks she feel resentful of the older children and adults in her home who do not contribute, so she forces them to pay her something toward household expenses. The rent is extremely cheap ($91 a month), since she lives in public housing, and the gas and electric and telephone are fairly reasonable (about $100 each), since they support eight family members.

Although Cora discussed her drug use with me at length, she never disclosed how much money she regularly spent on it, partly because she simply did not keep track. She paid her bills at the beginning of the month and then used the rest of her money to buy things as she needed them, in some months borrowing and giving her surplus to others when she could.

Note that Social Security is a relatively large amount in comparison with AFDC. This disparity reflects the difference between those populations deemed "deserving" of aid and those less "deserving." See M. Katz, *The Undeserving Poor* (New York: Pantheon Books, 1989).

32. During the previous month, the welfare office had notified all AFDC recipients that they would be receiving one check per month, on the first, rather than a partial check on the first and another partial check on the fifteenth. Cora told me that this would be disastrous for many women she knew who did not know how to budget their money, although she felt confident that it would have no effect on her.

33. Sociologists and psychologists have debated the etiology of higher rates of delinquency among poor children. Some attribute patterns of delinquency to poor parenting and suggest that the poor parenting skills are partly a result of high stress and few resources to deal with life's visissitudes (Larzelere and Patterson, 1990). Other researchers indicate that poor parents have less ability to provide consistent, supportive guidance to children and rely on punitive punishment more often than higher-income parents do (McLoyd, 1990). See R. Larzelere and G. Patterson, "Parental Management: Mediator of the Effect of Socio-economic Status on Early Delinquency," *Criminology* 28 (1990): 301–23. V. C. McLoyd, "The Impact of Economic Hardship on Black Families and Children: Psychological Distress, Parenting, and Socioemotional Development," *Child Development* 61 (1990): 311–46.

For a review of factors associated with the development of delinquency patterns among children in poverty, see R. J. Sampson and J. H. Laub, "Urban

Poverty and the Family Context of Delinquency: A New Look at Structure and Process in a Classic Study," *Child Development* 65 (1994): 523–40.

34. Lawrence Kohlberg has written extensively about the moral development of children and adults. Briefly, in Stages 1 and 2, children obey out of fear of authority and because of their orientation to punishment, obedience, and physical and material power. In Stage 3, their morality is bounded by interpersonal relationships in which goodness occurs in light of helping or pleasing others. The fourth stage of morality shifts to an orientation toward rules, and higher stages are marked by an orientation toward abstract principles of justice. Carol Gilligan countered Kohlberg's theory, suggesting that his hierarchy often leaves women at the lower rungs of the moral development ladder and that women's orientation to relationship is not only culturally defined and guided but also represents a very highly developed sense of morality.

Cora's morality is most notable for its orientation toward relationships, although it might also be argued that the rules that have been designed systematically leave out the poor, and therefore, her behavior is based on a quest for justice beyond externally defined rules and regulations.

For more details regarding issues of moral development, see C. Gilligan, *In a Different Voice* (Cambridge, MA: Harvard University Press, 1982); L. Kohlberg, *The Philosophy of Moral Development* (San Francisco: Harper & Row, 1981); J. M. Rich and J. L. DeVitis, *Theories of Moral Development* (Chicago: Thomas, 1985).

35. Center on Addiction and Substance Abuse, *Substance Abuse and Women on Welfare* (New York: Center on Addiction and Substance Abuse, June 1994). The authors point out that these estimates may be low, as they rely solely on self-reported data. Estimates from the U.S. Department of Health and Human Services, however, suggest that 4.5 percent of AFDC recipients have a substance abuse problem that may be "debilitating." See Jennifer Dixon, "Welfare Drug Abuse Charged, *Fresno Bee*, June 28, 1994, p. A4.

36. According to the Center on Addiction and Substance Abuse at Columbia University, 12 percent of AFDC women "consumed five or more drinks in one sitting at least two times in the past month, compared to six percent of non-AFDC women; 23 percent used an illicit drug in the past year, compared to 12 percent of non-AFDC women; 17 percent used marijuana in the past year compared to 8 percent of non-AFDC women; [and] 34 percent of AFDC mothers who abuse illegal drugs also abuse alcohol, compared to 17 percent of non-AFDC mothers." Center on Addiction and Substance Abuse at Columbia University, "Substance Abuse and Women on Welfare," June 1994, p. 3.

37. D. Besharov, "The Children of Crack: Will We Protect Them?" *Public Welfare*, Fall 1989, pp. 6–11; D. Besharov, "Crack Children in Foster Care," *Children Today*, July–August 1990, pp. 21–25.

38. These figures are based on the 1993 Regional Market Rate Survey of California Child Care Providers (California Child Care Resource and Referral Network, San Francisco). The rate is for full-time care for children ages two through five.

39. Waiting lists are kept separately by facility. After we called all the local

publicly subsidized child-care centers in Cora's neighborhood, we estimated an average waiting period of three years.

40. L. V. Klerman, "The Health of Poor Children: Problems and Programs," in A. C. Huston, ed., *Children in Poverty: Child Development and Public Policy* (Cambridge: Cambridge University Press, 1991), pp. 136–57.

41. Like Ana's son, Cora now has a large debt to pay, as she still owes the business school about $4,000 in tuition.

42. If Cora were working, she would qualify for the Earned Income Tax Credit, discussed in Chapter 3. This would give her about $1,000 in additional income if she worked full time. Although this additional sum would be helpful, it would still leave her well below the poverty line if she had a job that paid less than about $6.50 per hour.

43. Alex Kotlowitz has written a compelling book about the daily lives of children raised in the projects in Chicago. His book conveys a sense of the kind of false bravado that many children must assume in order to conquer their daily fears of being hurt by neighborhood thugs. See A. Kotlowitz, *There Are No Children Here: The Story of Two Boys Growing up in the Other America* (New York: Doubleday, 1991).

James Garbarino, Kathleen Kostelny, and Nancy Dubrow also provide evidence that what may appear to be bravado on the outside really masks stress that has lasting effects on young children. Coping with uncontrollable danger interrupts children's learning processes and compromises their psychological well-being. See J. Garbarino, K. Kostelny, and N. Dubrow, *No Place to Be a Child: Growing up in a War Zone* (Lexington, MA: Lexington Books, 1991).

For a review of the effects of poverty and other stressors on children's mental stability and social adjustment, see N. Garmezy, "Resilience in Children's Adaptation to Negative Life Events and Stressed Environments," *Pediatric Annals* 20 (1991): 459–66.

44. There are times when Cora's care of her children is neglectful. Her behavior, however, is not unusual when one considers the personal, economic, and environmental stresses she must face. Although most AFDC mothers do not mistreat their children, an examination of the child population served by child welfare service agencies revealed that about 45 percent of children come from AFDC families. Therefore, it is important to understand the differences between those AFDC families who do mistreat and those who do not mistreat their children.

One study examined these differences and found that although the mothers in both samples shared some characteristics, the mistreating mothers had lives that were "problem ridden." These problems included greater financial concerns, worries about their children, concerns about boyfriends or husbands, and concerns about their own mental health. The children were more likely to exhibit problems at home and at school. The mistreating mothers were also more likely to have had severe bouts with depression, more likely to have problems with drugs and/or alcohol, and more likely to be involved in abusive relationships with men. S. Zuravin and G. L. Greif, "Normative and Child-Maltreating AFDC Mothers," *Social Casework: The Journal of Contemporary Social Work*, February 1989, pp. 76–84.

45. A stronger predictor of teenage parenthood, particularly for African American teens, is being raised in a poor neighborhood. A girl's mother's use of welfare is less a determinant of future welfare use. S. E. Mayer and C. Jencks, "Growing up in Poor Neighborhoods: How Much Does It Matter?" *Science* 243 (1989): 1441–45.

46. Neurofibromatosis is also known as the "elephant man" syndrome. For details regarding the disease and an excellent bibliography of sources, see J. Van de Kamp, *Neurofibromatosis* (Bethesda, MD: U.S. Department of Health and Human Services, Public Health Service, National Institute of Health, 1987).

47. He claims that he cannot attend school with his current wardrobe, but the $100 shoes and the $80 pants he says he must have are beyond Cora's budget.

48. Life in the inner-city ghetto does not necessarily confer a lifetime of bad effects. Some studies show that certain family attributes can cushion the harsh effects of extreme poverty and antisocial surroundings. Jarrett found that factors such as strong parental supervision of youth, relationships with "conventional" families, pooled family resources, and flexible living arrangements may ameliorate some of the difficulties of living under extreme circumstances. For a review of some of the factors that may protect children and that may lead to "resiliency," see N. Garmezy, "Children in Poverty: Resilience Despite Risk," *Psychiatry* 56 (1993): 127–36; R. L. Jarrett, *A Comparative Examination of Socialization Patterns Among Low-Income African-Americans, Chicanos, Puerto Ricans, and Whites: A Review of the Ethnographic Literature* (New York: Social Science Research Council, 1990); S. S. Luthar and E. Zigler, "Vulnerability and Competence: A Review of Research on Resilience in Childhood," *American Journal of Orthopsychiatry* 61 (1991): 6–22; M. Radke-Yarrow and E. Brown, "Resilience and Vulnerability in Children of Multiple-Risk Families," *Development and Psychopathology* 5 (1993): 581–92; J. E. Richters and P. E. Martinez, "Violent Communities, Family Choices, and Children's Chances: An Algorithm for Improving the Odds," *Development and Psychopathology* 5 (1993): 609–27.

49. N. Glazer, "Education and Training Programs and Poverty," in S. H. Danziger and D. H. Weinberg, eds., *Fighting Poverty: What Works and What Doesn't* (Cambridge, MA: Harvard University Press, 1986), pp. 152–72.

Finding a Better Way

1. G. Duncan, *Years of Poverty, Years of Plenty* (Ann Arbor, MI: Survey Research Center, 1984).

2. The term *residual welfare population* has been used by many researchers. Rebecca Maynard specified the parameters of this population in a recent conference. Some estimate that the "residual" population includes about 20 percent of the total welfare population. See Urban Institute, *Self-Sufficiency and the Low-Wage Labor Market: A Reality Check for Welfare Reform* (Washington, DC: Urban Institute, April 12, 1994).

3. SSI, or Supplemental Security Income, is probably a more appropriate

source of income for women such as Darlene, but the eligibility criteria are very tight. SSI is currently available to the aged, the blind, and the disabled and has always been somewhat more generous than AFDC. Most agree that the disabled cannot help their circumstances, and expectations that they work are either very low or nonexistent. Although the mentally ill can be counted among the disabled if they have written documentation of their illness from a physician or practicing psychiatrist, the verification procedures are more onerous than they might be for AFDC. Once a person is certified as eligible, SSI is a lifetime entitlement unless the person's condition changes substantially.

A very small proportion of women on welfare are unable to take advantage of education or training programs; they also are severely challenged to obtain regular work in a private-sector or publicly supported job. For the small portion of the AFDC population that is mentally ill or disabled, SSI is probably a more appropriate income source.

4. According to Corbett, the welfare population can be divided into three general groups: About 30 percent of AFDC entrants are short-term users (less than three years on welfare); about 40 percent are intermediate users (between three and eight years on welfare); and about 30 percent are persistent welfare users. Corbett's analogy of the welfare population to an onion having many layers is instructive. He recommends programs targeted to women on various layers of this onion. See T. Corbett, "Child Poverty and Welfare Reform: Progress or Paralysis?" *Focus* 15 (1993): 1–17.

5. General Accounting Office, *Families on Welfare: Focus on Teenage Mothers Could Enhance Welfare Reform Efforts* (Washington, DC: General Accounting Office, 1994).

6. For a review of the state welfare reforms in the early 1990s, see M. Wiseman, "Welfare Reform in the States: The Bush Legacy," *Focus* 15 (1993): 18–36.

7. "HHS Grants Wisconsin Waiver to Time Limit AFDC; Other States Await Approval," *Welfare to Work*, November 8, 1993, p. 1.

8. Douglas Besharov describes the problems that may result from the two-year limit, and he questions whether this limit will be foolproof or whether numerous exemptions will water down the plan. See D. J. Besharov, "The End of Welfare as We Know It?" *The Public Interest* 111 (1993): 95–109.

9. M. J. Bane and D. T. Ellwood, "The Dynamics of Dependence: The Routes to Self-Sufficiency," unpublished manuscript (Cambridge, MA: Urban Systems Research and Engineering, 1983).

10. G. Garin, G. Molyneux, and L. DiVall, "Public Attitudes Toward Welfare Reform: A Summary of Key Research Findings," unpublished manuscript (Washington, DC: Peter D. Hart Research Associates & American Viewpoint, 1994), p. 2 (emphasis in original).

11. Studies in Washington, California, and Vermont show that even though many AFDC families leave welfare within two years (a large percentage, in fact, leave welfare within one year), many later return to the welfare rolls and, over their lifetimes, are on welfare for more than two years. For a discussion of state data, see M. Greenberg, *Beyond Stereotypes: What State AFDC Studies on Length of Stay Tell Us About Welfare as a "Way of Life"* (Washington, DC: Center for Law and Social Policy, 1993).

12. See Harrington for an excellent description of the changing American economy and the marginalization of workers: M. Harrington, *The New American Poverty* (New York: Penguin Books, 1984).

13. See D. Besharov, "Targeting Long-Term Welfare Recipients," in P. H. Cottingham and D. T. Ellwood, eds., *Welfare Policy for the 1990s* (Cambridge, MA: Harvard University Press, 1989), pp. 146–64; G. J. Duncan and S. D. Hoffman, "Teenage Underclass Behavior and Subsequent Poverty: Have the Rules Changed?" in C. Jencks and P. E. Peterson, eds., *The Urban Underclass* (Washington, DC: Brookings Institution, 1991), pp. 155–74.

14. C. Murray, *Losing Ground: American Social Policy 1950–1980* (New York: Basic Books, 1984).

15. E. Liebow, *Tell Them Who I Am* (New York: Free Press, 1993).

16. "Around the Nation, Olympia, Wash. *Welfare to Work*, June 21, 1993, p. 6.

17. This dichotomy can be seen in two counties in California currently being studied by the MDRC. Alameda County has made an effort to provide education and training opportunities to women on welfare through their GAIN program. The program focuses on preparing women for well-paying jobs. In Riverside County, the emphasis is on quick job placement and short-term services. Although early results from the recent MDRC study show greater benefits from the short-term approach, Alameda County officials still hope that long-term findings will reveal a better investment return from their approach. See Manpower Demonstration Research Corporation, *GAIN: Benefits, Costs, and Three-Year Impacts of a Welfare-to-Work Program* (New York: Manpower Demonstration Research Corporation, 1994).

18. Legislators might want to consider the benefits of extending the two-year limit for some proportion of the welfare population that is willing and able to take advantage of such an offer. For example, one option might be to allow women who are making good academic progress in school and who are taking courses that will qualify them for a marketable job to continue for four years. The cost of supporting this smaller group of women would be greater, but their contribution to society in the long run might be well worth the investment.

19. According to the *New York Times*, the percentage of full-time workers aged eighteen to twenty-four with below-poverty wages rose from 23 percent in 1979 to 47 percent in 1992. John DeParte, "Sharp Increase Along the Borders of Poverty," *New York Times*, April 1, 1994, p. A 18.

20. "Around the Nation, Boston," *Welfare to Work*, May 10, 1993, p. 6.

21. W. Kelso, *Poverty and the American Underclass: Changing Perceptions of the Poor in America* (New York: New York University Press, 1994).

22. Although many critics of "workfare" generally regard it as an unfair punishment for low-income women, there is growing support for the notion, on the basis of equity. Even the majority of low-income women on welfare support some form of work in exchange for welfare (although their support wanes unless the work has real value). See ibid.

23. "Most States Cut Efforts, Says Report," *Welfare to Work*, January 20, 1992, p. 6.

24. In 1992, California voters considered a proposal to cut welfare benefits by 10 percent and by an additional 25 percent after six months on aid. Although the proposal was not approved, California has made other, significant cuts in welfare benefits. One of the cuts, initially granted by the federal government, came under scrutiny by the federal courts and was overturned. In its July 13, 1994, ruling, *Beno* v. *Shalala*, the court found that the U.S. Department of Health and Human Services had not adequately considered objections to the 1992 waiver that dropped AFDC benefits below federal standards. This ruling will likely be appealed.

25. Garrett, Ng'andu, and Ferron examined data from the HOME instrument used in the National Longitudinal Survey of Youth (NLSY). The NLSY studies families over time and registers changes in family income, work patterns, and family life. These effects also were noted by Salkind and Haskins in their examination of the negative income tax experiments. See P. Garrett, N. Ng'andu, and J. Ferron, "Poverty Experiences of Young Children and the Quality of Their Home Environments," *Child Development* 65 (1994): 331–45; N. J. Salkind and R. Haskins, "Negative Income Tax: The Impact on Children from Low-Income Families," *Journal of Family Issues* 3 (1982): 165–80.

26. "Maryland Lawmakers Battle over Controversial `Family Cap' Penalty," *Welfare to Work*, February 28, 1994, p. 1.

27. One of the major proponents of this position is Charles Murray, "Welfare and the Family: The U.S. Experience," *Journal of Labor Economics* 11 (1993): 224–62.

28. According to the GAO, since 1976, the number of large families on AFDC decreased from about 22 percent of the welfare population to about 13 percent. General Accounting Office, *Families on Welfare: Sharp Rise in Never-Married Women Reflects Societal Trend* (Washington, DC: General Accounting Office, 1994).

29. A recent study by Mauldon and Miller shows that women on welfare are more likely to have tubal ligations than are women who do not receive AFDC. Their study also found that women on AFDC have almost the same number of children as do women who do not receive AFDC, and they plan to have about the same number of children. However, women on AFDC are more likely to report having had an unwanted pregnancy than are women who do not receive welfare. See J. Mauldon and S. Miller, "Child-Bearing Desires and Sterilization Among United States Women: Patterns by Income and AFDC Recipiency," unpublished manuscript (Berkeley, CA: Graduate School of Public Policy, 1994).

30. According to Rank, "Each additional year on welfare lowers the probability of giving birth by .62 to 1." M. Rank, *Living on the Edge: The Realities of Welfare in America* (New York: Columbia University Press, 1994), p. 76.

31. "Around the Nation, Des Moines, Iowa," *Welfare to Work*, May 24, 1993, p. 7.

32. "Around the Nation, Carson City, Nev.," *Welfare to Work*, June 7, 1993, p. 7.

33. J. Levin-Epstein, *Drop-out Rates and Income Status* (Washington, DC: Center for Law and Social Policy, 1994).

34. W. F. McMahon, M. Thomas, S. B. White, and J. F. Zipp, *Do School Attendance Rates Vary Between AFDC and Non-AFDC Support Children?* (Milwaukee: Urban Research Center, University of Wisconsin, September 1989).

35. J. Pawasarat, L. Quinn, and F. Stetzer, *Evaluation of the Impact of Wisconsin's Learnfare Experiment on the School Attendance of Teenagers Receiving Aid to Families with Dependent Children* (Milwaukee: Employment and Training Institute, University of Wisconsin, February 1992).

36. Centers of Disease Control, "Preschool Children at High Risk for Measles: Opportunities to Vaccinate," *American Journal of Public Health* 83 (1993): 662–67.

37. E. George, *Needling the System: Welfare Agency Approaches to Preschool Immunization* (Washington, DC: Center for Law and Social Policy, 1993).

38. J. Levin-Epstein and M. Greenberg, *The Rush to Reform: 1992 State AFDC Legislative and Waiver Actions* (Washington, DC: Center for Law and Social Policy, November 1992).

39. Zill and associates suggest that the home environments for AFDC and non-AFDC poor children are less "satisfactory" with regard to "injury prevention and health promotion" than are those for non-poor families. See N. Zill, K. A. Moore, E. W. Smith, T. Stief, and M. J. Coiro, "The Life Circumstances and Development of Children in Welfare Families: A Profile Based on National Survey Data," unpublished manuscript (Washington, DC: Child Trends, October 1991).

40. For a discussion of the Wisconsin reforms, see Isabel Wilkerson, "Wisconsin Welfare Plan: To Reward the Married," *New York Times*, February 12, 1991, p. A16. An article in the *Wall Street Journal* states that since Norplant was introduced into the United States in 1991, more than 700,000 women have had the drug surgically inserted. The cost of Norplant, however, is a matter of controversy. The drug and insertion kit cost $350, a charge not fully reimbursed by Medicaid. See Elyse Tanouye, "Norplant's Maker Draws Sharp Criticism on Pricing of Long-Acting Contraceptive," *Wall Street Journal*, September 1, 1993, pp. B1–B2.

41. "Around the Nation, Annapolis, Md.," *Welfare to Work*, July 19, 1993, p. 7.

42. "Around the Nation, Trenton, N.J.," *Welfare to Work*, October, 11, 1993, p. 6.

43. "Around the Nation, Springfield, Ill.," *Welfare to Work*, December 6, 1993, p. 7.

44. A. de Tocqueville, *Democracy in America* (Garden City, NY: Doubleday, 1969 [originally published 1848]), p. 550.

45. For a description of the effects of returning to work, for a sample of welfare recipients, see N. Gilbert, J. D. Berrick, M. K. Meyers, *GAIN Family Life and Child Care Study* (Berkeley, CA: Family Welfare Research Group, 1992).

46. Families also receive a work-expense "disregard" of $90 a month and a child-care "disregard" (for those parents paying child-care expenses of $200 per month for infants and $175 for other children).

Some states (e.g., California, Illinois, Michigan, Minnesota, Missouri, New Jersey, South Carolina, Utah, Vermont, and Wisconsin) have been granted permission from the federal government to change the time limits on the AFDC work disregards. For example, as of September 1, 1993, California's state law changed, and women were able to obtain the "30 and a third" until their income was enough that they were no longer eligible for AFDC.

47. One study found that the average job welfare recipient was paid about ten cents over the minimum wage. Such jobs typically lasted about ten or eleven months. See Institute for Women's Policy Research, *Combining Work and Welfare: An Alternative Anti-Poverty Strategy* (Washington, DC: Institute for Women's Policy Research, 1993).

48. "Around the Nation, Atlanta," *Welfare to Work*, May 24, 1993, p. 7.

49. J. Cramer, "Births, Expected Family Size, and Poverty," in J. Morgan et al., eds., *Five Thousand American Families: Patterns of Economic Progress* (Ann Arbor, MI: Survey Research Center, 1974), vol. 2, pp. 279–318.

50. According to government sources, teen parents are the poorest of the welfare population. Although the proportion of all teenage welfare mothers has remained small (about 7 percent of the welfare population was under the age of twenty in 1969, which had increased to 7.6 percent as of 1992), they have their own needs that must be attended to. See General Accounting Office, *Families on Welfare: Focus on Teenage Mothers Could Enhance Welfare Reform Efforts* (Washington, DC: General Accounting Office, 1994); House Ways and Means Committee, *1994 U.S. Government Green Book: Overview of Programs* (Washington, DC: U.S. Government Printing Office, 1994).

51. The Clinton administration's welfare proposal provides significant funding toward preventing teenage pregnancy, through media messages and increased education regarding pregnancy prevention (Work and Responsibility Act of 1994).

52. Some research shows that living with grandparents may provide a buffering effect for young families, so that households can more effectively promote socioemotional health for children. (Furstenberg, 1976; Furstenberg, Brooks-Gunn, & Morgan, 1987; Horwitz, Klerman, Kuo, & Jekel, 1991; Kellam, Ensminger, & Turner, 1977). More recent studies, however, show that the presence of grandparents in the home may not have a strong effect on young parents (Moss & Carver, 1992; Wasserman, Brunelli, & Raub, 1990). See F. F. Furstenberg Jr., *Unplanned Parenthood: The Social Consequences of Teenage Childbearing* (New York: Free Press, 1976); F. F. Furstenberg Jr., J. Brooks-Gunn, and P. Morgan, *Adolescent Mothers in Later Life* (Cambridge: Cambridge University Press, 1987); S. M. Horwitz, L. V. Klerman, H. S. Kuo, and J. F. Jekel, "Intergenerational Transmission of School-Age Parenthood," *Family Planning Perspectives* 23 (1991): 168–72; S. G. Kellam, M. E. Ensminger, and R. J. Turner, "Family Structure and the Mental Health of Children," *Archives of General Psychiatry* 34 (1977): 1012–22; G. Wasserman, S. A. Brunelli, and V. A. Raub, "Social Supports and Living Arrangements of Adolescent and Adult Mothers," *Journal of Adolescent Research* 5 (1990): 54–66.

53. Although health-care reform was promised in the early days of the Clinton administration, it is now unclear whether such legislation will be passed in the foreseeable future. Currently, families on welfare qualify for health insurance under Medicaid, and many workers in some professions have

employer-sponsored support. But the working poor are often left out, and it is this group that is in most desperate need of health-care reform.

I do not pretend to be an expert on health-care reform and will leave the details to those better informed, but it seems clear that many of our policies for the poor provide all-or-nothing options. If families fall below a set income level, they qualify for assistance, but once their income exceeds a certain amount, their support is immediately cut. A more rational approach that recognized the slow progression in workers' income over time might provide a sliding fee scale for Medicaid coverage. Any working family in the United States whose employer did not provide health-care insurance would be allowed to buy Medicaid. Low-income families would qualify for full coverage. As their family income rose, families would be required to pay a share of the cost. This option would not have a time limit. The current regulations for transitional Medicaid coverage under the JOBS program allow for twelve months of medical support. But after a year of work, employees rarely receive a guarantee that they will get health insurance or a raise. The time-limited approach is arbitrary, forcing women to choose between going back on AFDC or taking a chance with their child's health. The latter alternative is untenable; all Americans, regardless of their income, should have access to health care for their children.

54. *JOBS-Supported Child Care.* If women are to participate in programs such as JOBS, we must find a way to lessen their child-care burden. Breaks in child care, such as those Sandy describes, are common and may have negative developmental consequences for children (Gilbert, Berrick, & Meyers, 1992). From the time a woman begins her JOBS program, she should be given a seamless child-care system so that her child can benefit from continuous care.

Transitional Child Care. Offering twelve months of transitional child care is a first step toward easing the burden that accompanies a change from welfare receipt to full-time employment. But this approach does not offer the security that many working families need during those first critical years when they are trying to escape poverty. Some evidence suggests that low-income families spend approximately 30 percent of their income for child care (single parents spend 50 percent), whereas child-care costs for middle-income families are far lower (10 percent) (Hofferth, Brayfield, Deich, & Holdomb, 1991). A study conducted some time ago also indicated that two years of child-care benefits were essential to creating a lasting benefit for women who had recently left the welfare rolls (Hosni, 1979). For some families, it may take longer.

Many women like Sandy would combine welfare with work if they were given a chance, yet child-care costs are prohibitive. In addition, because the eligibility rules for TCC are so limited, very few women qualify for assistance. But if our goal is to help get women off welfare, then TCC must be offered to any woman who works, regardless of whether she is completely free of AFDC.

Sandy's suggestions about easing the transition from welfare to work are also very good. Essentially, she suggested a sliding-scale approach to child care. Like my earlier recommendations for health-care insurance, child care should be provided to any low-income working family. As their income rose, working mothers would pay a share of cost.

Child-Care Tax Credit. For a single, simplified child-care system, the current Child and Dependent Care Tax Credit could also be revised to assist low-income working families with child-care expenses. Currently, parents who earn at least $10,000 annually are eligible for a tax credit of up to 30 percent on $2,400 in child-care expenditures. This credit is deducted from the family's tax liability, assuming that the family pays taxes. Families who do not pay taxes because of low-income status are not eligible for the credit. Because the child-care tax credit cannot be refunded, it is of no use to many low-income families. The primary beneficiaries of the policy are, instead, middle-class families. In fact, spending under the child-care tax credit tripled during the 1980s, totaling nearly $4 billion in assistance to middle-income families (Besharov & Tramontozzi, 1989; Robins, 1989).

By making the tax credit refundable, low-income families would be given substantial assistance with their child-care burden. The symbolic gesture of helping the poor along with the middle class would also send a strong message to the American public about the value we place on all families.

Streamlined Categorical Child-Care Programs. Currently, a number of targeted, categorical programs are available for small groups of low-income families. Separate eligibility criteria are often listed for these different programs, creating a bewildering array of very limited possibilities for families. These resources and funding streams should be integrated and administered by a single agency.

Under the integrated system, any low-income working mother would qualify for a voucher allowing her to choose the center or family day care of her choice. The voucher would be accepted as cash, ensuring a choice of child care and avoiding some of the costs associated with government-funded child care. With the government's increasing involvement in the child-care business, however, federal child-care standards should be established to ensure at least a minimal level of safety and security for these children.

See D. J. Besharov P. N. Tramontozzi, "Federal Child Care Assistance: A Growing Middle Class Entitlement," *Journal of Policy Analysis and Management* 8 (1989): 313–18; Gilbert, Berrick, and Meyers, *GAIN Child Care and Family Life Study*; S. L. Hofferth, A. Brayfield, S. Deich, and P. Holdomb, *National Child Care Survey, 1990* (Washington, DC: Urban Institute Press, 1991); D. Hosni, "An Economic Analysis of Child Care Support to Low-Income Mothers," unpublished manuscript (Orlando: University of Central Florida, 1979); P. K. Robins, "Federal Financing of Child Care: Alternative Approaches and Economic Implications," paper presented at the Economic Implications and Benefits of Child Care Conference, Racine, WI, January 1989.

55. In 1988, the federal government went a long way in improving the child-support enforcement system in the United States. First, under the Family Support Act, the states were required to develop routine income-withholding mechanisms so that all absent parents would have child-support payments taken from their wages once a child-support order was handed down. Second, the act required states to follow established guidelines for determining

child-support payments based on income and assets. Third, it strengthened paternity requirements, encouraging the states to establish paternity for children born outside marriage, to obtain the Social Security numbers of both parents at the time of the birth, and to offer federal financial incentives for the states to provide blood tests to establish paternity in contested situations (Garfinkel & McLanahan, 1990). Although these changes were helpful, we are still a very long way from having a child-support system that works. See I. Garfinkel and S. S. McLanahan, "The Effects of the Child Support Provisions of the Family Support Act of 1988 on Child Well-being," *Population Research and Policy Review* 9 (1990): 205–34.

56. Before the 1993 budget law was passed by the Clinton administration, the phaseout for the EITC was set at $22,000. Under the new law, the EITC will phase out at $23,760 for families with one child and $25,300 for families with two children.

Further expansion might include increasing the base rate of the EITC and adjusting it for family size. The EITC currently returns approximately 18.5 percent on the first $7,760, diminishing to zero percent as income increases. Under the new law, the EITC will return about 26 percent on the first $7,750, rising to 34 percent on the first $6,000 by 1995. Although this is a substantial improvement from before, the new law will still leave a single parent with two children, working full time at the minimum wage, right at the poverty level.

Most Americans do not think that a family can survive at the poverty line; they believe that the official poverty line is set too low. A study conducted in 1990 found that when asked, What amount of weekly income would you use as a poverty line for a family of four (husband, wife, and two children) in this community? the average figure reported by the American public was about 24 percent higher than the official poverty line. As good informants about the cost of living in the United States, their responses should be taken seriously. The combination of work with the EITC should move families as close as possible to the "new" poverty line created by the American public.

57. The minimum wage increased in 1991 (to $4.25 per hour), although a full-time job at that rate still raises only one person out of poverty. A family of two would remain about $600 below the poverty line, and a family of three would be short by $2,300.

58. If women must rely on AFDC for a time, we must make the system fair so that they are not forced to commit welfare fraud. Rebecca's housing choice is not extravagant. She lives in a one-bedroom apartment in a marginal neighborhood where rents are about $150 below the market rate. Even so, Rebecca's rent consumes more than 90 percent of her monthly welfare grant. The remaining few dollars cannot cover regular expenses such as cleaning supplies, clothing, or transportation. For most women, living on the amount of money provided through AFDC and food stamps is unrealistic. Without additional income or other supports, women are forced to find illegal means of caring for their families.

One option to make living on welfare more realistic would be to give Section 8 housing vouchers to any woman working, going to school, or in a training program while on AFDC. Section 8 is preferable to public housing, as women can use the voucher anywhere in their community. Landlords willing to accept Section 8 vouchers are partially paid by the renter (who pays 30 percent of her income toward rent, and so when her income rises, so will her copayment); the remainder of the rent is paid by the government. Section 8 vouchers help disburse low-income housing throughout the community so that such women can choose a neighborhood where they feel comfortable and relatively safe. Housing in better neighborhoods often means better schools for children and offers a buffer against the negative consequences of a poor education (Kaufman & Rosenbaum, 1992; Rosenbaum, 1991; Rosenbaum & Popkin, 1991; Rosenbaum, Popkin, Kaufman, & Rusin, 1991). Finally, Section 8 vouchers guard against the development of publicly supported ghettos, offering low-income children the opportunity to play alongside middle-income children in their yards and at school.

See J. E. Rosenbaum, "Black Pioneers—Do Their Moves to Suburbs Increase Economic Opportunity?" *Housing Policy Debate* 2 (1991): 1179–1214; J. Kaufman and J. E. Rosenbaum, "The Education and Employment of Low-Income Black Youth in White Suburbs," *Educational Evaluation and Policy Analysis* 14 (1992): 229–40; J. E. Rosenbaum and S. J. Popkin, "Employment and Earnings of Low-Income Blacks Who Move to Middle-Class Suburbs," in C. Jencks and P. Peterson, eds., *The Urban Underclass* (Washington, DC: Brookings Institution Press, 1991), pp. 342–56; J. E. Rosenbaum, S. Popkin, and J. Rusin, "Social Integration of Low-Income Black Adults in Middle-Class White Suburbs," *Social Problems* 38 (1991): 448–62.

59. According to William Julius Wilson (1987), jobs would have an effect on the culture, on people's standard of living, on women's choices about single parenthood, and on men's criminal activity. Jobs are the only source of legitimate income in the United States among low-income people. Our efforts to legitimize and therefore legalize people's work effort might do more than criticisms and declarations have about how people ought to behave.

But jobs may not be enough. Many Americans believe that poverty is the result of laxity, that if people simply applied themselves to the task, they would find a job and then everything would be fine. But finding a job does not provide an avenue out of poverty for millions of men and women. In 1986, about 3.5 million employed heads of families remained in poverty. One million of them had full-time, year-round jobs. The statistics are much more depressing for female-headed households. About one in five families headed by a single working woman is caught in poverty (Levitan, Belous, & Gallo, 1988). This suggests that jobs that pay a living wage will be a major part of real welfare reform. See S. Levitan, R. S. Belous, and F. Gallo, *What's Happening to the American Family?* (Baltimore: Johns Hopkins University Press, 1988); W. J. Wilson, *The Truly Disadvantaged: The Inner City, the Underclass, and Public Policy* (Chicago: University of Chicago Press, 1987).

60. Martin Tolchin, "Welfare Overhaul: Right Timing for a War Dance," *New York Times*, October 3, 1988, p. A18.

61. Jonathan Marshall, "Welfare Incentive Program is Working, Study Reports, *San Francisco Chronicle*, April 20, 1993, p. 12.

62. A. C. Huston, "Children in Poverty: Developmental and Policy Issues," in A. C. Huston, ed., *Children in Poverty: Child Development and Public Policy* (Cambridge: Cambridge University Press, 1991), pp. 1–22.

Study Methods

1. N. Gilbert, J. D. Berrick, and M. Meyers, *GAIN Family Life and Child Care Study* (Berkeley, CA: Family Welfare Research Group, 1992).

2. Regarding the validity of ethnographic samples, Mead writes, "The validity of the sample depends not so much upon the number of cases as upon the proper specification of the informant, so that he or she can be accurately placed, in terms of a very large number of variables—age, sex, order of birth, family background, life-experience, temperamental tendencies, political and religious position, etc. . . . Within this extensive degree of specification, each informant is studied as a perfect example, an organic representation of his complete cultural experience." M. Mead, quoted in J. C. Johnson, *Selecting Ethnographic Informants* (Newbury Park, CA: Sage, 1990), p. 22.

3. D. L. Jorgensen, *Participant Observation: A Methodology for Human Studies* (Newbury Park, CA: Sage, 1989), p. 30.

4. H. R. Bernard, *Research Methods in Cultural Anthropology* (Newbury Park, CA: Sage, 1988), p. 177.

5. M. Burawoy, "The Extended Case Method," in M. Burawoy et al., eds., *Ethnography Unbound: Power and Resistance in the Modern Metropolis* (Berkeley and Los Angeles: University of California Press, 1991), pp. 271–90; R. F. Ellen, ed., *Ethnographic Research: A Guide to General Conduct* (New York: Academic Press, 1984); O. Werner and G. M. Schoepfle, *Systematic Fieldwork* (Newbury Park, CA: Sage, 1987).

6. M. Bulmer, "The Value of Qualitative Methods," in M. Bulmer, with K. G. Banting, S. S. Blume, M. Carley, and C. Weiss, eds., *Social Science and Social Policy* (Boston: Allen & Unwin, 1986), pp. 80–204.

7. D. M. Fetterman, *Ethnography: Step by Step* (Newbury Park, CA: Sage, 1989).

8. W. J. Wiener and G. C. Rosenwald, "A Moment's Monument," in R. Josselson and A. Lieblich, eds., *The Narrative Study of Lives* (Newbury Park, CA: Sage, 1993), pp. 30–58.

9. Jorgensen, *Participant Observation*.

10. J. P. Spradley, *The Ethnographic Interview* (New York: Holt, Rinehart & Winston, 1979).

11. S. M. Miller, "The Participant Observer and `Over-rapport'," in G. J. McCall and J. L. Simmons, eds., *Issues in Participant Observation* (Reading, MA: Addison-Wesley, 1969), pp. 87–89.

12. E. Sawyer, "Methodological Problems in Studying So-Called 'Deviant' Communities," in J. Ladner, ed., *The Death of White Sociology* (New York: Random House, 1973), pp. 361–79; Spradley, *The Ethnographic Interview*; R. H. Wax, "Gender and Age in Fieldwork and Fieldwork Education: No Good Thing Is Done by Any Man Alone," *Social Problems* 26 (1979): 509–22.

13. Jorgensen, *Participant Observation*.

14. G. Rosenthal, "Reconstruction of Life Stories," in R. Josellson and A. Lieblich, eds., *The Narrative Study of Lives* (Newbury Park, CA: Sage, 1989), pp. 59–91.

15. Jorgensen, *Participant Observation*.

16. Ibid.

17. Rosenthal, "Reconstruction of Life Stories."

Index

Index